AF470047

Other than the photographer's own surviving notes, the following sources have provided valuable background information during the compiling of this volume. In instances where our research has thrown up conflicting information, we have trusted Tom Williams' own hand-written notes, recorded at the time, so we apologise in advance for any potential errors or misinformation.

Peto's Register of Great Western Railway Locomotives Volume One. *Irwell Press ISBN 1 871608 50 3*

Great Western Steam in Shakespeare Country. *Pixton ISBN 978 1 905505 13 5*

Railway Nostalgia around Warwickshire. *Hibbs ISBN 0 9518557 4 3*

www.sixbellsjunction.co.uk

www.brdatabase.info

www.warwickshirerailways.com

The National Railway Museum

We would also like to thank the following individuals for their assistance with this project:

Dick Blenkinsop, Brian & Gordon England, Ashley Pettifer, Andy Tinkler, Richard Howarth,
Mike Collins, Terry Dorrity, Mike Musson, Michael Whitehouse
and last but not least, the late John Jennings.

The 12-hour clock was still in use on British Railways when the vast majority of these images were taken and is therefore used in all titles. Also, where we are certain of the camera and film type used, it is duly stated in the captions, along with the shutter speed and aperture, if recorded by the photographer.

The copyright holders regret that it is not currently possible to supply individual print copies of any of the images published within.

Copyright for all colour slides taken by T E Williams, including those 'lent' or submitted for duplication but not returned, remains with O & P Williams.

Compiled by Phillip & Owen Williams

Publication design & slide restoration by Phillip Williams

Copyright: IRWELL PRESS LIMITED ⓒ 2021

ISBN 978-1-911262-30-5

First published in the United Kingdom in 2021 by Irwell Press Limited, 59A, High Street, Clophill, Bedfordshire MK45 4BE
Printed by Akcent Media Limited

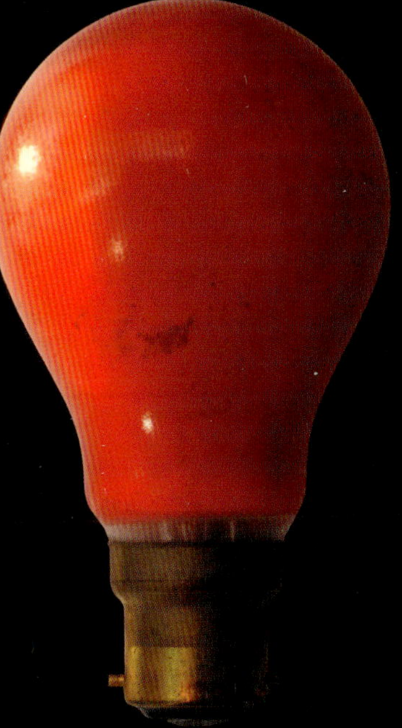

There's not really very much that I can add to what I've said previously, other than to perhaps highlight a couple of differences between this book and previous volumes. As Dad, in my opinion, was as much an artist as he was a photographer, several images that had previously been discounted, have now been re-evaluated from the perspective of the *mood* that they evoke. Blurring is a contentious issue amongst photographers: it can be an enemy as much as it can also be a friend and several of the photos we've decided to include, exhibit motion blur (whether intentional or consequential) to great effect. Such images won't please everyone, but they'll certainly create a feeling of *being there*. In my opinion, all that a still image can hope to achieve within the context of 'capturing the moment', is to elicit a sense of being in the photographer's shoes. The sheer sensation of witnessing a hurtling mass of iron and steel *can* remain forever animated within the confines of a piece of celluloid, with the assistance of blurring.

Another aspect of Dad's artistry was his willingness to take risks when faced with extreme lighting conditions. As much as his wage packet didn't allow him to shoot film willy-nilly, his faith in his own abilities was rarely shaken. Indeed, often the single limiting factor was the film in his camera. Slide film has an inherent inability to cope with extreme contrast and occasionally, purely as a consequence of Dad's shooting into the sun, or having sunlight reflected from a locomotive's polished contours directly into the lens, a great photo was potentially spoiled. In such instances, I've employed a method of double-scanning: initially exposing for the highlights and secondly for the shadows. These two scans, after a degree of manipulation, are then combined to create a 'best of both'. Some may argue that this process is little more than cheating, but in this digital world, where does cheating begin and where does it end? I've not painted anything in that wasn't already there and I've certainly not painted anything out, other than damage and debris. All that has happened is that tonal range has been increased in washed-out highlights and filled-in shadows. This process is, or so I'd like to think, little more than an expansion on choosing a grade of paper on which to print from a conventional b/w negative. Darkroom techniques were rarely considered cheating. Indeed, they were just *part of the art*: perhaps now just one of the many *lost* arts, thanks to so-called progress. I wasn't going to mention the dreaded *'C' word*, but ironically, if it hadn't been for *Lockdown* constraints, I wouldn't have had the time to spend on this whole process: so in the words of Eric Idle, *'Always look on the….'*, etc., etc.

Phillip Williams
Stratford-upon-Avon,
January, 2021

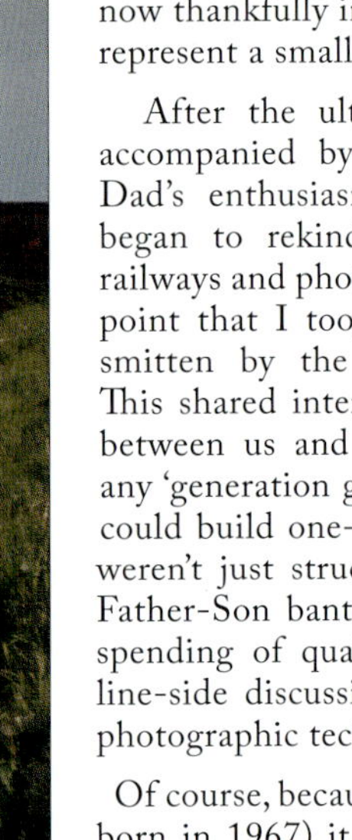

Above: Worcester's recently-overhauled **6820 Kingstone Grange** passes under the *A3102 Bath Road* bridge just outside Wootton Bassett on the South Wales and Bristol line with an empty coaching stock working. Those of you familiar with Dick Blenkinsop's excellent book, *Silhouettes of the Great Western* will recognise this scene. Dad is standing behind Dick and makes certain to compose his version of the scene accordingly! *14/5/60 (Kodachrome)*

It's been quite strange really: whilst trying to gain inspiration to formulate something to write here, I thought I'd thumb through the previously published volumes and I'm still staggered by the number of photographs that I don't recall ever seeing before in slide-form prior to the process of digitisation and restoration. It's doubly strange when one considers that I actually *grew up* with these slides; revisiting them from time to time, carefully extracting them from their boxes in the loft and returning them just as carefully. I can only imagine that this is down to the restoration process itself; reinstating natural colours and minimising garish casts caused primarily by the passage of time. Of course, these colour images now thankfully immortalised in print, only represent a small tip of a large iceberg.

After the ultimate passing of steam, accompanied by an inevitable hiatus in Dad's enthusiasm, he slowly but surely began to rekindle his hunger for both railways and photography and it was at this point that I too, as a young lad, became smitten by the same life-long passion. This shared interest forged a strong bond between us and more than made up for any 'generation gap'. It also meant that we could build one-to-one conversations that weren't just structured around the typical Father-Son banter. It also guaranteed the spending of quality time together at the line-side discussing both locomotives *and* photographic techniques.

Of course, because of my age-group (I was born in 1967) it was this second phase of Dad's railway photography that interested me the most and forged my fascination for *'Westerns'* in particular. Indeed, amongst his later colour output, there's an almost equivalent volume of early *BR blue* diesel captures dating from 1973, right up to the time of his death in April 1980. I occasionally wonder what might happen to this fine body of work once Phillip has completed the digitisation and restoration process, as I have no children and I'd like to think that they won't just be shoved away in some store room somewhere, never to be seen again. One thing's for certain: they won't be sold off piecemeal like many other photographic collections.

We hope that you enjoy this latest volume and although it may be the last in this series, rest assured that many more colour photographs by T.E.Williams will see the light of day if we have our way.

Owen Williams
Barnstaple,
January, 2021

Contents

Introduction iii

1 | The *'Great Way West'*: Paddington to Bristol 1

2 | The *'Birmingham line'* through Warwickshire 11

3 | Named Expresses *on the 'Western'* 23

4 | Holidays in South Devon 31

5 | Specials *&* Irregular Workings 41

6 | The Cotswolds *& Vale of Evesham* 55

7 | Inter-regional Workings 63

8 | Freight, Parcels *&* Ironstone 73

9 | Locals *&* Semi-fasts 81

10 | Journeys to *'foreign'* parts 89

11 | Stratford-upon-Avon *& Shakespeare Country* 107

12 | The *Western Region*: On Shed 117

13 | Numerical index of Locomotives 124

Cover photographs:

SLIDE 952 | Sporting the slotted bogie, Old Oak's **6005 King George II** puts some smoke against a clear blue sky as it makes the climb through Budbrook towards Hatton with the 2.10pm Paddington to Birkenhead. *6005* was fitted with this unique assembly in late 1958 and it was retained well into 1961. *3/10/59 (Kodachrome)*

SLIDE 333 | The remnants of the newly-relaid goods loop litter the cutting here as **3440 City of Truro** thunders up the final stretch of Hatton Bank with the return leg of an *SLS* special train from Swindon Works to Wolverhampton (Low Level) *(see also slide 310 on page 45). 16/6/57 (Kodachrome)*

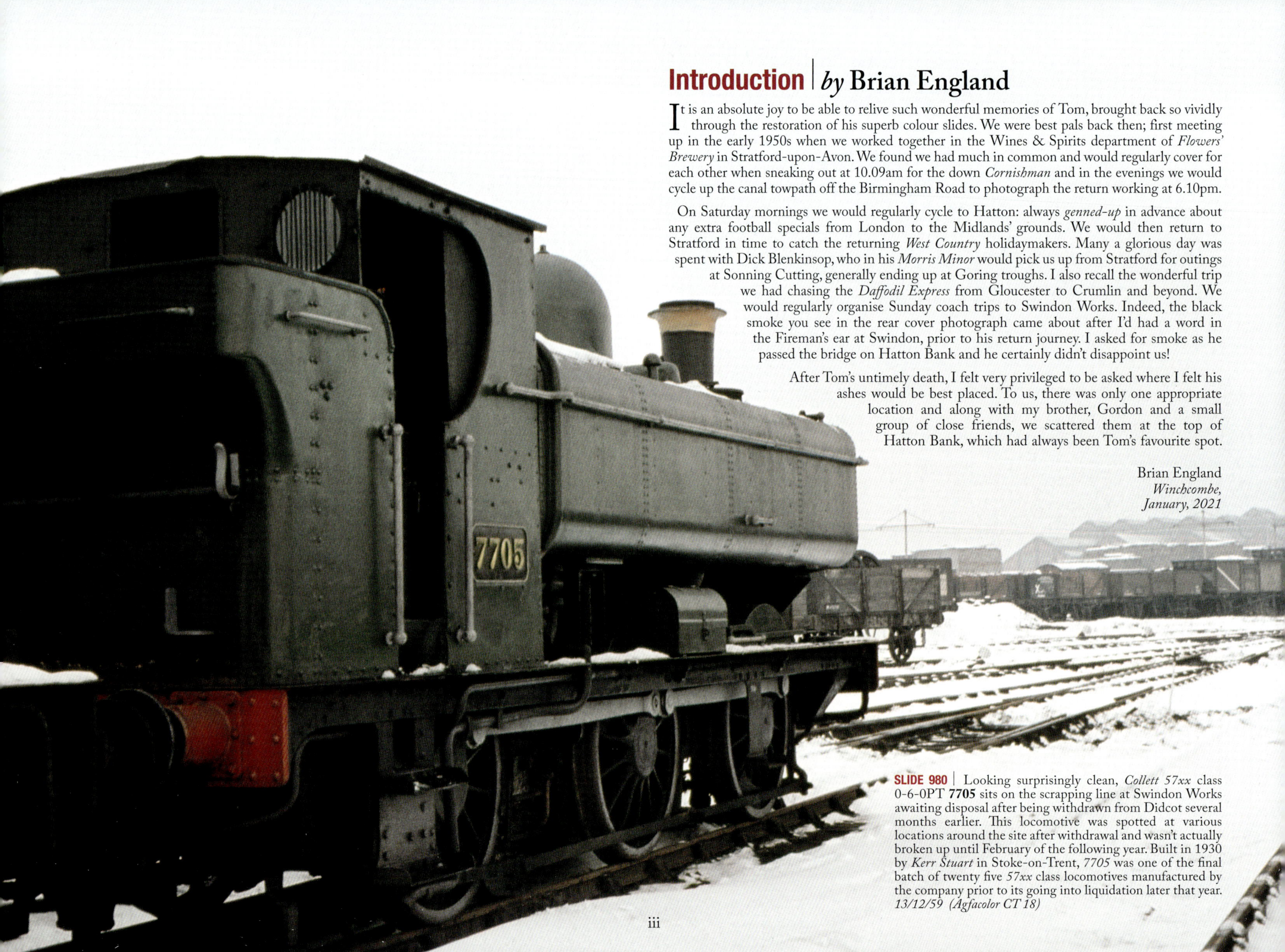

Introduction | *by* Brian England

It is an absolute joy to be able to relive such wonderful memories of Tom, brought back so vividly through the restoration of his superb colour slides. We were best pals back then; first meeting up in the early 1950s when we worked together in the Wines & Spirits department of *Flowers' Brewery* in Stratford-upon-Avon. We found we had much in common and would regularly cover for each other when sneaking out at 10.09am for the down *Cornishman* and in the evenings we would cycle up the canal towpath off the Birmingham Road to photograph the return working at 6.10pm.

On Saturday mornings we would regularly cycle to Hatton: always *genned-up* in advance about any extra football specials from London to the Midlands' grounds. We would then return to Stratford in time to catch the returning *West Country* holidaymakers. Many a glorious day was spent with Dick Blenkinsop, who in his *Morris Minor* would pick us up from Stratford for outings at Sonning Cutting, generally ending up at Goring troughs. I also recall the wonderful trip we had chasing the *Daffodil Express* from Gloucester to Crumlin and beyond. We would regularly organise Sunday coach trips to Swindon Works. Indeed, the black smoke you see in the rear cover photograph came about after I'd had a word in the Fireman's ear at Swindon, prior to his return journey. I asked for smoke as he passed the bridge on Hatton Bank and he certainly didn't disappoint us!

After Tom's untimely death, I felt very privileged to be asked where I felt his ashes would be best placed. To us, there was only one appropriate location and along with my brother, Gordon and a small group of close friends, we scattered them at the top of Hatton Bank, which had always been Tom's favourite spot.

Brian England
Winchcombe,
January, 2021

SLIDE 980 | Looking surprisingly clean, *Collett 57xx* class 0-6-0PT **7705** sits on the scrapping line at Swindon Works awaiting disposal after being withdrawn from Didcot several months earlier. This locomotive was spotted at various locations around the site after withdrawal and wasn't actually broken up until February of the following year. Built in 1930 by *Kerr Stuart* in Stoke-on-Trent, *7705* was one of the final batch of twenty five *57xx* class locomotives manufactured by the company prior to its going into liquidation later that year. *13/12/59 (Agfacolor CT 18)*

1 | The *'Great Way West'*: Paddington to Bristol.

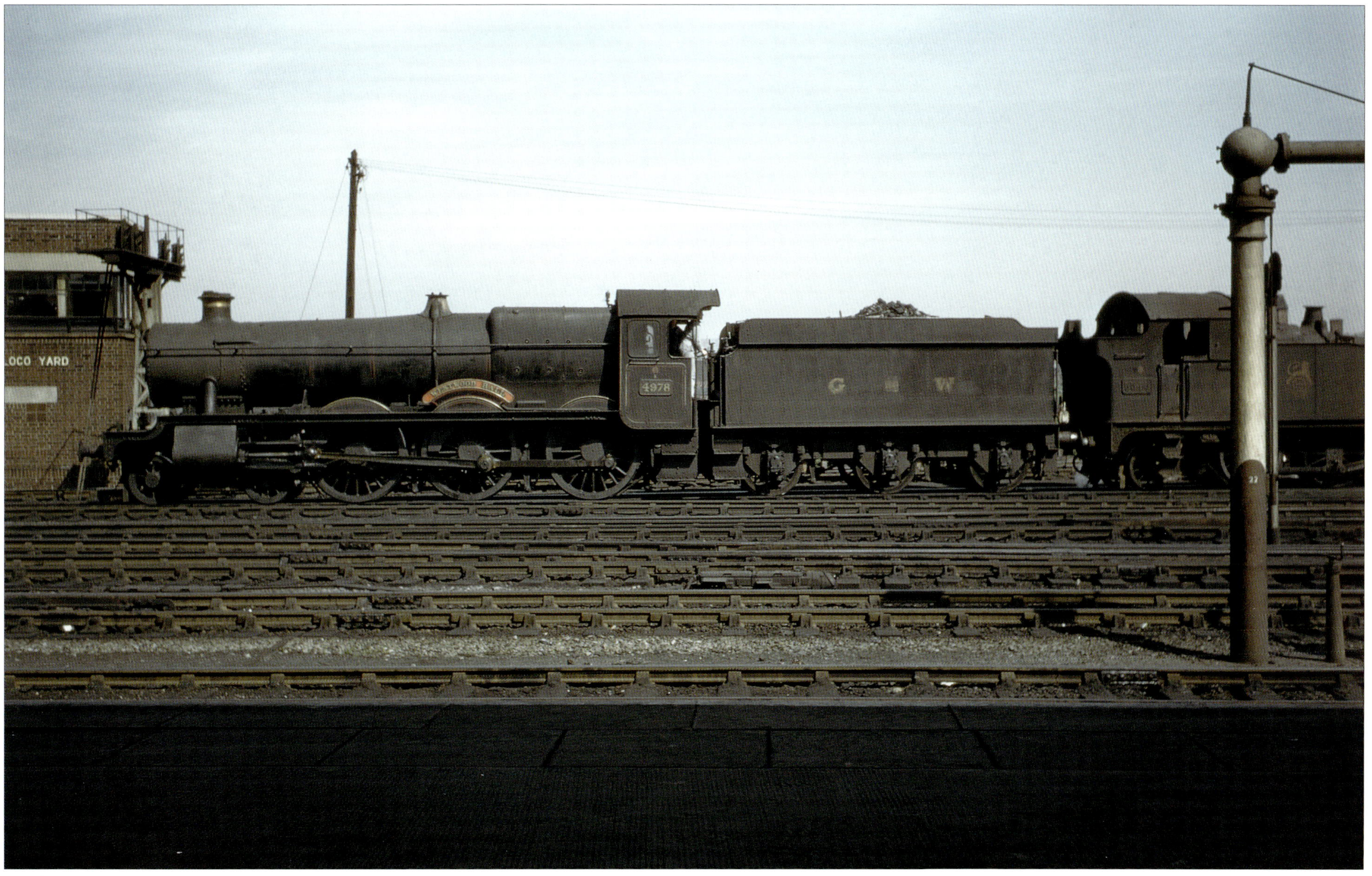

SLIDE 06 | Laira's **4978 Westwood Hall** displaying a most unlikely mixture of liveries stands at the entry to the locomotive yard at Bristol Temple Meads awaiting its next duties. Red-painted nameplates (and indeed numberplates) were relatively short-lived on the *Western Region*; the practice becoming official procedure in November 1949, but ceasing in April 1952. It is curious though, that the numberplates on *4978* have not been similarly treated. If a model maker were to build and exhibit a locomotive turned out as we see here, he'd have to be pretty certain about having corroborating evidence in order to avoid the scorn of his peers! The presence of a tender in pre-1948 condition may purely be down to the jocular or perverse attitude of a handful of ex-*GWR* men at Swindon. The *4575* class tank next to the *Hall* is **5510**, shedded at Swindon when this photograph was taken. ?/5/54 *Agfa Silette (Kodachrome)*

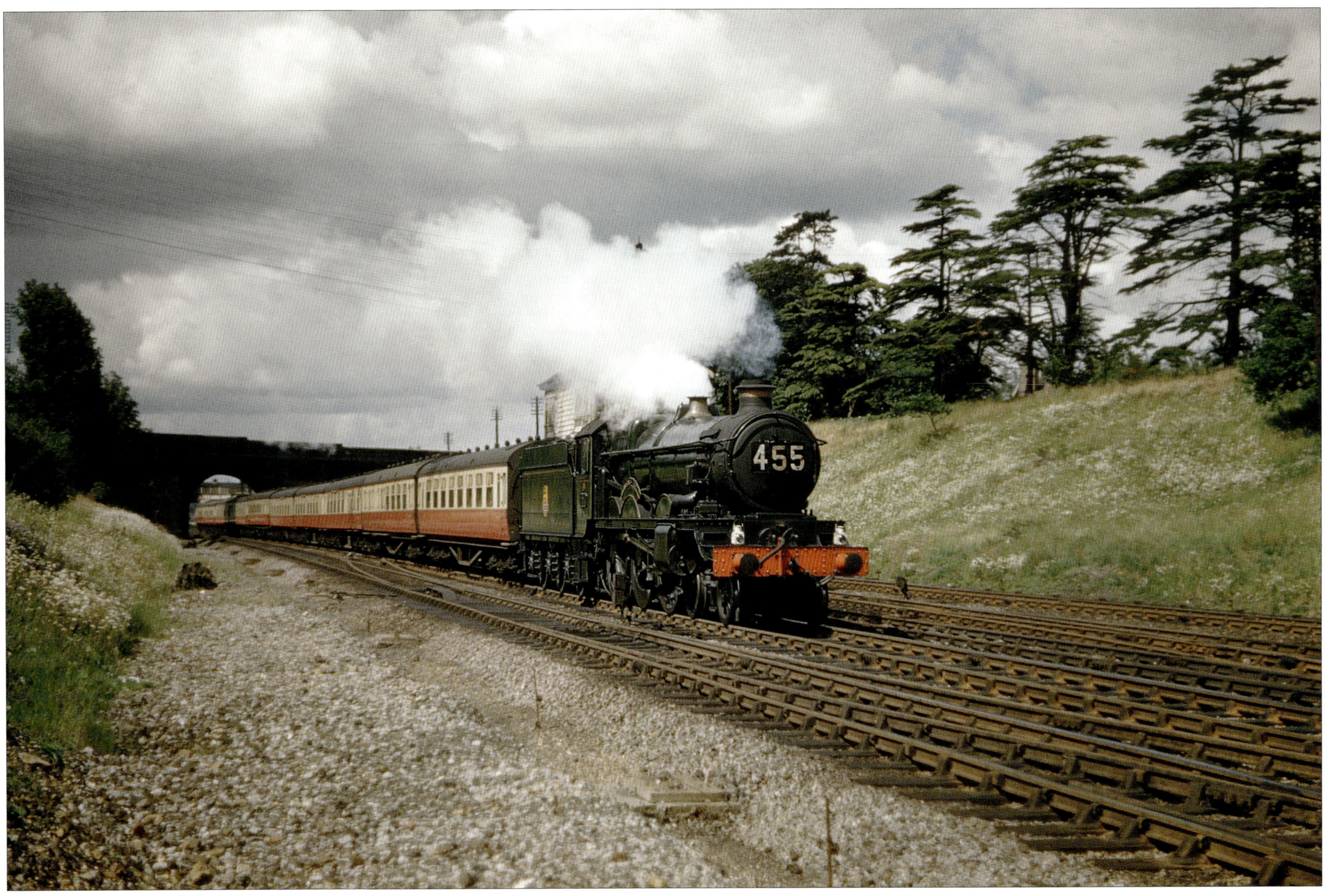

SLIDE 285 │ In stark contrast to the previous image, Bristol Bath Road's pristinely turned out **7014 Caerhays Castle** at the head of the 8.20am Weston-super-Mare to Paddington service almost smothers Twyford East Signal Box with steam as it threads the *Waltham Road* bridge: the distinctive station footbridge just visible beyond the end of the train. Pictured here still in possession of its single chimney and fresh from a heavy general overhaul at Swindon, *7014* was one of only five of its class to be fitted with the rather unsightly *Davies & Metcalfe* valveless lubricator assembly (fitted to the side of the smokebox) which regardless of any benefits, undoubtedly spoiled the clean lines of these iconic locomotives. This apparatus is also known to have been fitted to **4087**, **4088**, **5084** and **7013** (ex-**4082**). *11/6/57 (Kodachrome)*

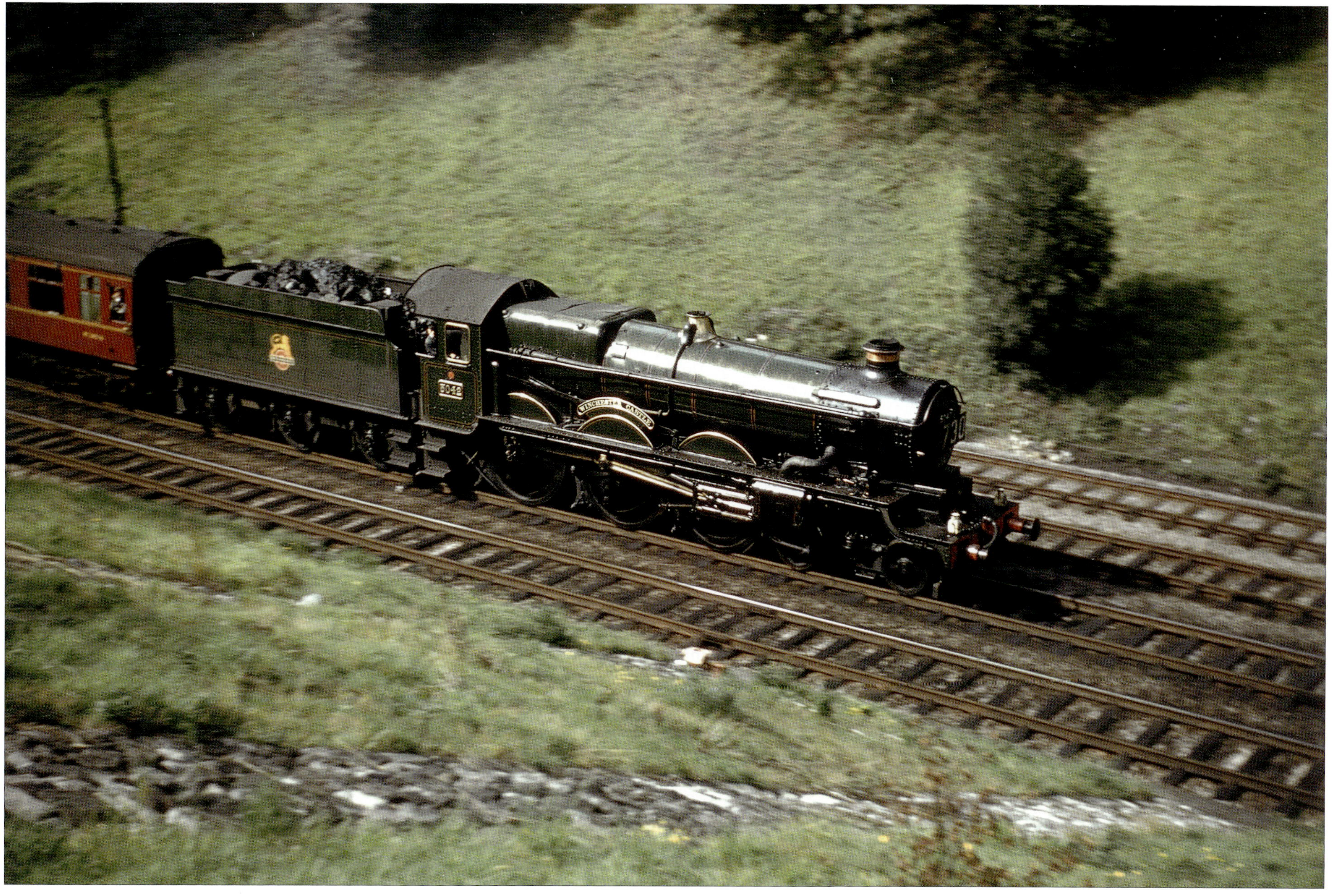

SLIDE 434 | Horton Road's **5042 Winchester Castle** is captured at speed in Sonning Cutting on the 11.45am SO Cheltenham to Paddington. On two consecutive Sundays in July 1956, this locomotive and classmate **5018 St Mawes Castle** took part in stress tests on the *Severn Railway Bridge* (of the former *Severn & Wye Railway*). The largest locomotives that had previously been allowed over the bridge (with special authorisation) were the 43xx class *Moguls*, but post-Nationalisation, plans were drawn up to re-evaluate the bridge's future potential. Initial tests involved a 500 ton load of ballast wagons being shunted onto the bridge by the double-headed *Castles* with strain gauges closely monitoring any small movements in the bridge. The double-headed *Castles* (*5018* piloting) next made several slow runs across the full length of the bridge. The full evaluation resulted in extensive strengthening work being carried out over the next four years, prematurely curtailed when in October 1960, the bridge was struck by two barges causing a partial collapse and rendering the whole building project commercially unviable. Five men also lost their lives. *7/9/57 Leica IIIA (Kodachrome)*

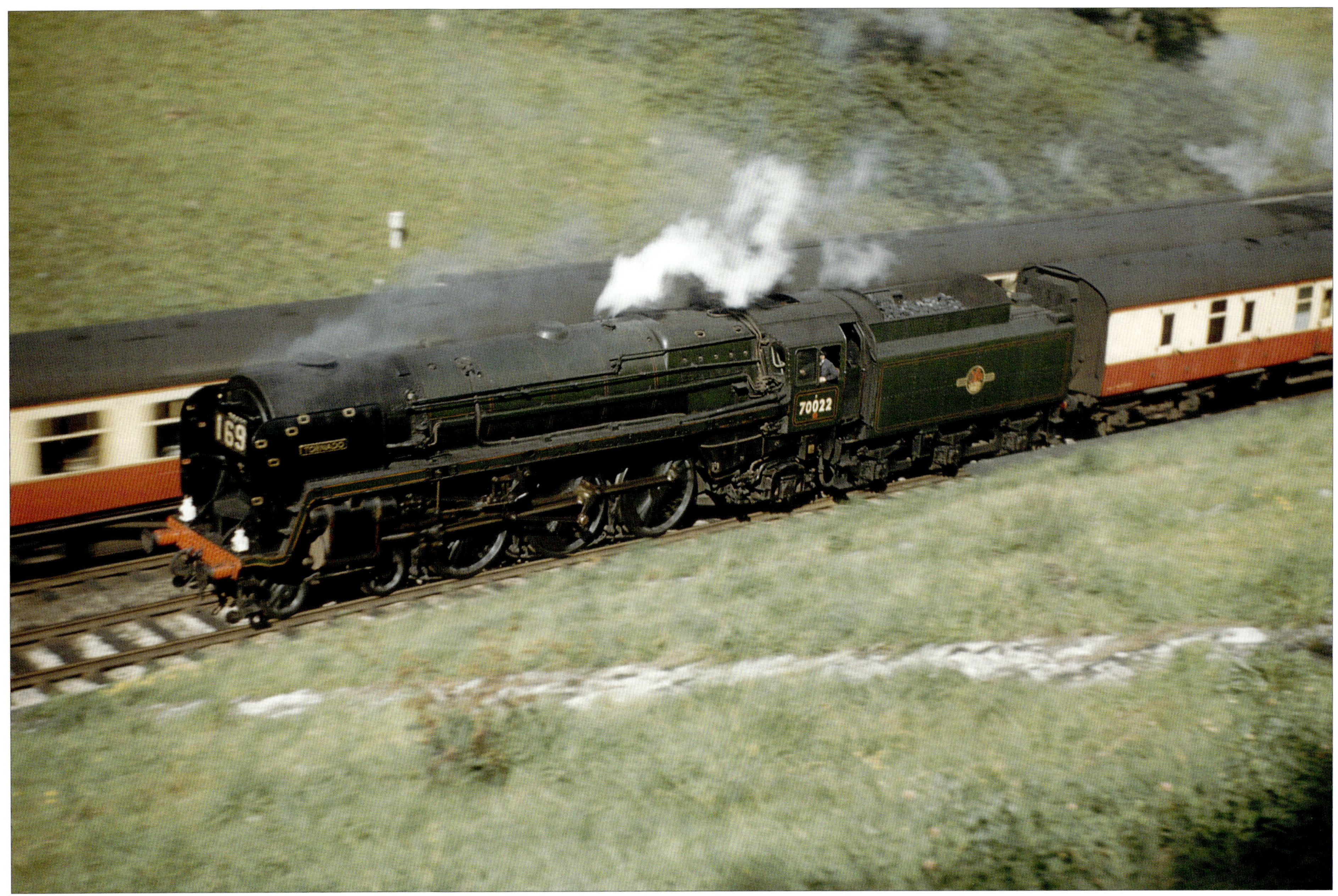

SLIDE 436 | Several minutes later, Cardiff Canton-based *BR Standard* class 7 **70022 Tornado** thunders past the photographer with the 1.55pm Paddington to Pembroke Dock service. The distinctive brass-lined handholds cut into the smoke deflectors of *Western Region* members of this class came about as a result of a serious accident at Milton, near Didcot on November 20th 1955, resulting in the derailment of a ten-coach excursion train from South Wales hauled by Canton's **70026 Polar Star**. The Driver's failure to see signals, partly as consequence of his left-hand seating position, compounded by the positioning of the smoke deflector handrails, resulted in the train entering a low-speed crossover at an estimated 50mph. The derailing locomotive slewed down the embankment, taking the leading coaches with it. There were eleven fatalities and over one hundred injured. *(See also slide 1466 on page 95). 7/9/57 Leica IIIA (Kodachrome)*

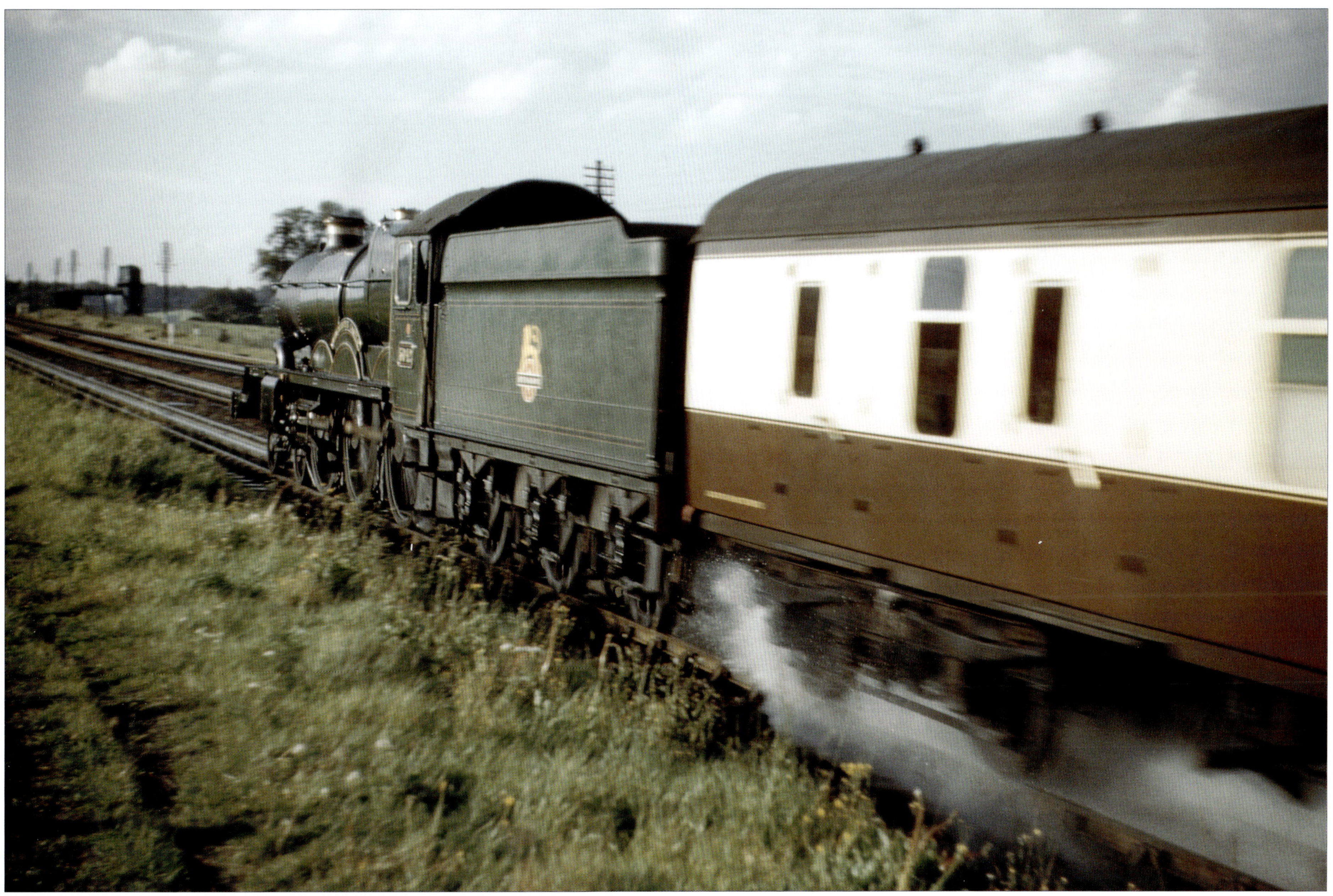

SLIDE 446 | **5042 Winchester Castle**, one of the last of its class to be withdrawn from service, is captured here on an unidentified down express thundering over Goring Troughs. As *slide 434* reproduced on page 3 will testify, taken earlier on the same day, this is a return trip for *5042*, but unfortunately the photographer did not record the specific working. At this moment, the train is a matter of seconds from crossing the River Thames via the *Gatehampton Railway Bridge* near Lower Basildon. This largely brick-built structure was designed by and erected under the auspices of Isambard Kingdom Brunel in 1838 and was contemporary with the *Maidenhead Railway Bridge* and *Moulsford Railway Bridge* along the same stretch of line. *7/9/57 Leica IIIA (Kodachrome)*

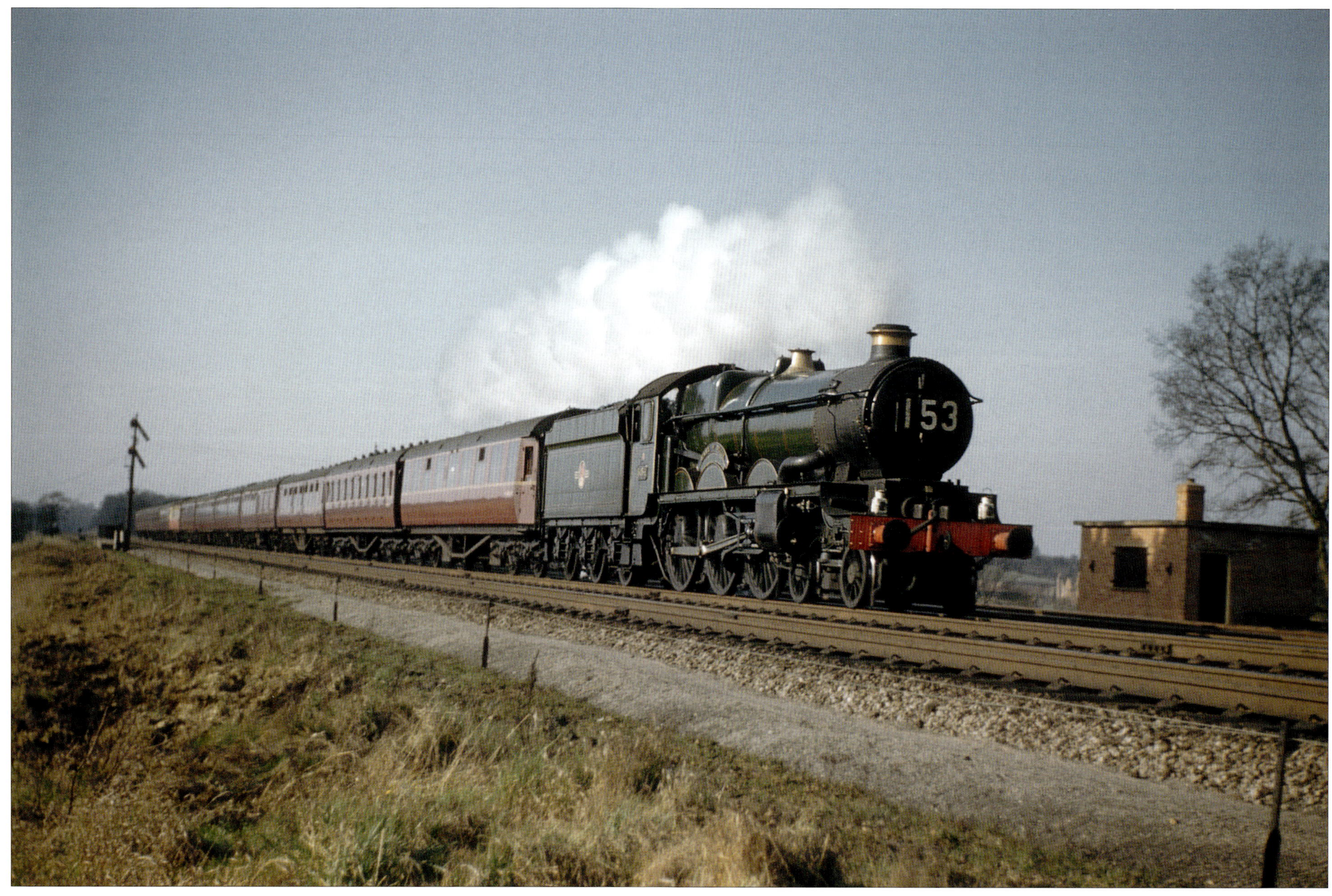

SLIDE 748 | *Castle* class **5054 Earl of Ducie** approaches Twyford with the 8.20am Weston-super-Mare to Paddington. This locomotive was also observed later in the day heading the 1.15pm return service. Interestingly, at a time when many members of the *Castle* class were receiving the new double chimney at the point of overhaul, several of the class were still having standard single chimneys fitted as replacements for their original 'tall' chimneys. *5054* was one such locomotive which was observed still in possession of its original chimney as late as September 1958. As is evident by the condition of the locomotive in this image, supported by existing records, the chimney was almost certainly replaced during a recent heavy intermediate overhaul at Swindon between December 1958 and January 1959, at which point a replacement boiler and tender were also fitted. *28/2/59 Leica IIIA 1/200th F2.5 (Kodachrome)*

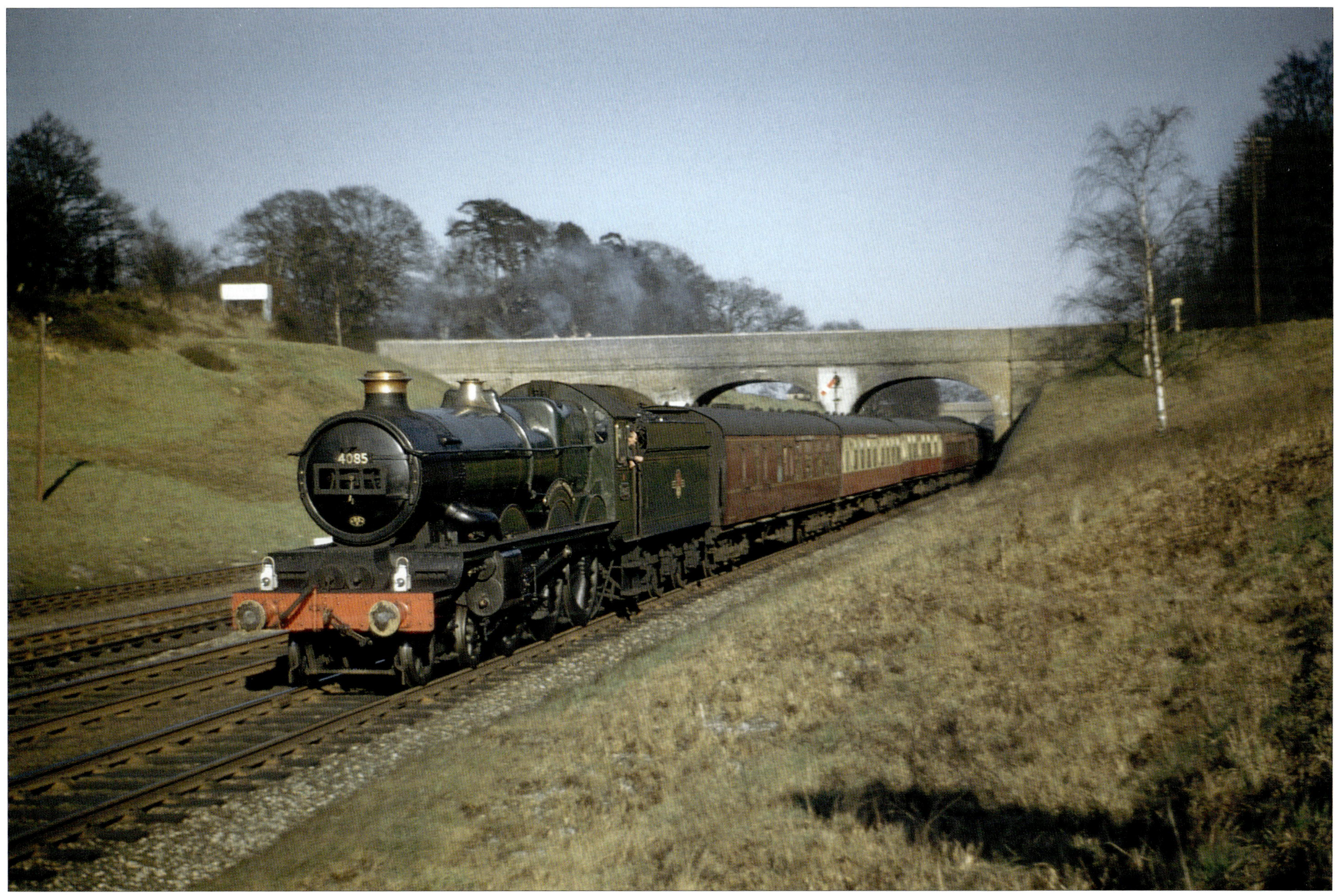

SLIDE 760 | A prime example of a photographer using the crisp light of a low Winter sun to great effect: Gloucester Horton Road's **4085 Berkeley Castle** looking in pristine condition threads the *Stanlake Lane* bridge, Ruscombe, near Twyford with the 2.15pm Paddington to Cheltenham. Note the white-washed brickwork designed to increase the visibility of the signal arm. Despite looking ex-works in this photograph, the condition of the locomotive here must be purely down to the cleaners at Horton Road, as *4085* hadn't visited Swindon for overhaul since August of the previous year *(see slide 775 on following page). 28/2/59 Leica IIIA 1/500th F2 (Kodachrome)*

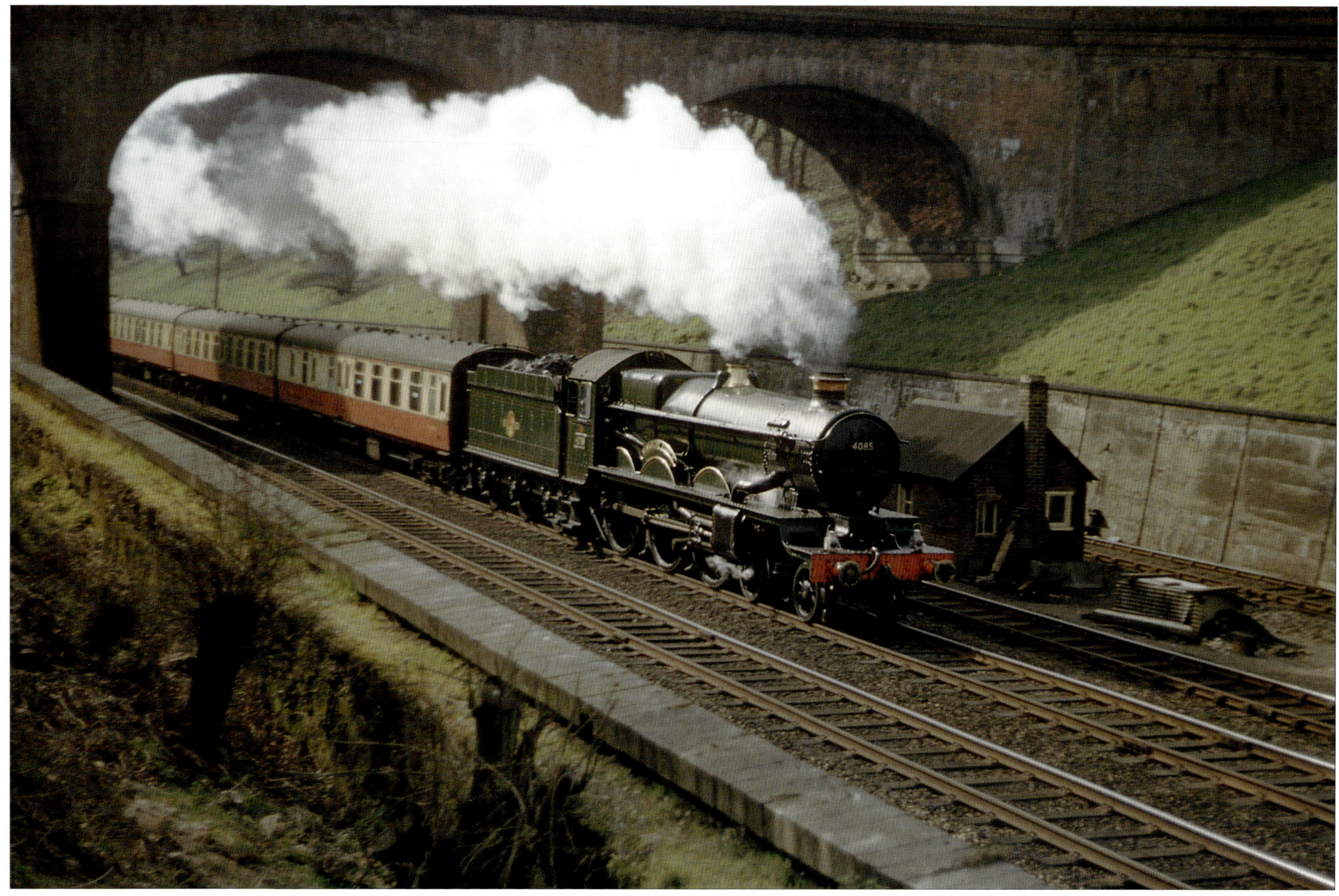

SLIDE 775 | On yet another visit to the Reading area a month later, equally favourable weather serves the photographer well. Again, Horton Road's **4085 Berkeley Castle** is captured in fine fettle passing the Ganger's hut situated beneath the imposing *Bath Road* bridge, Sonning: this time the train is the 11.45am Cheltenham to Paddington. This was to be the final year working out of Gloucester for *4085*: it was reallocated to Worcester in February 1960 where it remained for six months, prior to ending its days at Old Oak Common *(see also slide 111 on page 36)*. *31/3/59 Leica IIIA (Kodachrome)*

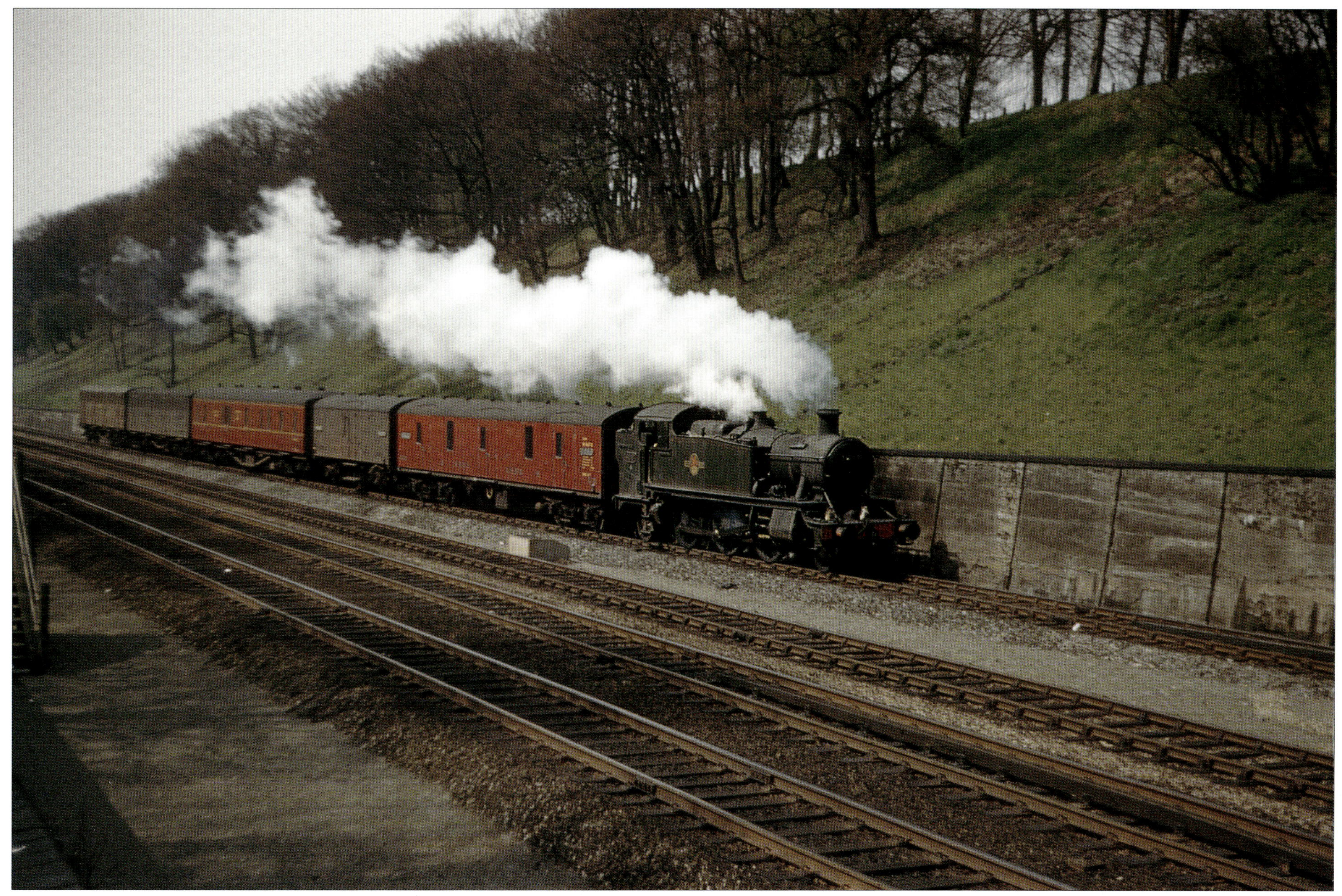

SLIDE 1009 | Captured just a few hundred yards from the location of the previous image, but almost exactly a year later, *Collett 2-6-2T* **6152** makes its way along Sonning Cutting on the up relief line with a Reading to Paddington parcels train. Built between 1931 and 1935 the *61xx* class totalled seventy locomotives, most of which worked their entire service lives within the *London Division*, though twenty or so travelled further afield in their later years. First entering service in February 1933 and spending most of its days working out of Slough, *6152* spent its final days at Didcot from where it was withdrawn in January 1962, making the short journey to Swindon for disposal just a few weeks later. *19/4/60 Leica IIIA (Kodachrome)*

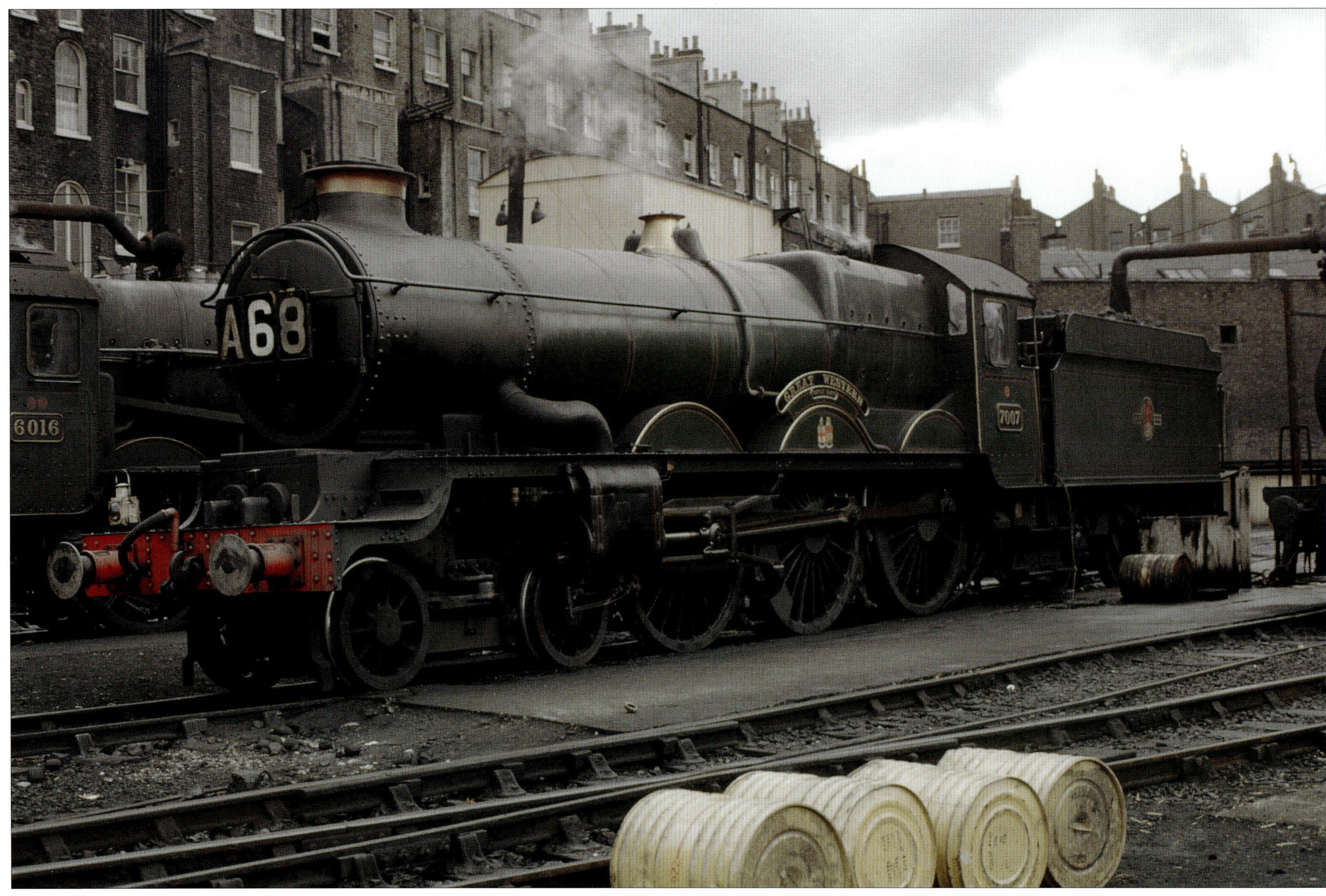

SLIDE 1528 | *Castle* class **7007 Great Western** is serviced at Ranelagh Bridge yard, prior to heading home to Worcester with the 5.15pm *Cathedrals Express*. Stafford Road's **6016 King Edward V** is visible in the background having just taken on water prior to returning home on the 5.15pm from Paddington. Note in the foreground the distinctive pale yellow barrels of *Alfloc* boiler feed water treatment. This mixture of compounds was developed in the early 1950s by *ICI* in conjunction with *BR* to minimise limescale build up, discourage corrosion and prevent foaming: all undesirable and potentially damaging in the long-term to any heated water system. The boiler tubes of Wolverhampton-based locomotives were particularly prone to scaling due to the notoriously hard water in the *Black Country*; ironically, perfect for brewing beer but a curse to an engineer! *(See also slide 743 on page 118)* *19/8/62 (Kodachrome)*

2 | The *'Birmingham line'* through Warwickshire.

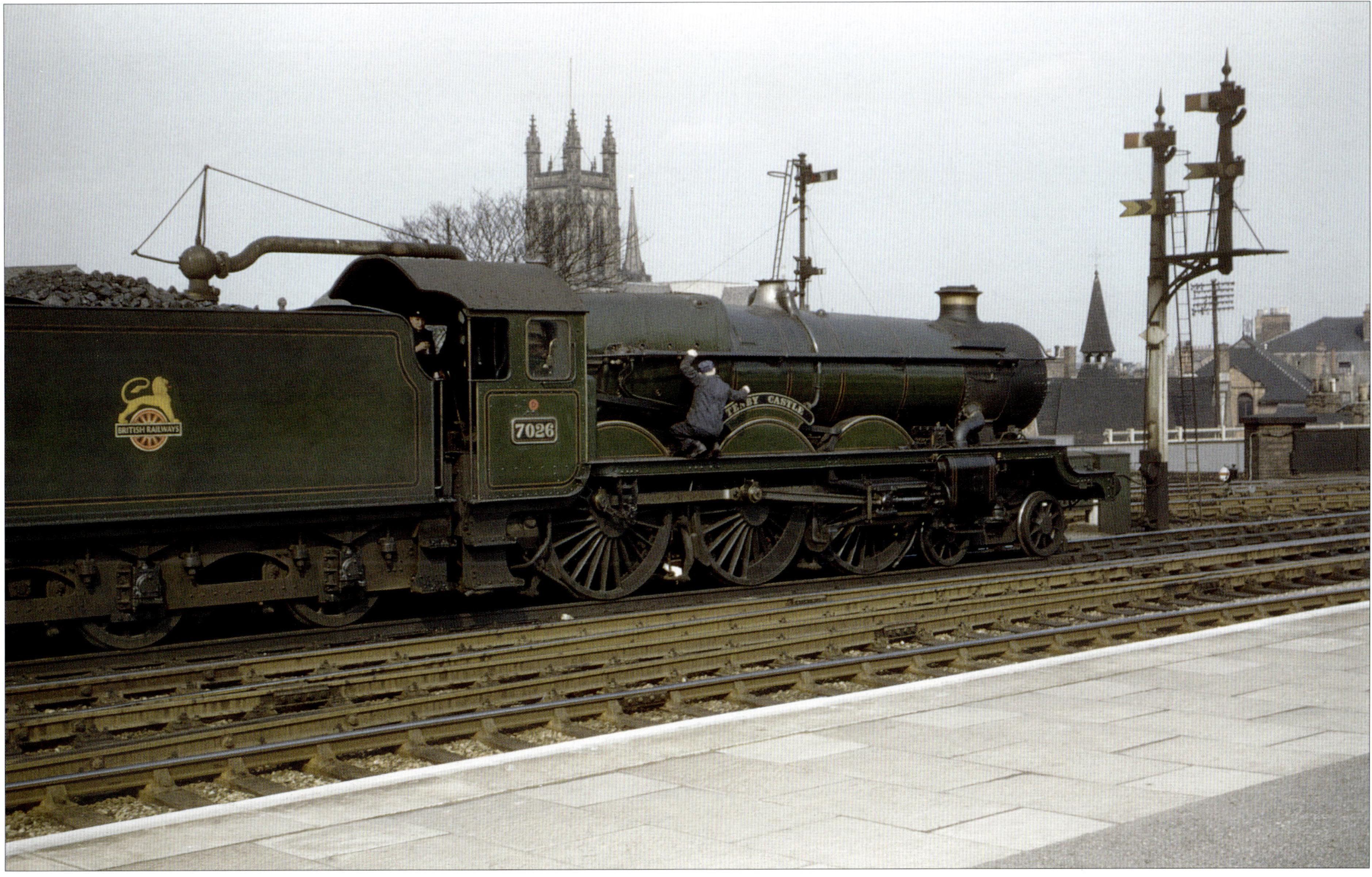

SLIDE 07 | The tower of *All Saints' Parish Church*, one of the largest parish churches in England, silently presides over the comings and goings as Stafford Road's **7026 Tenby Castle** on an afternoon Wolverhampton to Paddington express sits in the up main platform at Leamington Spa General awaiting the 'right away'. Meanwhile, the Fireman is taking the opportunity to take an oil can around the lubricators. Note in the background, the distinctive *LNWR* signal post that stood at the eastern end of the adjacent *LMR* Leamington Avenue Station which was ultimately destined to close in 1965 as part of the Beeching modernisation programme. The station and associated infrastructure would be demolished and the site completely levelled in 1977 as part of a redevelopment scheme. *?/5/54 Agfa Silette (Kodachrome)*

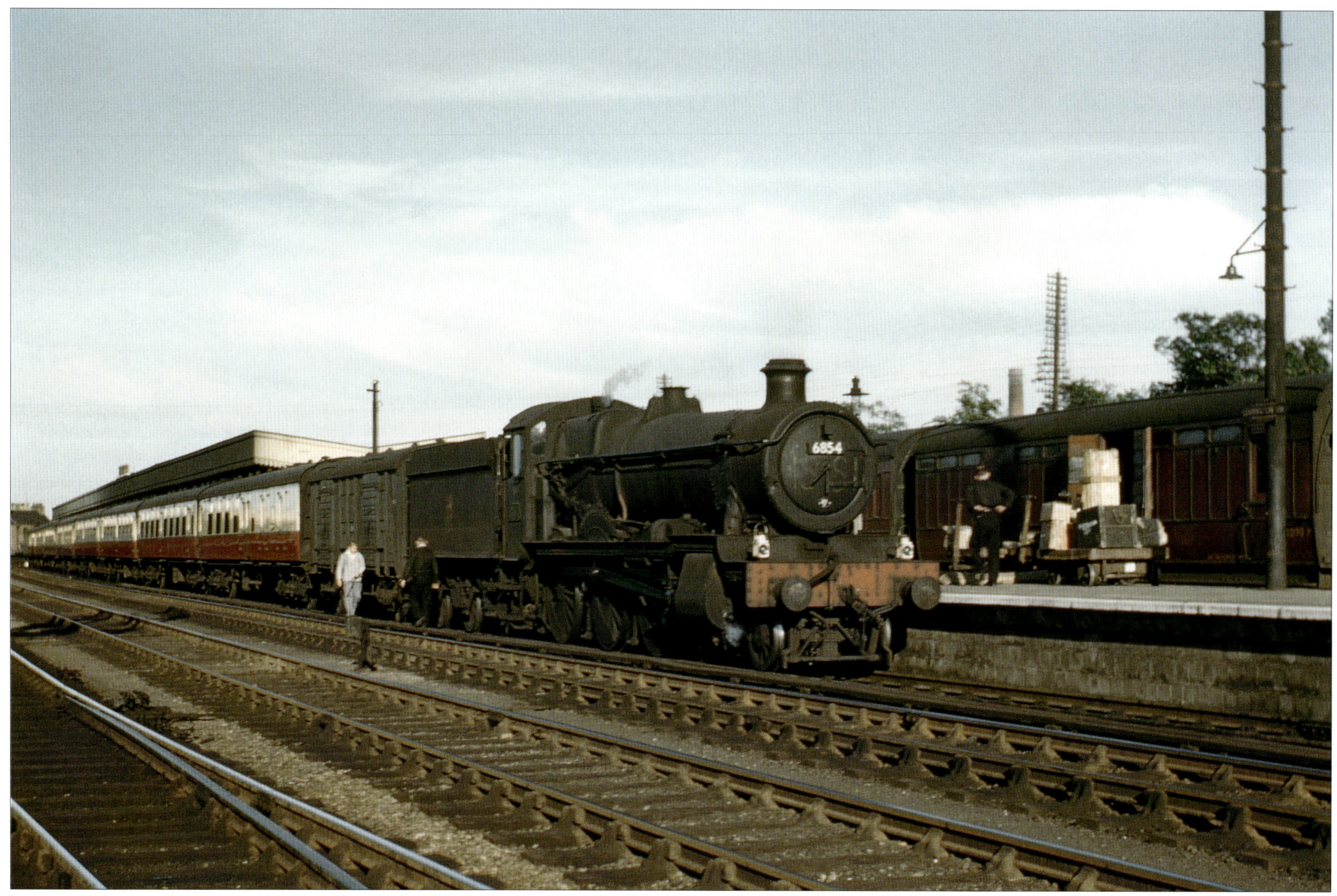

SLIDE 342 | Not the sharpest of photographs, but one that is full of detail and interest. Oxford's **6854 Roundhill Grange** on an unidentified north-bound express stands in the down platform at Leamington Spa General. It is the start of the holiday season and an ex-*SR* utility van has been added to the train to expand luggage capacity. Meanwhile, local Wheeltapper, Bert Smith and his mate go about their business utilising the planking that has been laid along the points rodding for this very purpose. Across the platform, a Porter contemplates the feasibility of moving a precariously balanced load of assorted parcels and carriage cases. Note the ageing ex-*LNWR* and ex-*LMS* vans on the unidentified parcels train which unfortunately the photographer failed to record: possibly because the locomotive had already been taken off. *19/6/57 (Kodachrome)*

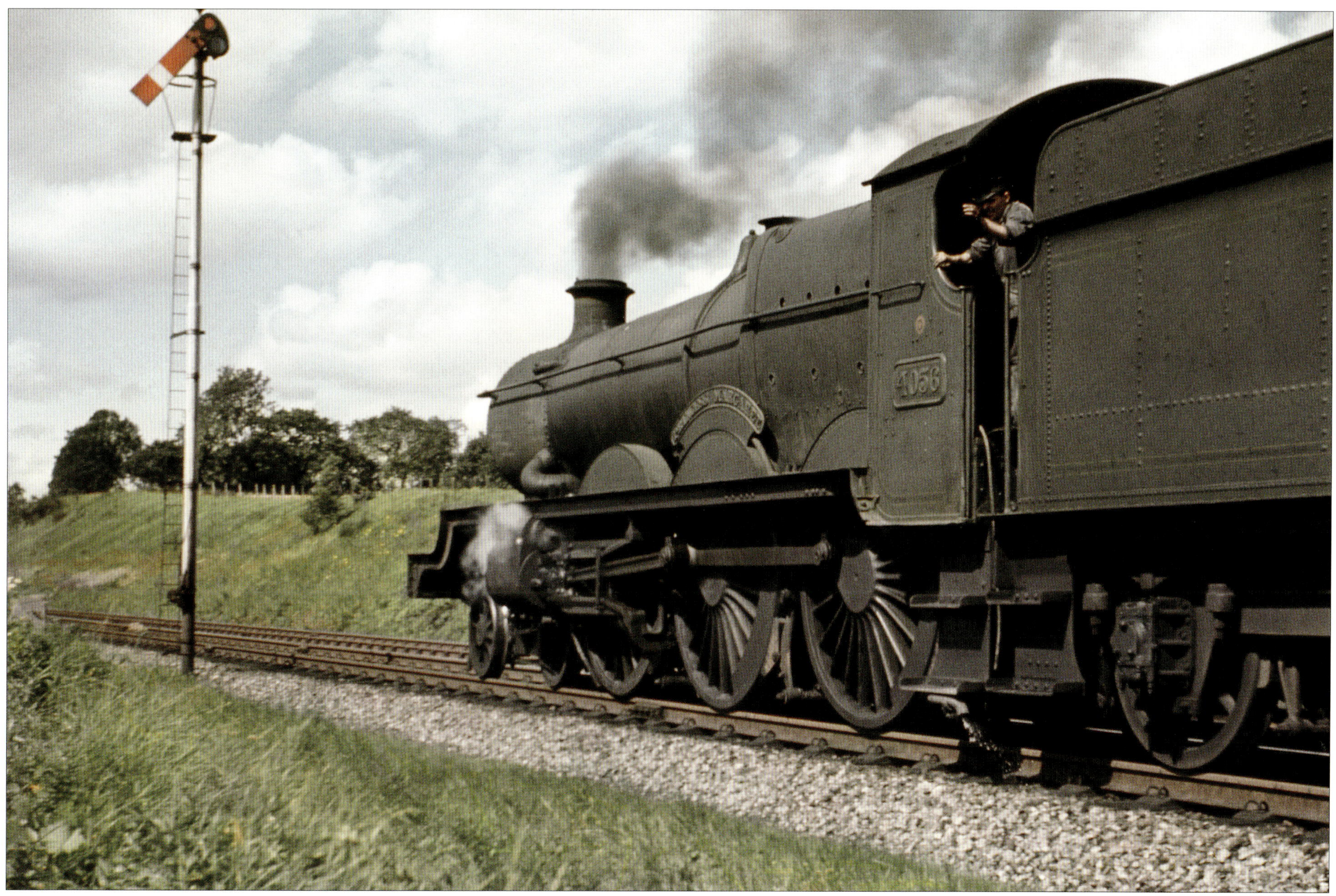

SLIDE 410 | This wave from the Fireman has perhaps a more profound significance than at first meets the eye. On what is certainly its final visit to the area, *Star* class **4056 Princess Margaret** has inexplicably turned up at the head of the 9.25am Weymouth to Wolverhampton service. It is pictured here having just run through Hatton North Junction on the approach to the cutting south of Shrewley, only two months away from withdrawal. In a pretty unkempt condition, it is almost certain that very little attention has been paid to the cleaning of this locomotive since the previous year when it hauled an *SLS* (Midland Area) special from Birmingham Snow Hill to Swindon, via Kidderminster, Hereford and Severn Tunnel Junction. On that occasion, it had been spruced up at Tyseley and had *GW*-style transfers applied to the buffer beam. Why *4056* turned up on this Wolverhampton train and how it worked its way back home to Bath Road, is a complete mystery. It was eventually broken up at Swindon during November 1957 after a creditable recorded mileage of 2,074,338. *24/8/57 Leica IIIA 1/500th F3.5 (Agfacolor CT 18)*

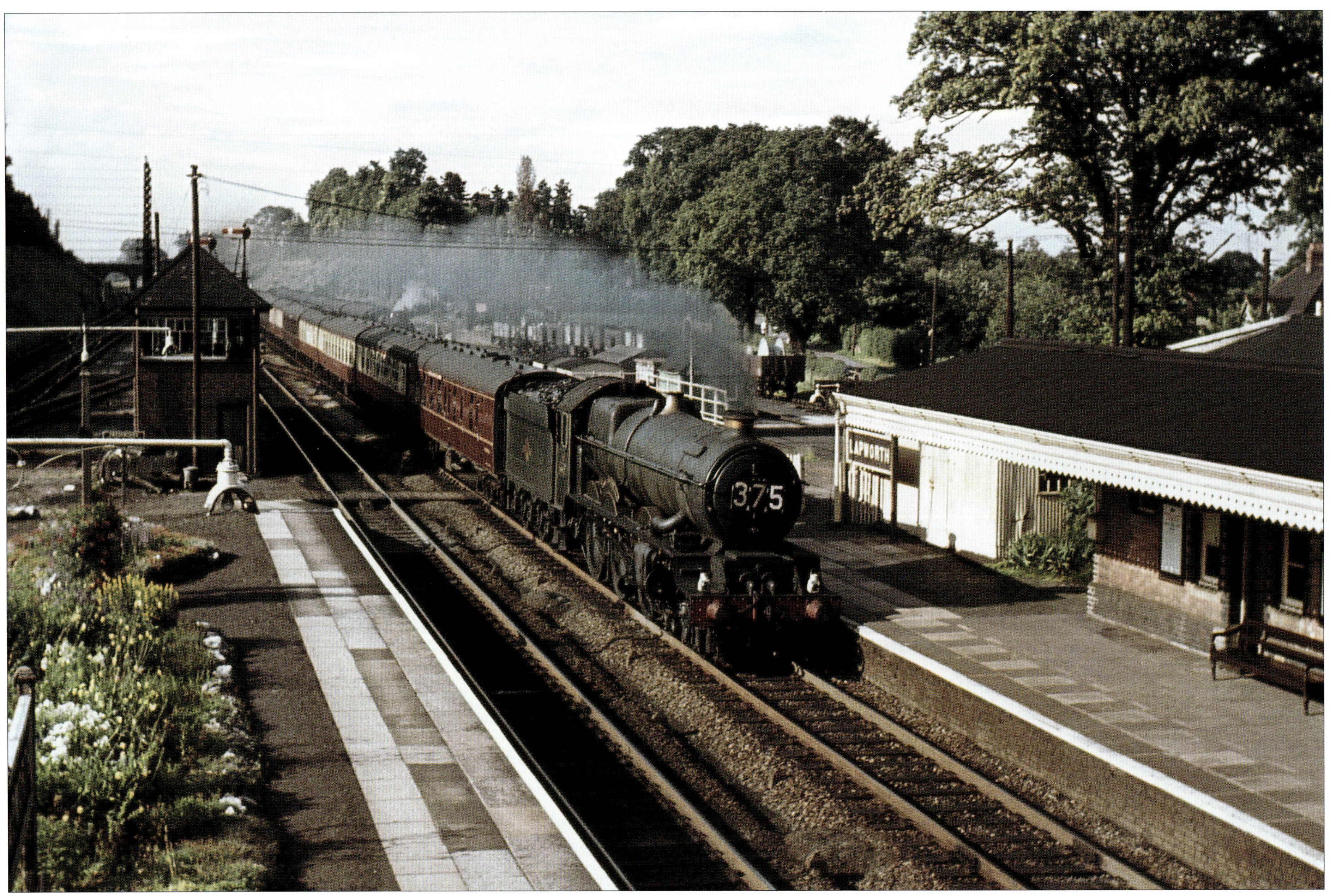

SLIDE 550 | At approximately 6.10pm on this fine Friday evening, the driver of Old Oak's **6012 King Edward VI** has shut off steam as it thunders through Lapworth Station on the 2.35pm Birkenhead to Paddington. Meanwhile, *5101* class 2-6-2T **4103** on an all-stations stopping service from Birmingham Snow Hill waits patiently in the up refuge siding for the giant to pass before resuming its journey to Leamington Spa General as empty stock. Lapworth Station was originally opened in 1854 as Kingswood; named after the village it serves, but its name was changed in May 1902 to avoid confusion with a station of the same name near Reigate in Surrey. Photograph taken from the station footbridge. *18/7/58 Leica IIIA 1/500th F4.5 (Agfacolor CT 18)*

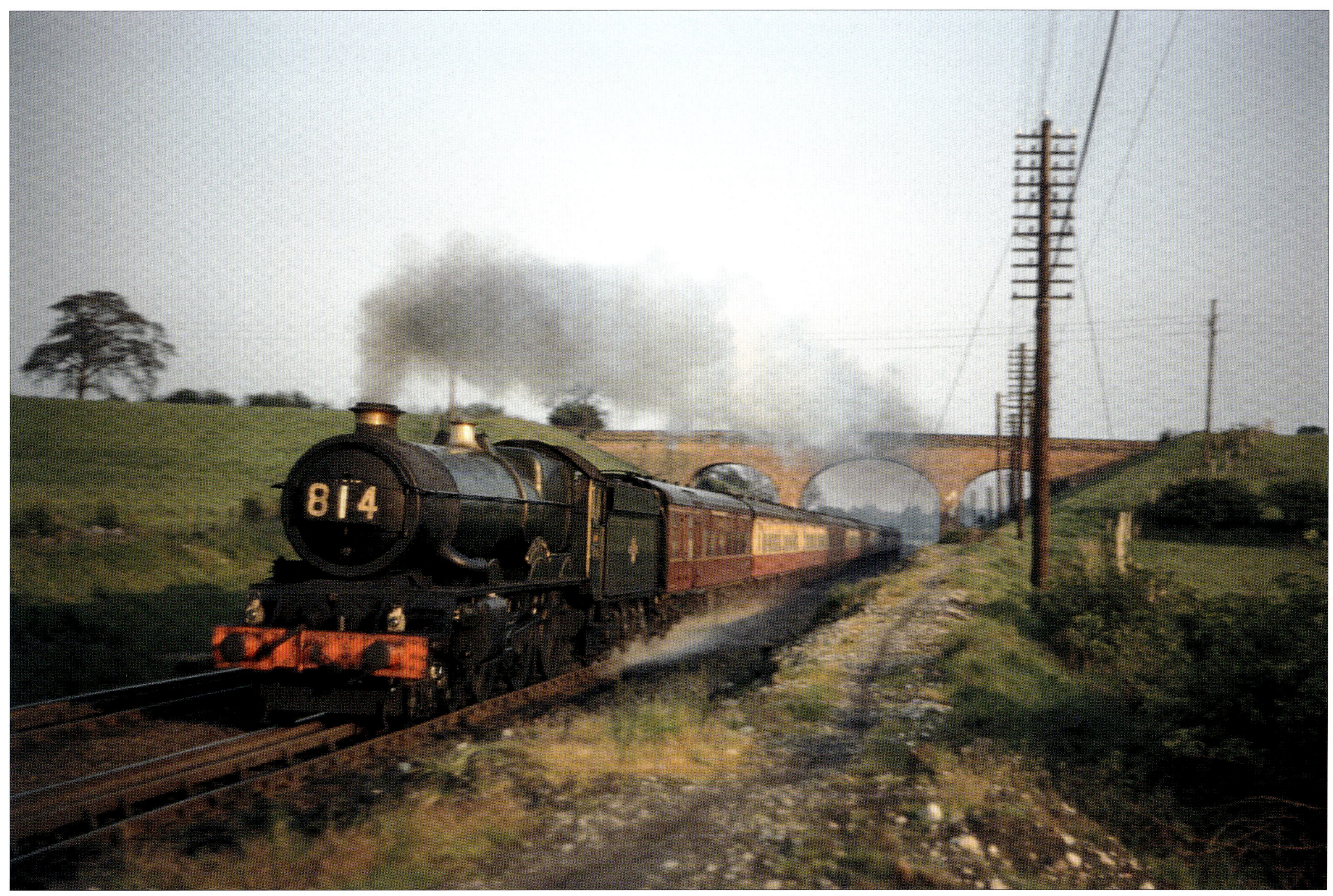

SLIDE 818 | **6017 King Edward IV** on the 5.10pm SX Paddington to Wolverhampton has just been reallocated from Laira to Stafford Road and is captured here in the fading daylight, just catching the final rays of the sun as it takes water at speed on Rowington troughs between Hatton and Lapworth. The *Finwood Farm* bridge in the background of this shot (that carried the Rowington to Lowsonford footpath) was demolished in the late 1980s as a part of the *M40* motorway construction plan, linking Oxford and Birmingham. Its demolition necessitated the construction of a new bridge, which now carries a re-routed *Finwood Road* over both the *M40* and the main line. Ironically, a short section of this new road partly occupies the track bed of the short-lived Rowington to Henley-in-Arden branch line. *6/5/59 Leica IIIA (Kodachrome)*

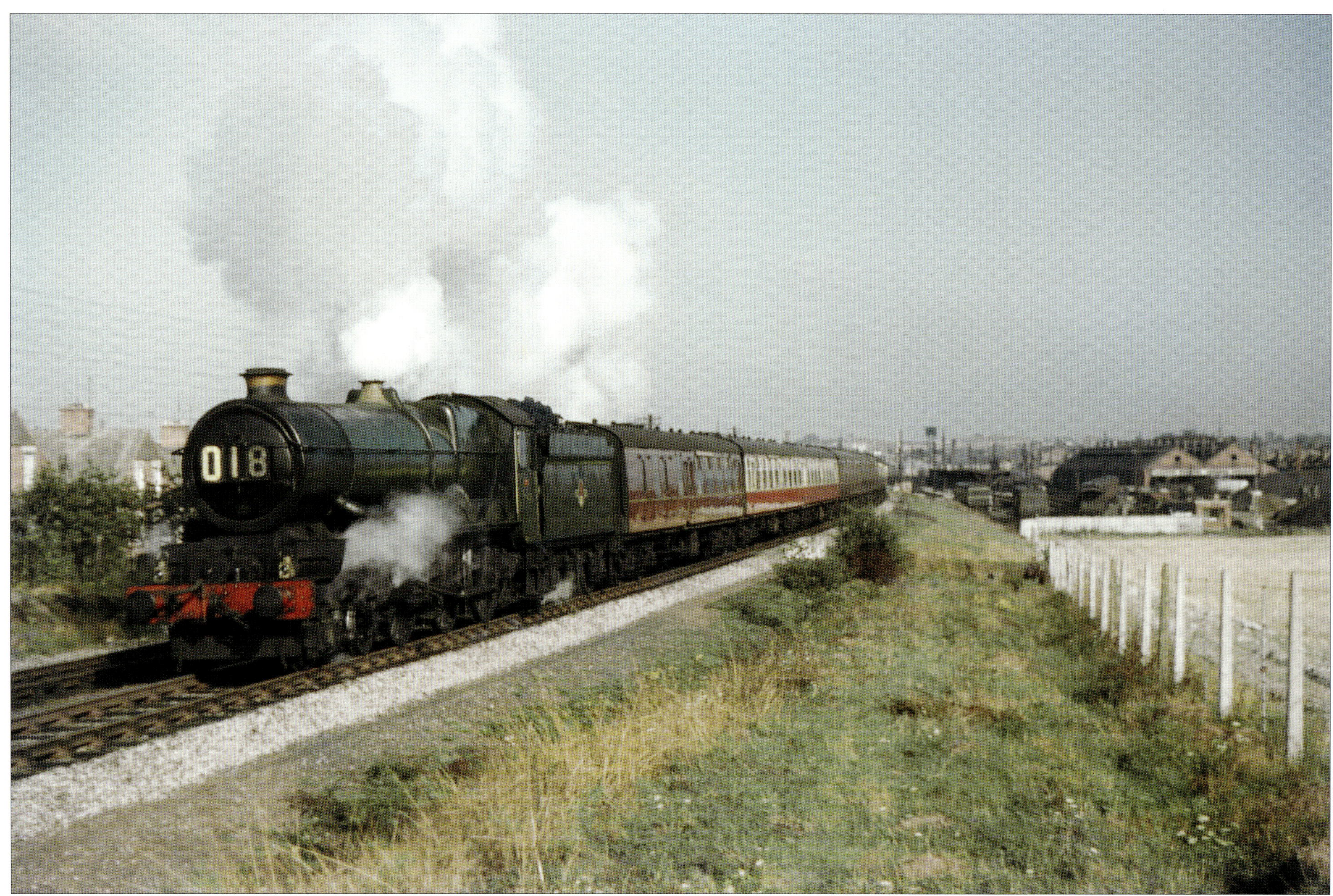

SLIDE 929 | Stafford Road's **6022 King Edward III** on the 7.30am Shrewsbury to Paddington accelerates away from its last stop at Leamington Spa General, passing the ex-*GWR* locomotive shed (on the far right) as it heads south towards Whitnash. The dark shape just visible behind the roof apices is the 45,000 gallon water tank situated on top of the brick-built coaling stage, which is unfortunately totally obscured in this image. The shed and supporting infrastructure here dated from 1905 and occupied the almost wedge-shaped expanse of ground separating the ex-*GWR* Leamington to Banbury main line from the ex-*LNWR/LMS* Leamington to Rugby branch line, which curved away in an easterly direction at this point after both running parallel at the location we see pictured in *slide 1180* on page 18. The shed at Leamington officially closed on June 12th 1965. *5/9/59 (Ilford 'D')*

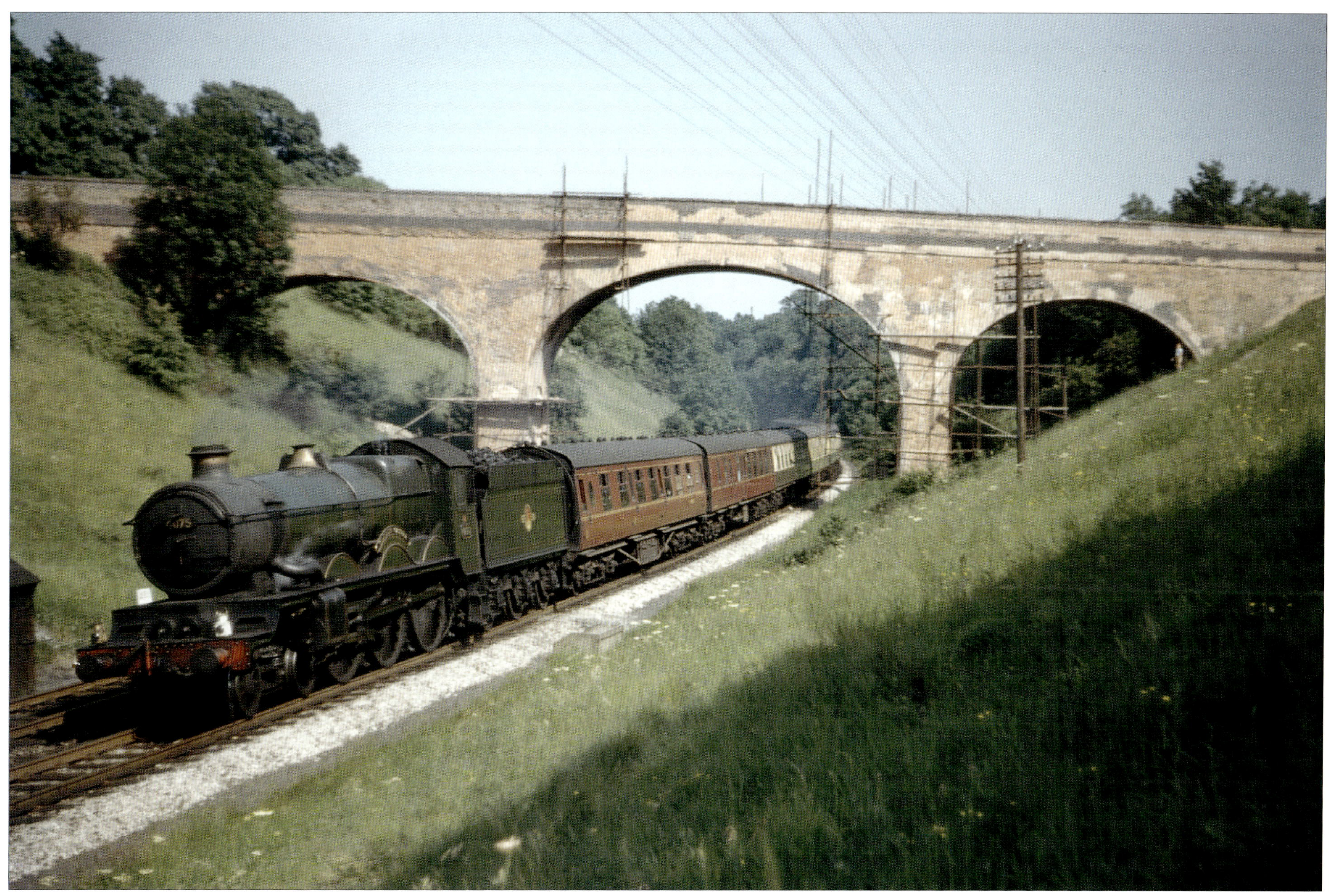

SLIDE 1067 | The *Bull Ring Farm* access bridge, approximately six hundred yards north-west of Harbury Tunnel appears to be undergoing repairs to its brickwork as Old Oak Common's **4075 Cardiff Castle** runs out of the cutting with an unidentified down Saturday morning express. One of the deepest cuttings in the country when it was originally constructed, the civil engineering at this location has continually given cause for concern, with wet winters regularly causing slippage to the earthworks; one of the most disruptive in recent times occurring in January 2015, when the movement of over 300,000 tons of earth and stone caused a six-week closure of the main line *(see also slide 167 on page 107).* 4/6/60 *(Kodachrome)*

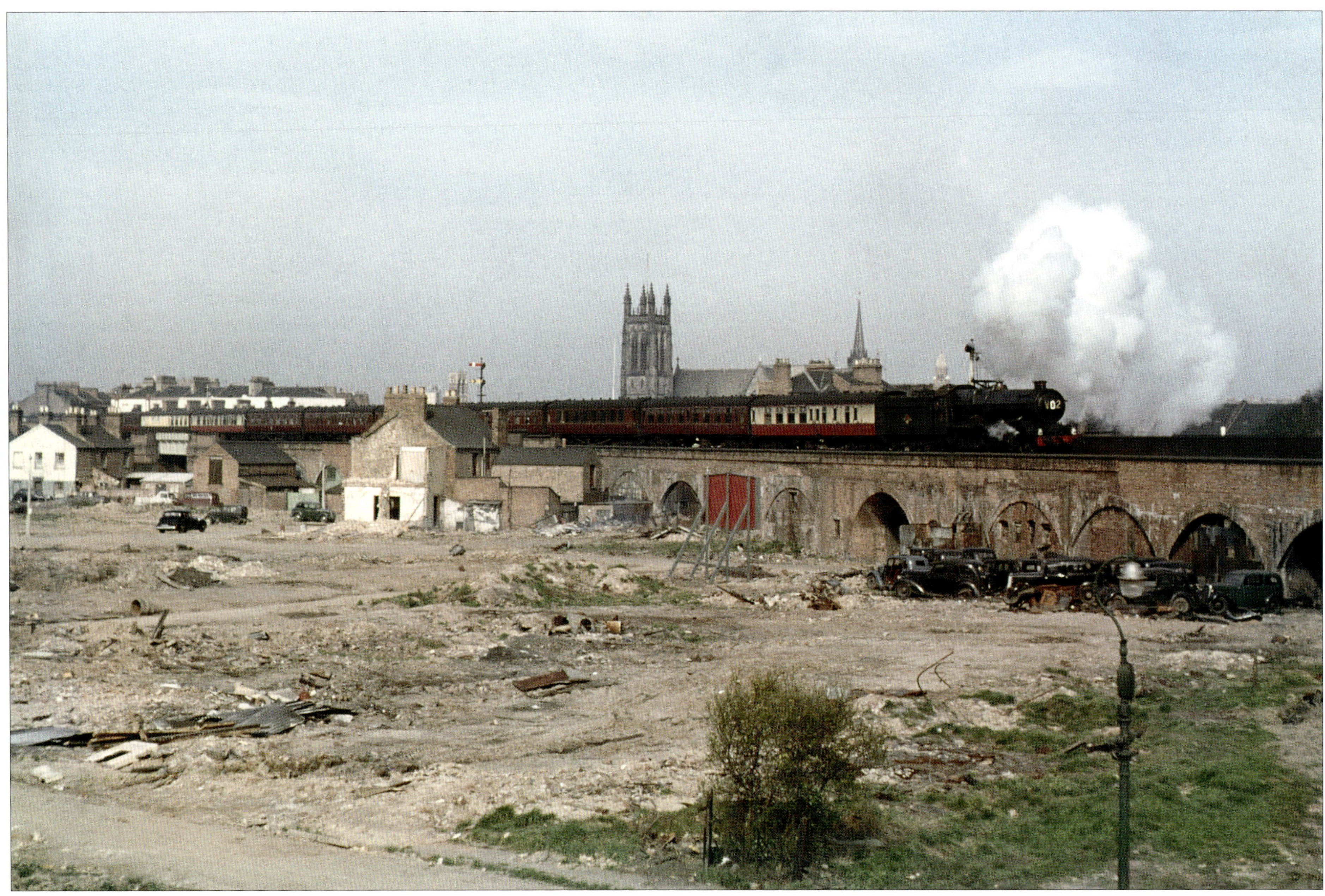

SLIDE 1180 | **6005 King George II** accelerates the 6.30am Birkenhead to Paddington, south from Leamington Spa over one of the two massive brick viaducts: the other carrying the ex-*LNWR/LMS* line to Rugby. The train is about to pass Leamington Spa South Junction Signal Box. There is much detail in this image, painting a picture of a skyline in a state of flux. In the background we see the ever-present tower and spire of the *All Saints' Parish Church* and in the foreground, what was once residential terracing recently levelled for the building of the *Althorpe Industrial Estate*. The solitary building that the train is passing behind that seems to be making a defiant last stand, is the soon-to-be demolished *White Lion* public house which stayed open for business for many months after this image was captured. Photograph taken from the canal footbridge close to the eastern corner of the *Flavel Eagle Foundry*. *11/3/61 (Perutz)*

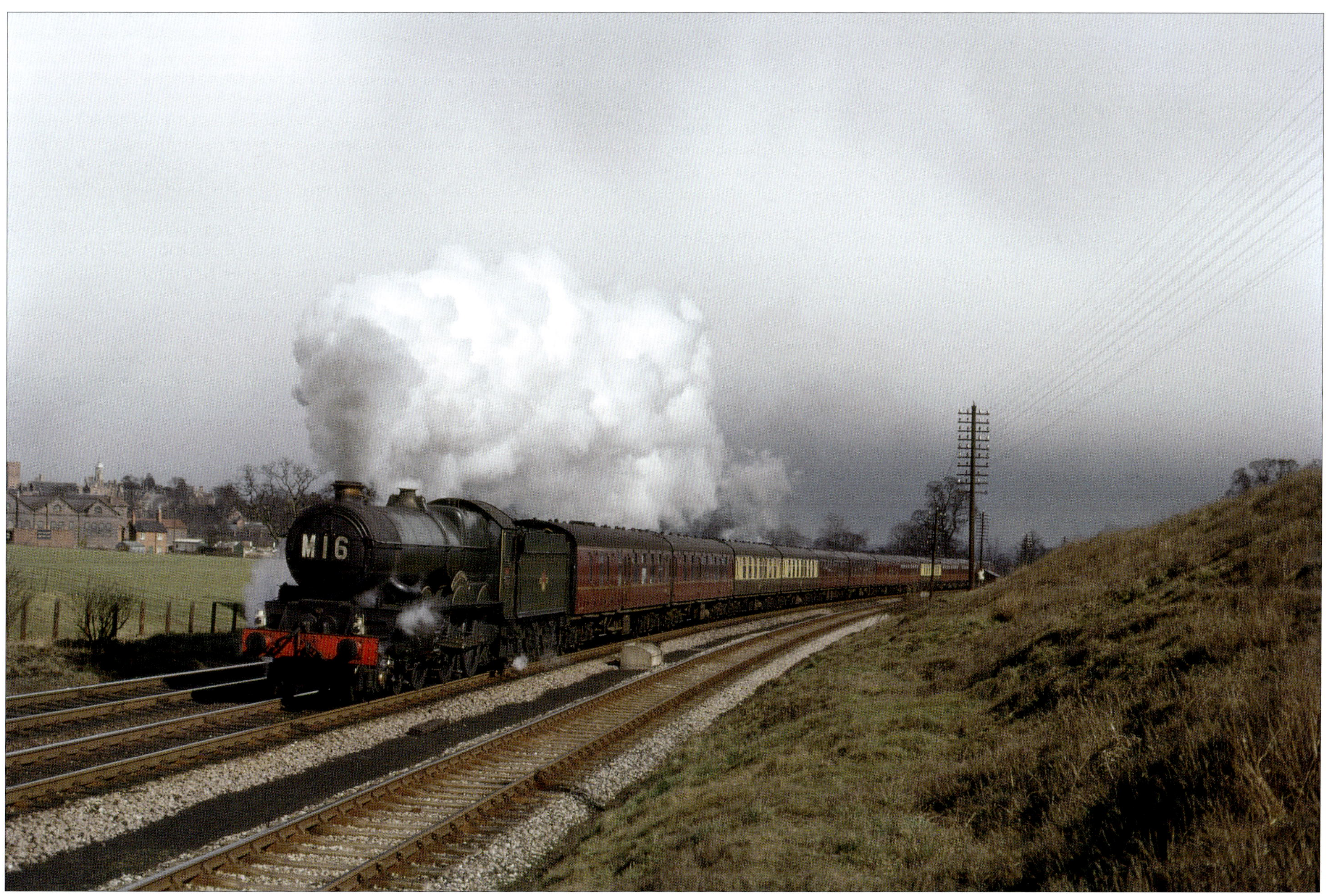

SLIDE 1207 | Minus its shed allocation plate, but otherwise looking a true thoroughbred, Stafford Road's **6027 King Richard I** enters the great cutting on Hatton Bank, north-west of Warwick with the 1.10pm Paddington to Birkenhead. On the left horizon we see the *Grand Union Canal* workshop buildings, overlooked by the bell tower of *Hatton Central Hospital*. The route availability for the *Kings* had substantially increased by this time, which had involved fundamental modifications to key structures north of Wolverhampton; primarily the platform clearances at Codsall Station, plus the lifting of weight restrictions on Shifnal Viaduct after a process of rebuilding; both of these actioned during the 1950s. As a result, it is possible that *6027* worked through to Shrewsbury, but still may have been taken off at Wolverhampton (Low Level), as would always have been the case historically. *31/3/62 (Kodachrome)*

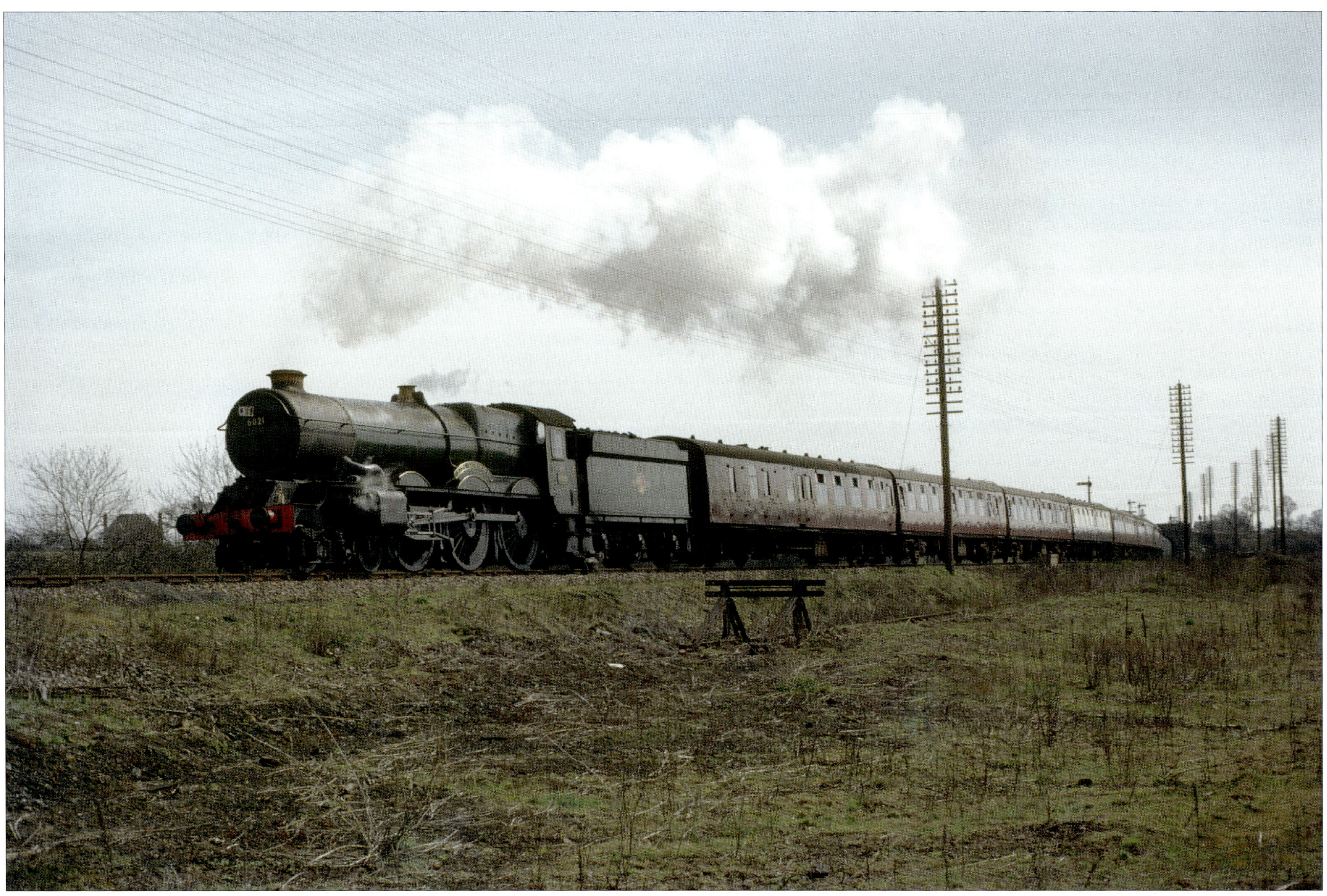

SLIDE 1316 | Old Oak Common's **6021 King Richard II** has topped Hatton Bank and leans into the north-westerly curve between the station and Hatton North Junction with the 9.10am Paddington to Wolverhampton. Although not immediately obvious from this photograph, *6021* is the final custodian of the unique slotted bogie assembly seen on the front cover image of **6005** captured almost three years previously. The expanse of rough ground in the foreground of this image was originally one of the *GWR* tip sidings and the site of Hatton Middle Signal Box, rendered obsolete in 1936 by the building of a new box (the second incarnation of Hatton's South Box) on the station's island platform, hidden in this image by the end of the train and the minor road bridge in the distance. The branch line to Stratford-upon-Avon is just out of view, curving off to the right. *?/4/62 (Kodachrome)*

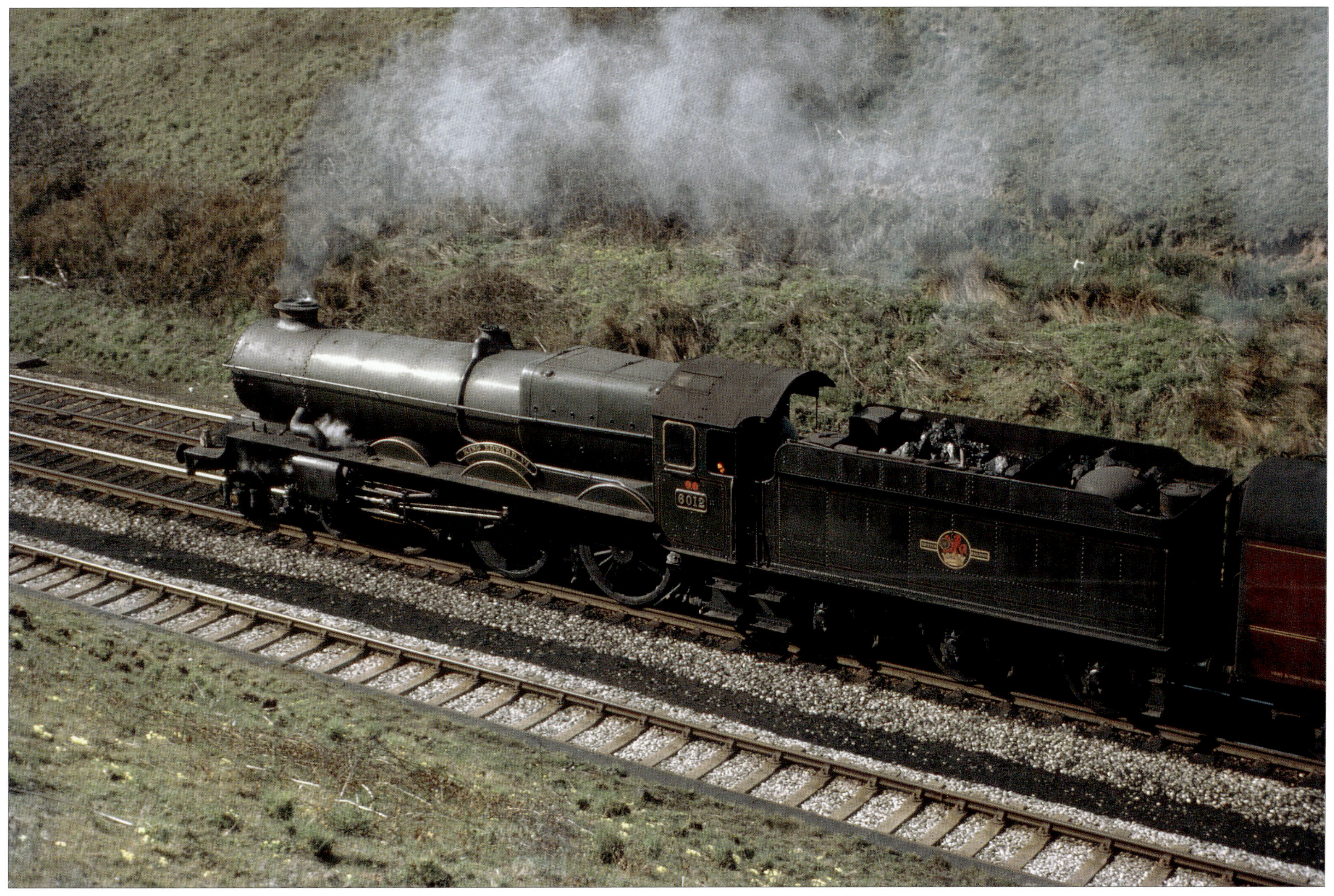

SLIDE 1323 | Photographed from the brow of the great cutting at Hatton, **6012 King Edward VI** is caught heading confidently up the bank towards the down distant signal with just a trace of steam leaking from its inside cylinders. The crew will be fully occupied at this point in the climb and indeed, the barely-visible Fireman appears to be putting his back into launching another shovel-full of coal into his fire. Built at Swindon in April 1928, *6012* spent almost all its *BR* days alternating between Laira and Old Oak Common before moving to Stafford Road in March 1962, from where it was withdrawn in September 1962 and sold as scrap to *Cox & Danks* of Langley Green, Oldbury almost exactly a year later. Ironically, *Cox & Danks* only disposed of a dozen steam locomotives in total: *Castle* class **5045 Earl of Dudley** and the rest, ex-Stafford Road *Kings*. *?/4/62 (Kodachrome)*

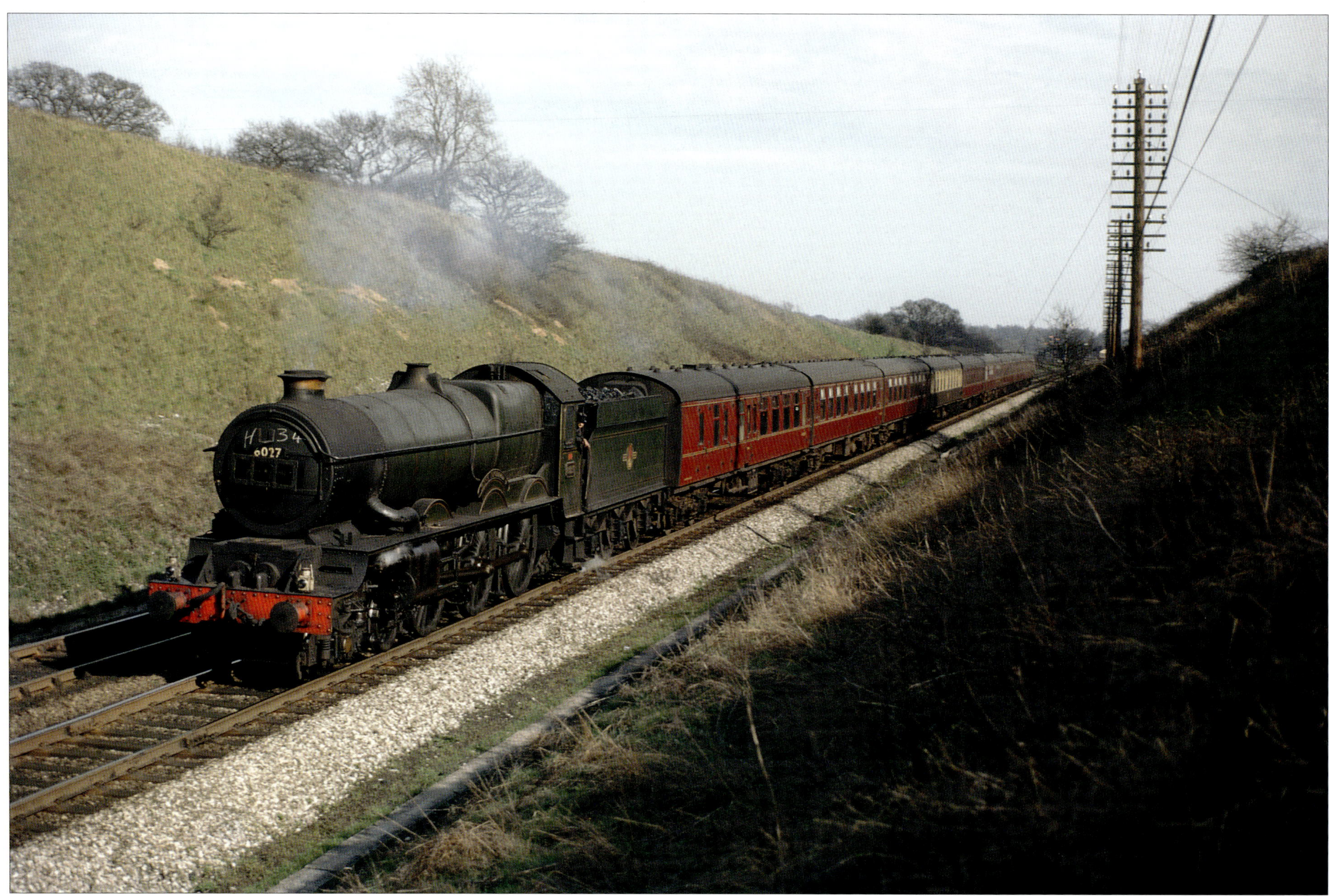

SLIDE 1324 | Minus its Stafford Road shed allocation plate, **6027 King Richard I** is approaching the Shrewley Common road bridge spanning the cutting between Hatton North Junction and the water troughs at Rowington on an unidentified Paddington to Wolverhampton working (the Hatton North Signal Box and associated signalling array is just visible in the distance). Although the locomotive is equipped with a frame to carry the reporting numbers, the smokebox has been chalked graffiti-style with it instead: an annoying trend towards the end of steam on the *Western Region*. Note in this photograph, the clear evidence that *6027* has been fitted with replacement front end half-frames: the large washer-like support discs riveted to the inside face of the protruding frame-ends to strengthen the lifting eyelets. Fourteen members of the class were treated to this preventative modification during overhaul at intervals throughout the 1950s *(see also slide 1387 on page 30)*. *?/4/62 (Kodachrome)*

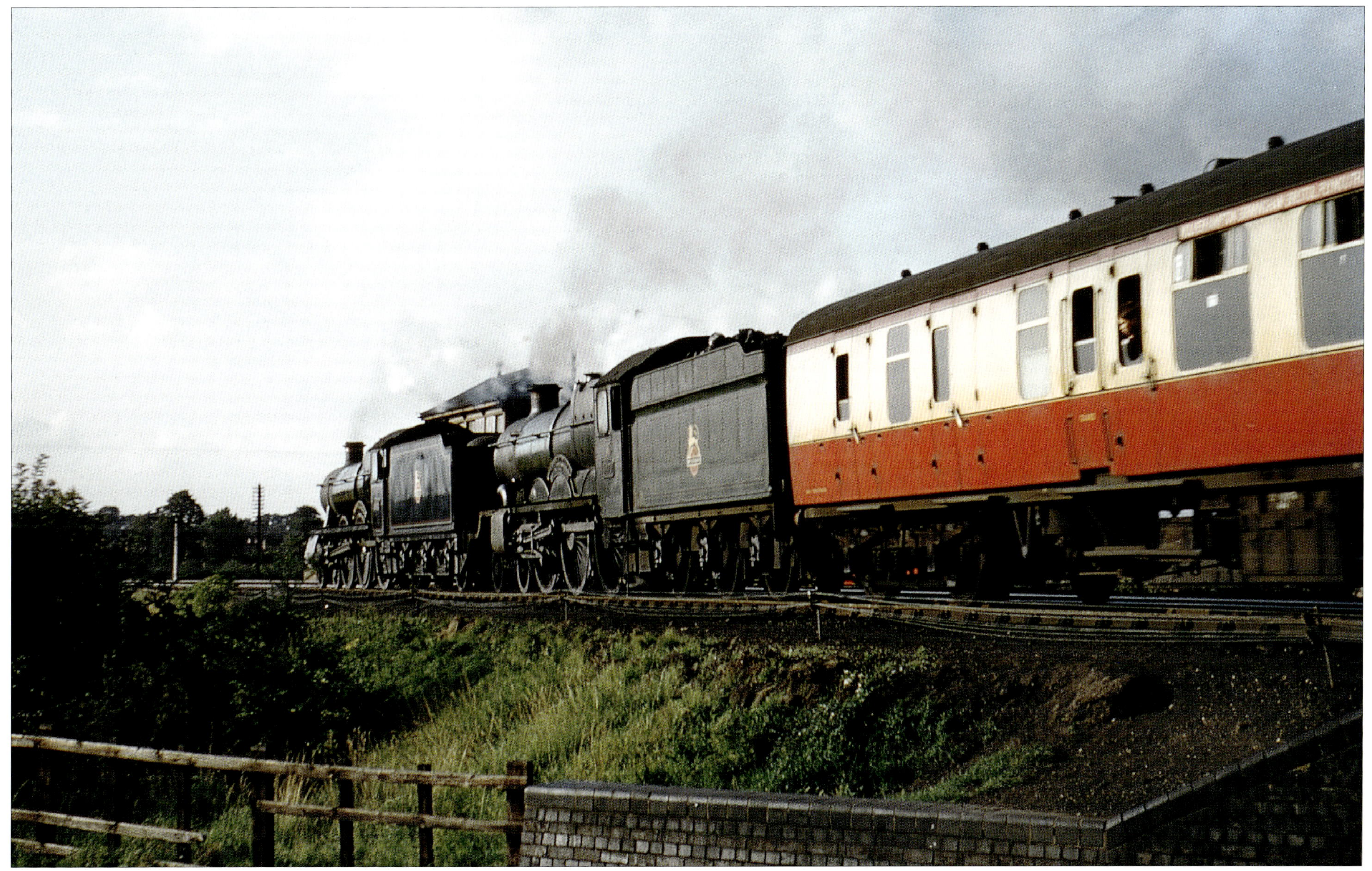

SLIDE 127 | Looking north from the banks of the *Stratford-upon-Avon Canal*, we see **4988 Bulwell Hall** assisting *Castle* class **5070 Sir Daniel Gooch** on the Penzance to Wolverhampton *Cornishman* service. The train is about to pass the Stratford-on-Avon East Signal Box on its climb up the bank through Bishopton to the village of Wilmcote, just over three miles away. *4988* was based at Tyseley between October 1955 and May 1958 and during this period was regularly observed at Stratford, particularly on piloting duties, assisting the more heavily loaded north-bound Summer passenger expresses. Ironically, both of these locomotives met their final fate during 1964: *4988* being broken up at Swindon where it had been built in 1931 and *5070* by *Bird's* of Risca, Newport. *17/8/56 Periflex 1/125th F5 (Kodachrome)*

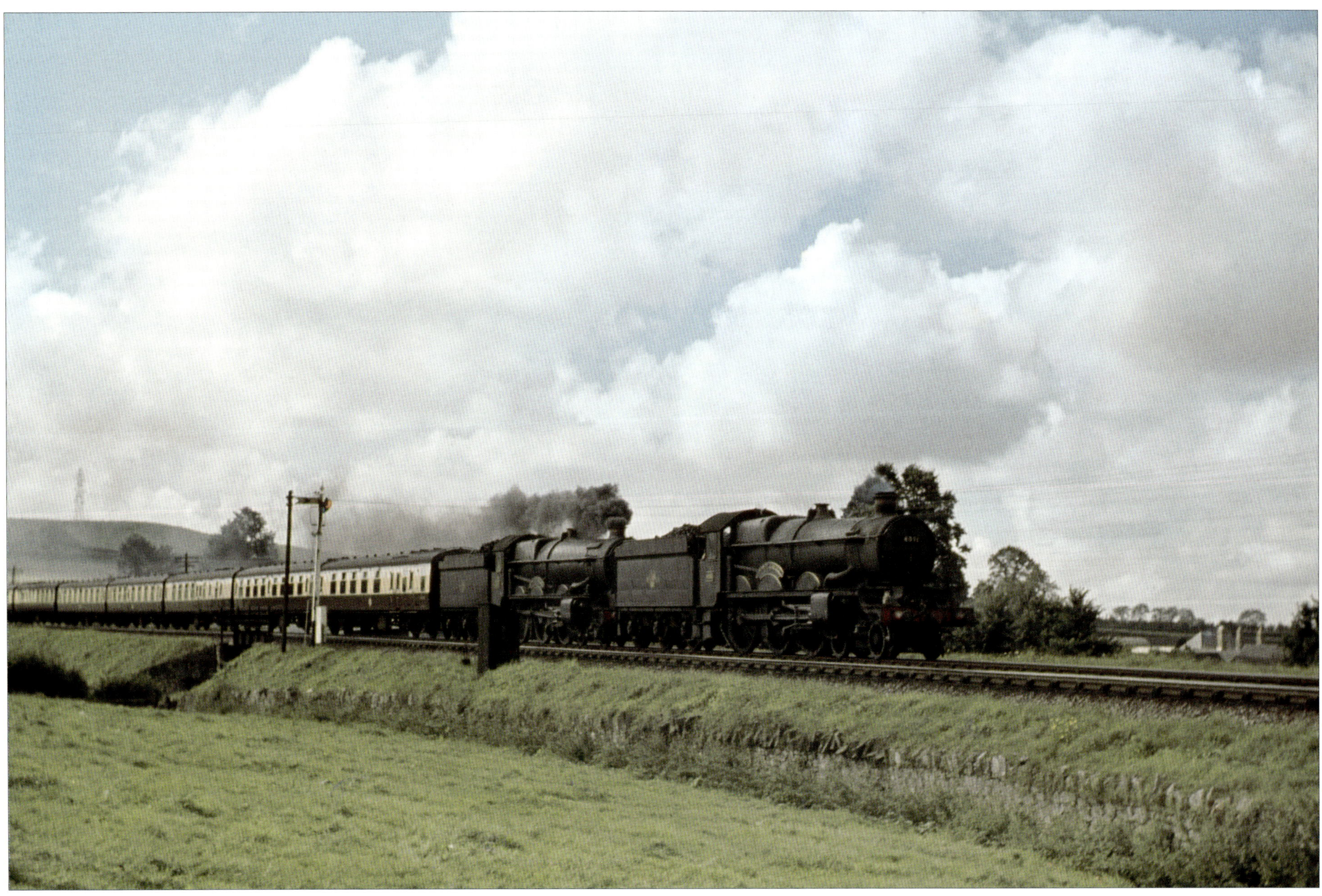

SLIDE 644 | Looking almost due-west towards Dainton hamlet, Teignbridge at around 1.45pm, Old Oak Common shedmates **4091 Dudley Castle** and **6022 King Edward III** are looking understandably grubby after a busy high-mileage Summer as they head down the bank towards Stoneycombe on the up *Cornish Riviera*, their train having just cleared Dainton summit. Just four months after this photograph was taken, *4091* was to become one of the first 'new build' *Castles* to be withdrawn for scrapping. 1959 proved not to be such a catastrophic year for *6022*, however. After spending almost four years at Old Oak Common, it was transferred to Stafford Road, Wolverhampton where it gave a good account of itself until withdrawal in September 1962. *3/9/58 Leica IIIA 1/500th F4 (Agfacolor CT 18)*

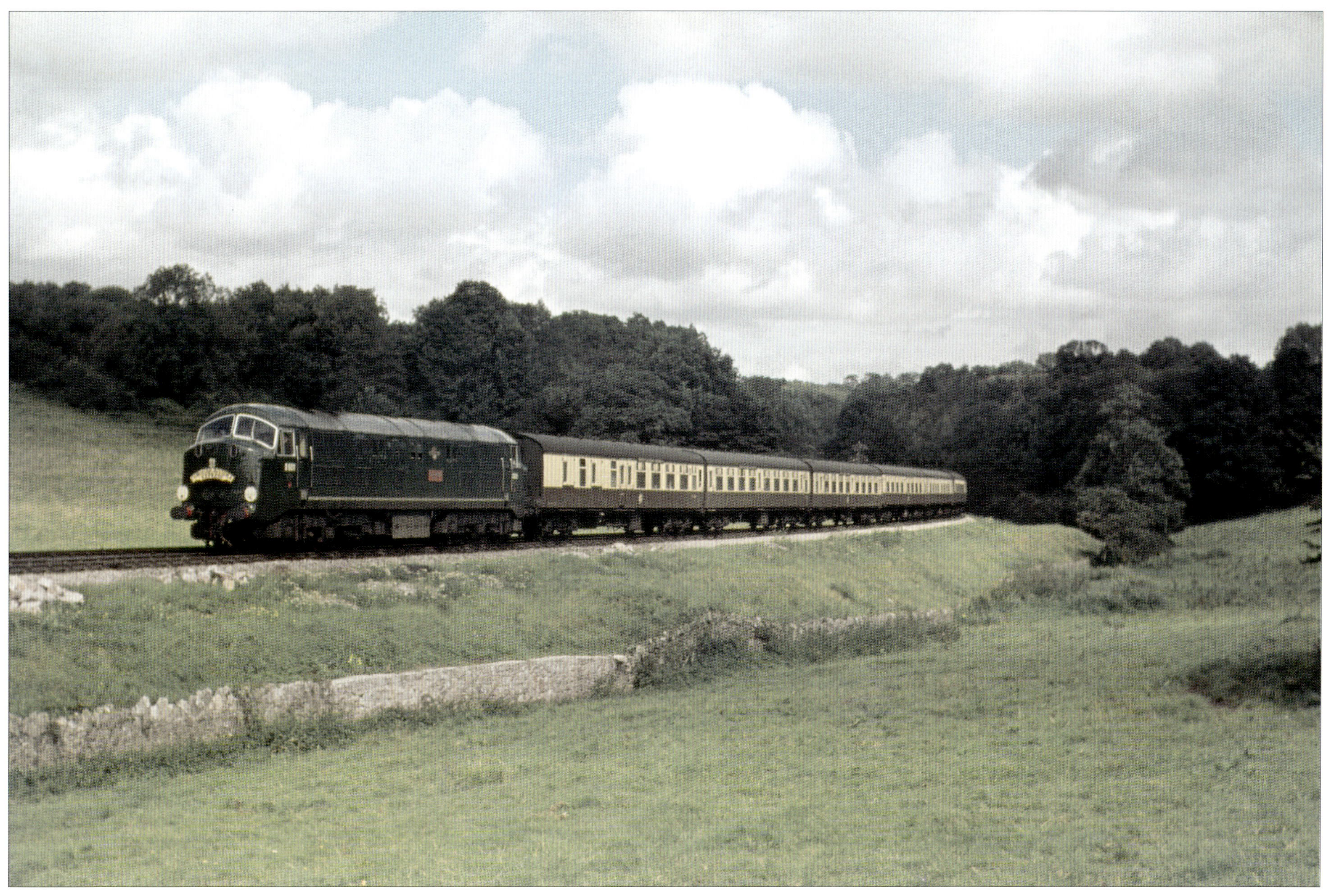

SLIDE 645 | Shortly after the previous image is captured, the distinctive growl of Laira's *D20/2 Warship* class **D601 Ark Royal** is heard rumbling up the tree-lined corridor over a minute before it comes into view, crawling unaided up the bank on the down working of the same service. It is almost certain that Tom Williams would have hesitated for a moment before choosing to release the shutter on this one, but it's important that he did as these two images together paint an accurate, if poignant picture of the state of express passenger services during what was to be a decade of fundamental change. Despite their regular deployment on such prestigious services as the *Riviera*, *Torbay Express* and *Mayflower*, this initial batch of five locomotives proved embarrassingly unreliable, to the consternation of *WR* top brass. *3/9/58 Leica IIIA 1/500th F4.5 (Agfacolor CT 18)*

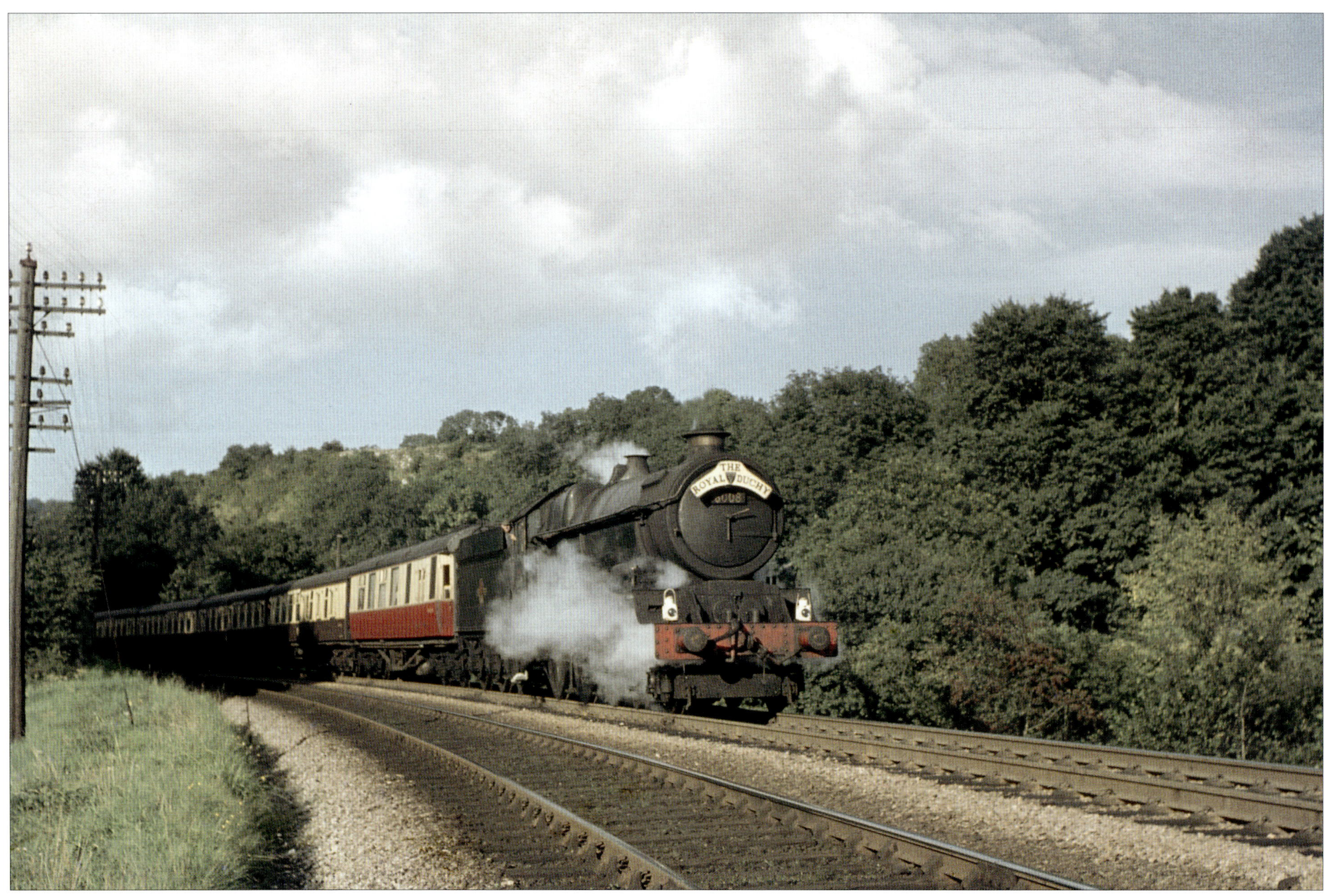

SLIDE 650 | Looking a little laboured in this shot, Laira-based **6008 King James II** on the 1.30pm Paddington to Penzance *Royal Duchy* service is caught here in the classic climbing pose, crawling out of the shadows and straight into the sun on its final approach to the north-easterly portal of Dainton Tunnel. The *King* will be taken off at the next stop at Plymouth North Road; most likely being replaced by a *Hall* or *Manor* class locomotive to haul the train the final 79½ miles westwards to Penzance. Dainton Tunnel at its eastern end was rarely chosen by photographers as a suitable location, due mainly to the often challenging lighting conditions: heavy shadows, compounded by sunlight regularly shining directly into the camera lens *(see slide 107 on page 35). 3/9/58 Leica IIIA 1/500th F4.5 (Agfacolor CT 18)*

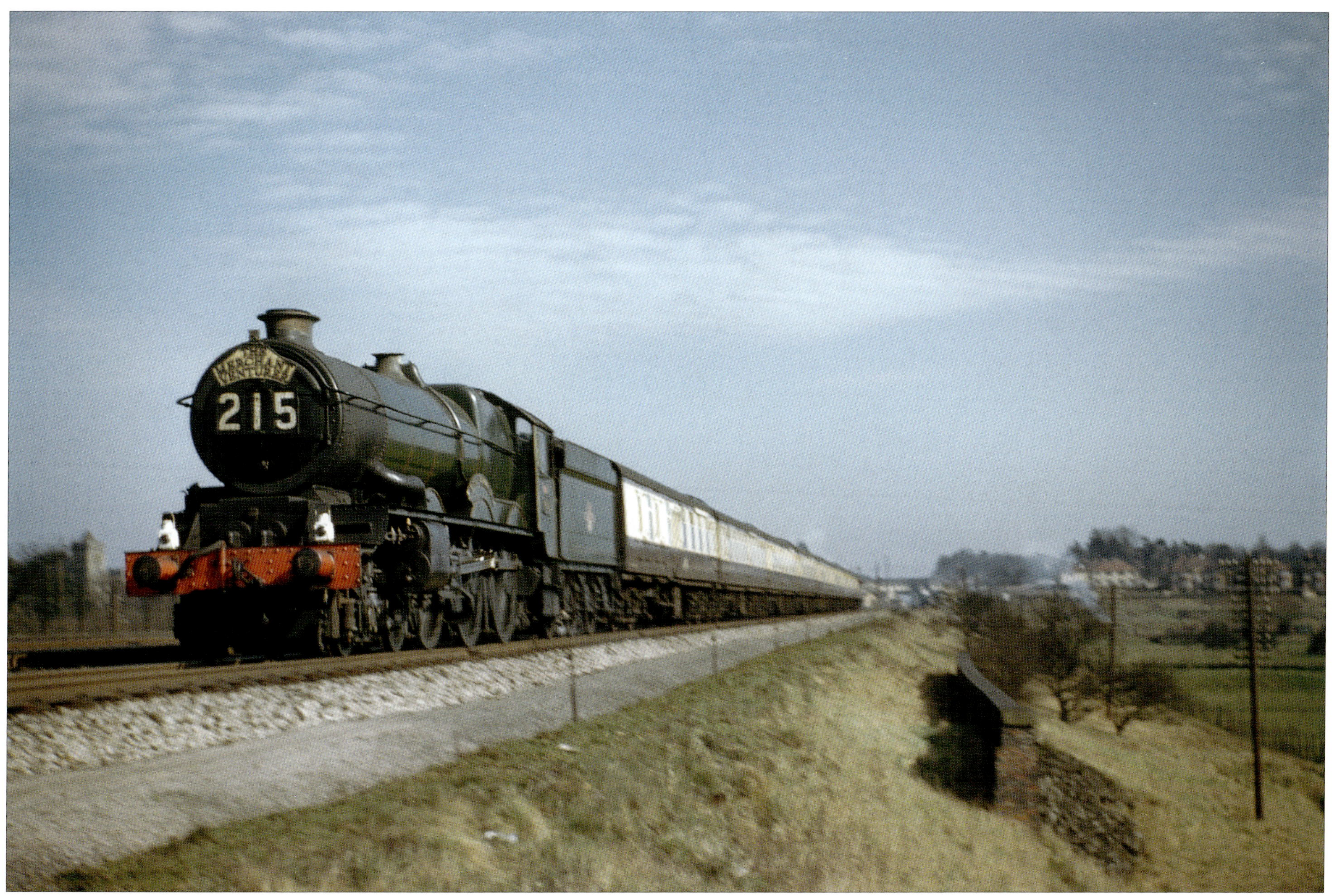

SLIDE 749 | Although normally a *Castle* turn, on this glorious Saturday morning the men at Old Oak Common have turned out **6019 King Henry V** for the 11.15am Paddington to Weston-super-Mare *Merchant Venturer* and it is caught here between Twyford and Sonning. Stopping only at Bath Spa and Bristol Temple Meads, the *King* will be changed for a more humble 4-6-0 for the last few miles to its destination. This service proved to be very popular, with the restaurant car staff being kept constantly busy serving luncheons throughout the journey: the majority of customers being businessmen. One could argue that these were the successors to the merchants of earlier times whose journeys between London and Bristol no doubt took considerably longer! Note the tower of *St Mary's Church*, Twyford, just visible on the left horizon. *28/2/59 Leica IIIA 1/200th F2.5 (Kodachrome)*

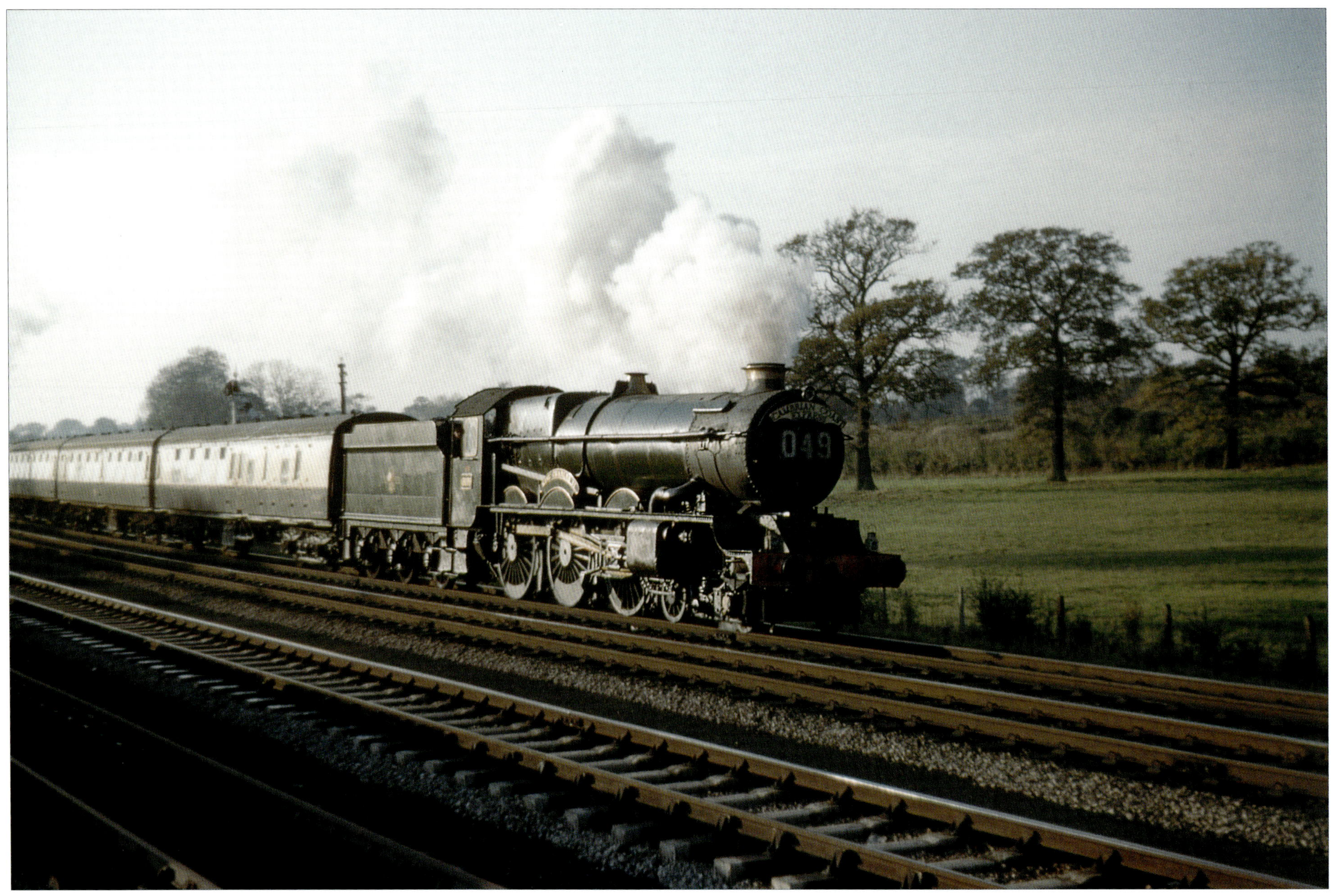

SLIDE 959 | With the low October sun creating a few technical challenges for the photographer, **6009 King Charles II** is captured hauling the up *Cambrian Coast Express* over the summit of Hatton Bank. A life-long Old Oak Common locomotive, *6009* had been historically deployed on the crack passenger services heading west out of the capital, until the gradual dieselisation of this route in the late 1950s created a natural displacement effect, resulting in *6009* turning up on north-bound services far more frequently. Of course, this displacement ultimately signified the beginning of the end for the whole *King* class and regardless of the impeccable work that these locomotives continued to put in during their twilight years, the writing was already on the wall. *6009* was withdrawn in September 1962 with a recorded service mileage of 1,932,102. Unfortunately, Tom did not record the exact date of this image, though we believe it to be a weekday afternoon. *?/10/59 (Kodachrome)*

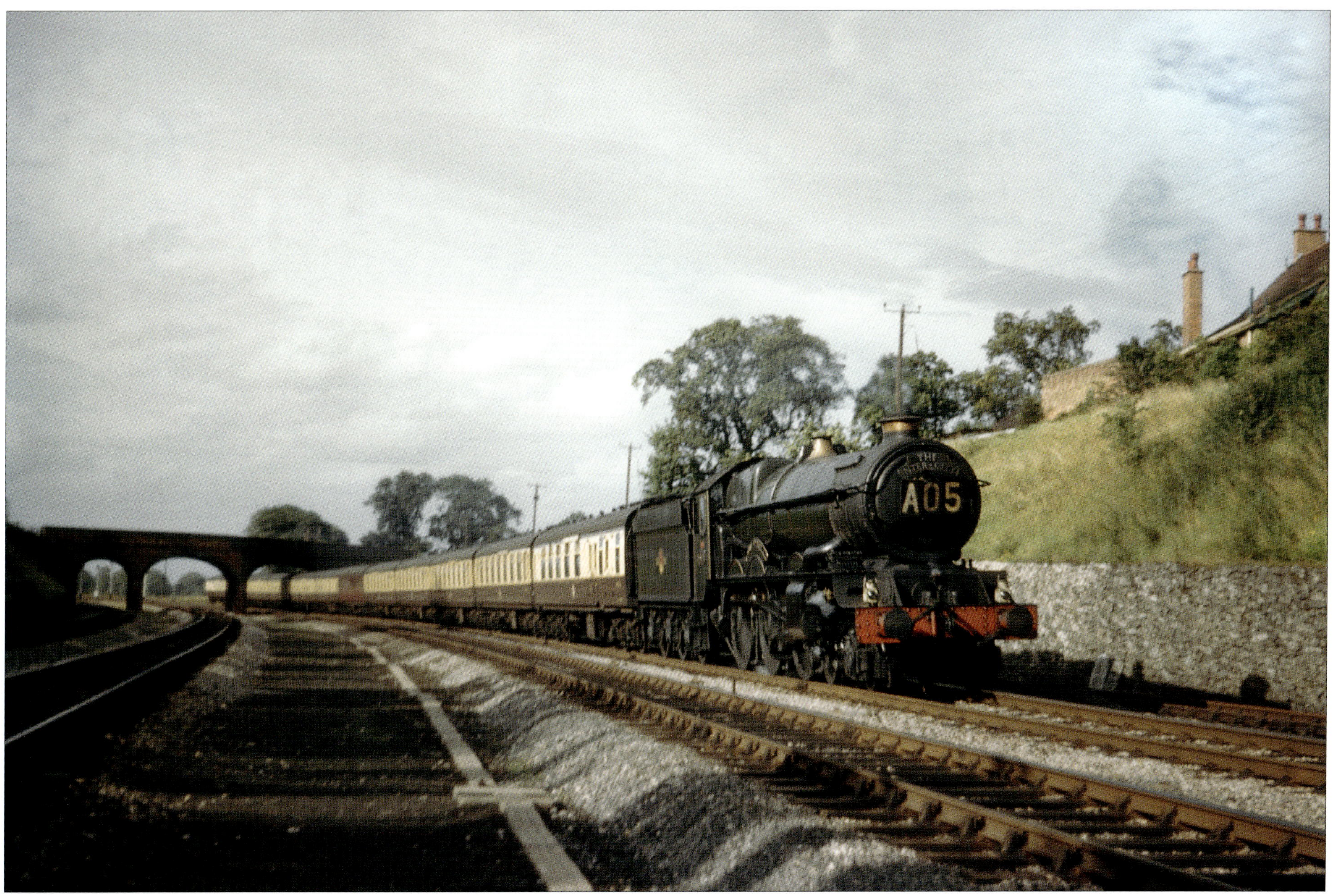

SLIDE 1112 | Old Oak Common's **6024 King Edward I** is captured here threading the *Rising Road* overbridge, just north of Lapworth Station with the up *Inter City* service on a day when strengthening coaches appear to have been provided to increase capacity. As in the case of classmate **6009 King Charles II**, *6024* wasn't a regularly observed performer on the 'Birmingham' line until comparatively late in its service life; initially working out of Newton Abbot and Laira before moving to Old Oak Common in late 1954. In October 1961, it found itself one of the 'replacement' locomotives following the migration of Cardiff Canton's *Britannias* to the *LMR*. At the same time, classmate **6010 King Charles I** was to take the same path, along with a handful of *Castle* and *Hall* class locomotives. *21/8/60 (Kodachrome)*

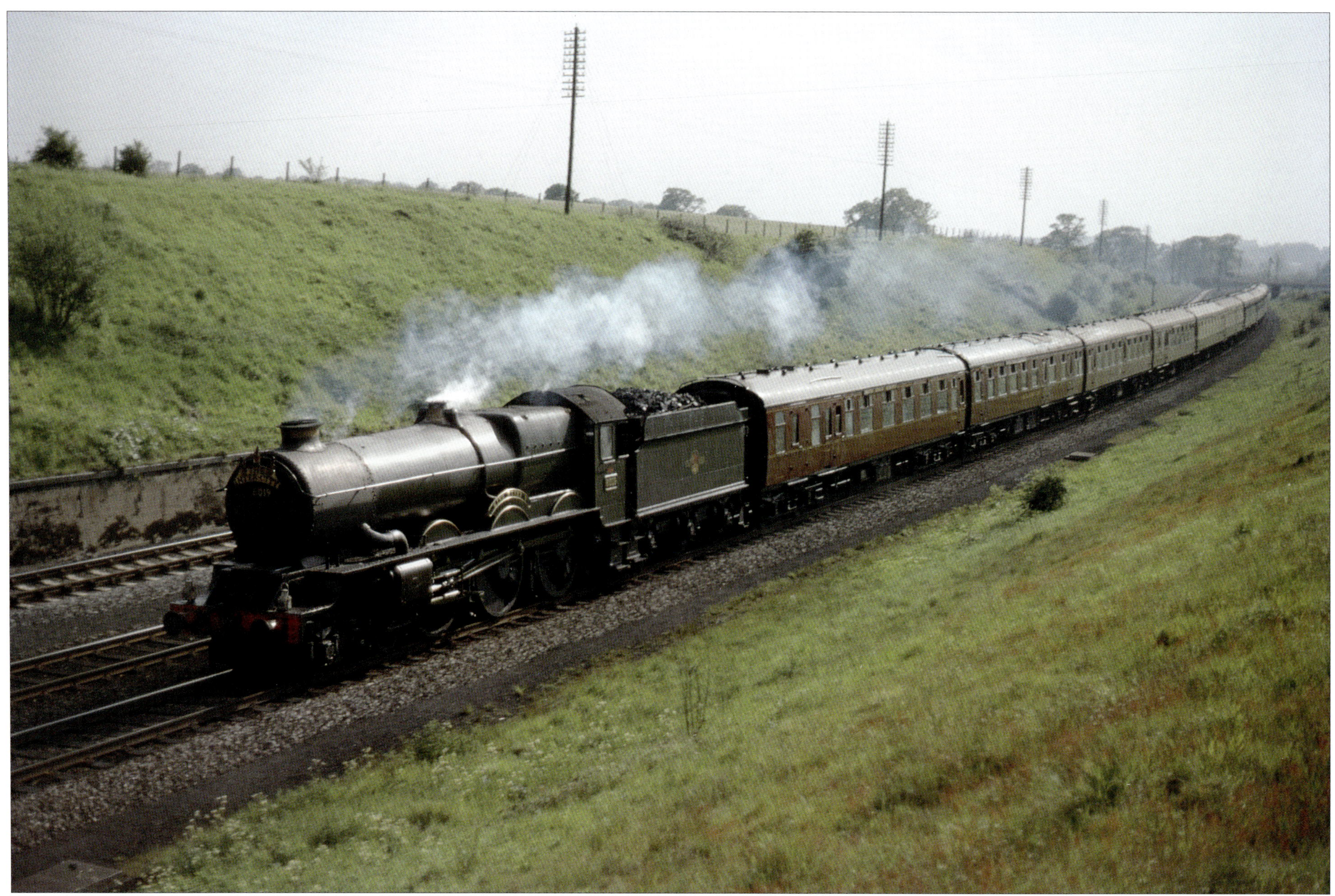

SLIDE 1387 | With the late afternoon sun creating a few potential challenges for the photographer, Old Oak's **6019 King Henry V** cruises down Hatton Bank with the up *Inter City*. This locomotive was unique in so far as it was the only *King* to have its inside valve covers extended, without actually receiving new front end half-frames. The reason for this is unclear, but was most likely the result of an extensive examination of the locomotive's frames (during overhaul), which had historically revealed their propensity to fracture, potentially resulting in a failure whilst running at speed. Indeed, cracks had begun to manifest themselves in the frames of many other class members; presumably a consequence of the many years of high mileage and heavy loadings. We must assume, however, that *6019's* frames were found to be in good shape. Note that in this image the later, more elaborate style of cast headboard is being displayed, in contrast to the earlier more Spartan design seen in *slide 1112* on the previous page. *31/5/62 (Kodachrome)*

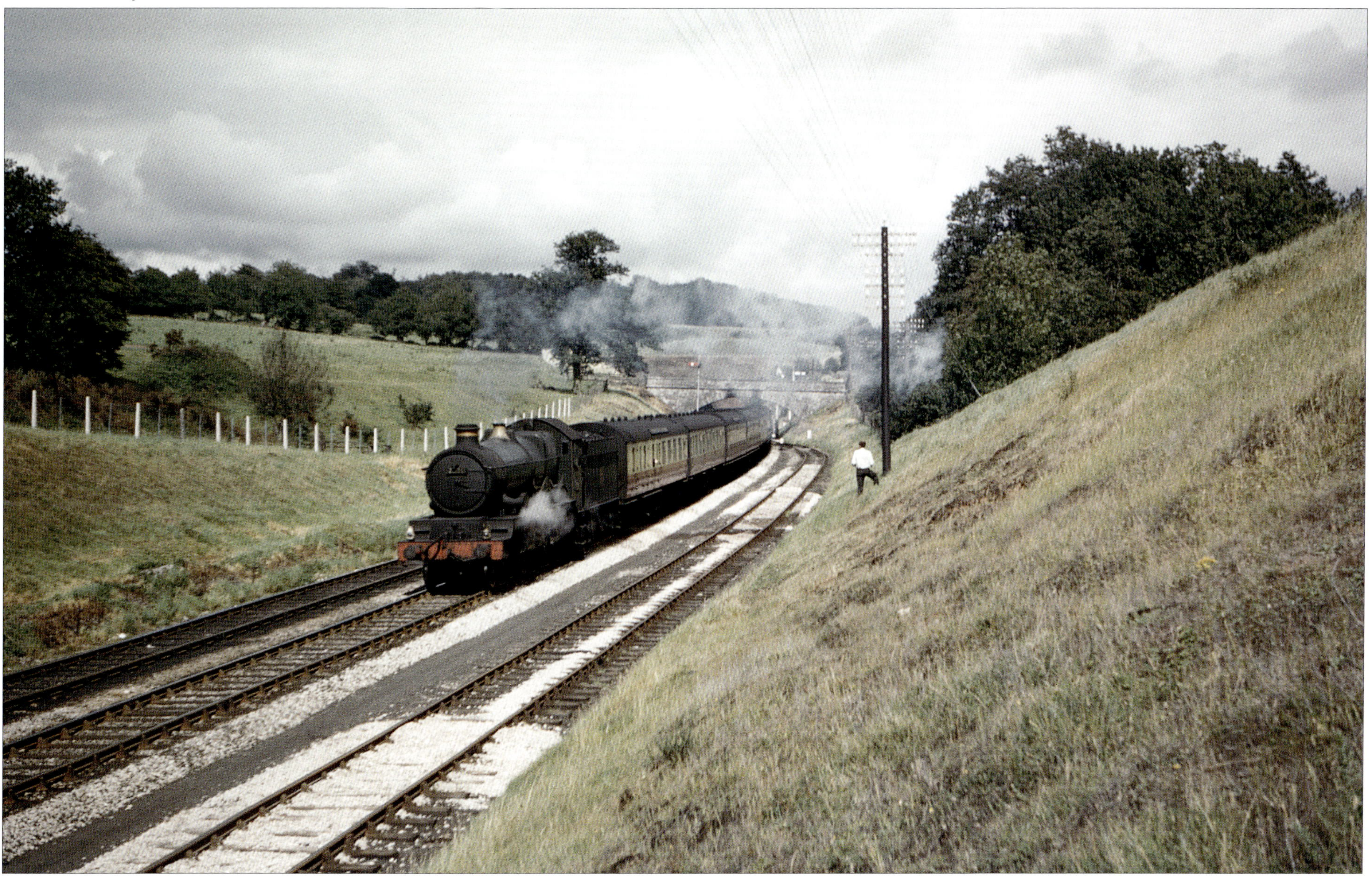

SLIDE 74 | Newton Abbot's *Castle* class **7000 Viscount Portal** has just left the western portal of Brunel's Whiteball Tunnel on the Somerset-Devon border and is beginning the twenty-mile descent to Exeter on a Kingswear express. This 1,000 yard long tunnel opened in 1844, allowing traffic to pass beneath the white sandstone of the *Blackdown Hills* between Exeter and Taunton. The tunnel's generous bore-width (originally built to accommodate broad-gauge traffic) has always been lauded by successive generations of engineers who have continually had to conduct repairs, generally associated with the tunnel's vintage and chemical erosion accelerated by over a century of acidic locomotive exhaust residues attacking its lining. In this image, the tunnel portal is partially hidden by the span of the stone occupation bridge, also dating from broad-gauge days. Also hidden behind this bridge on the right-hand side is the original wooden signal box which, due to an accident with a Tilley lamp just three months after this photograph was taken, was all but destroyed by fire. The line in the foreground is the down goods loop which was regularly utilised by banking locomotives resting between turns. *3/8/56 Periflex 1/125th F4.5 (Kodachrome)*

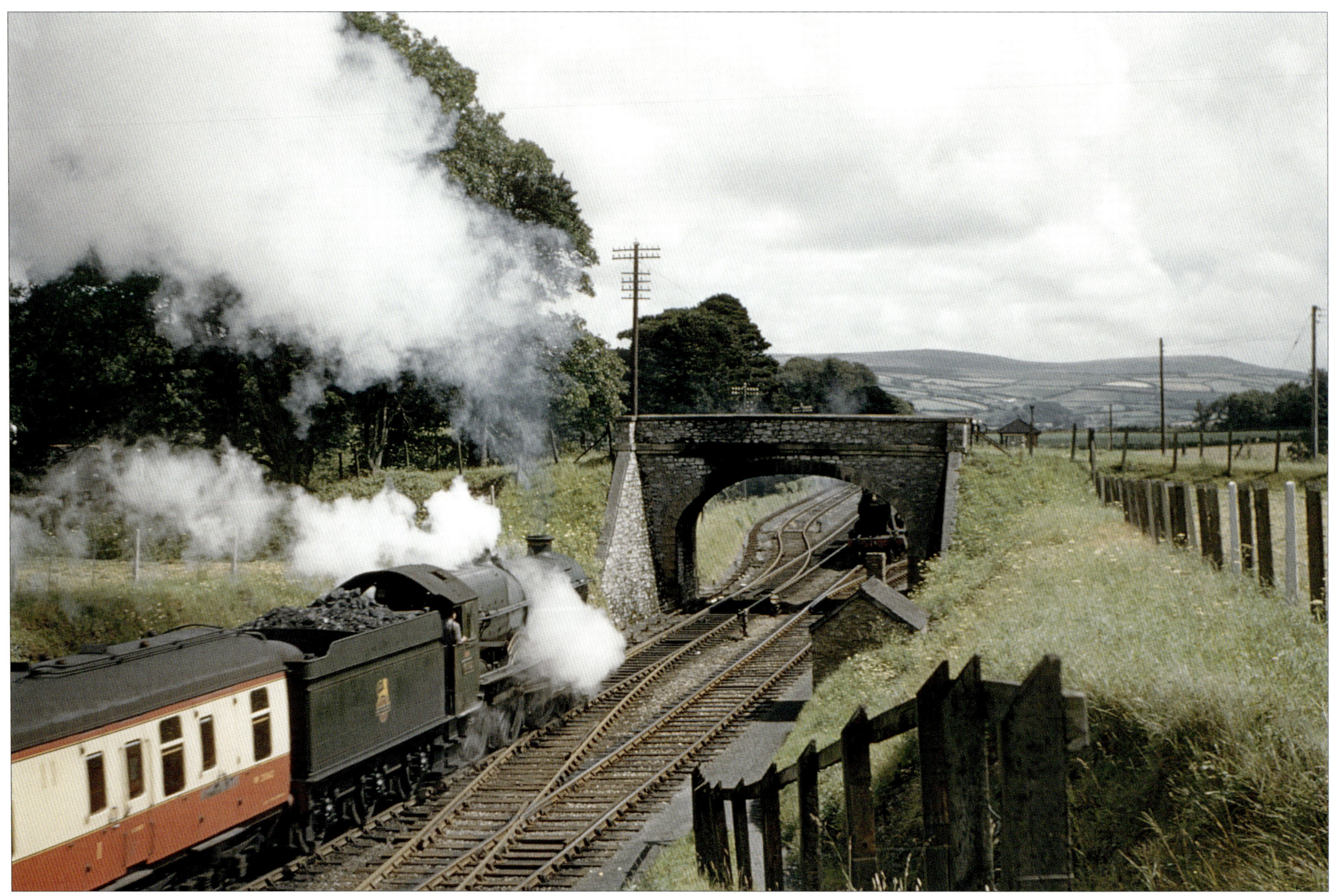

SLIDE 87 | Old Oak Common's **6003 King George IV** is looking rather laboured as it hauls an unidentified Plymouth to Paddington express (probably the 12.05pm) up Hemerdon Bank, east of Plympton, towards *Moor Bridge* with the signal box and running loops beyond. Meanwhile, Newton Abbot-based *Churchward/Collett 2884* class **3864** slows its approaches with a down mixed freight, in preparation for stopping to allow the pinning down of the brakes on its unfitted charge, prior to a controlled westward decent. Despite the shroud of escaping steam, it is evident in this shot that *6003* is still in possession of the final type of wider, sleeveless single chimney which had been fitted two years previously. This will be replaced by the final style of cast double chimney during April of the following year during a heavy general overhaul. *5/8/56 Periflex 1/125th F4.5 (Kodachrome)*

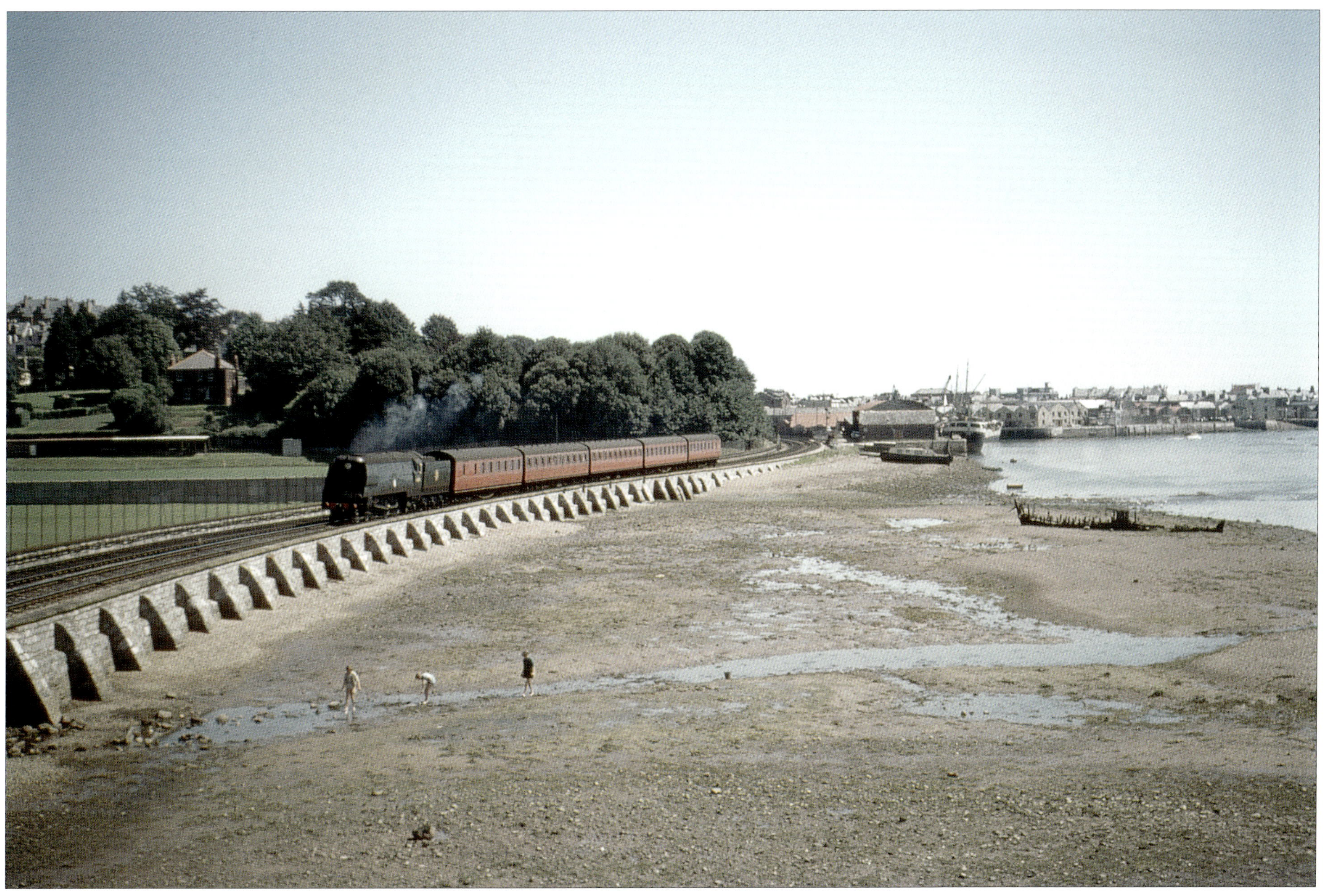

SLIDE 96 | Photographed from the *Teignmouth & Shaldon Bridge* and still in un-rebuilt condition, Exmouth Junction-based *Bulleid West Country/Battle of Britain* class **34014 Budleigh Salterton** is on *foreign* territory as it heads west along the north bank of the Teign Estuary towards Newton Abbot with an unidentified Exeter to Plymouth working. Built at Brighton Works and entering service in 1945 as *21C114*, this locomotive was less than two years away from an Eastleigh rebuild when the above photograph was taken. It was eventually withdrawn from Salisbury Shed in March 1965 and sold to *R.S.Hayes*, Tremain's Yard, Bridgend where it was broken up in May of the following year. *8/8/56 Periflex 1/250th F3.5 (Kodachrome)*

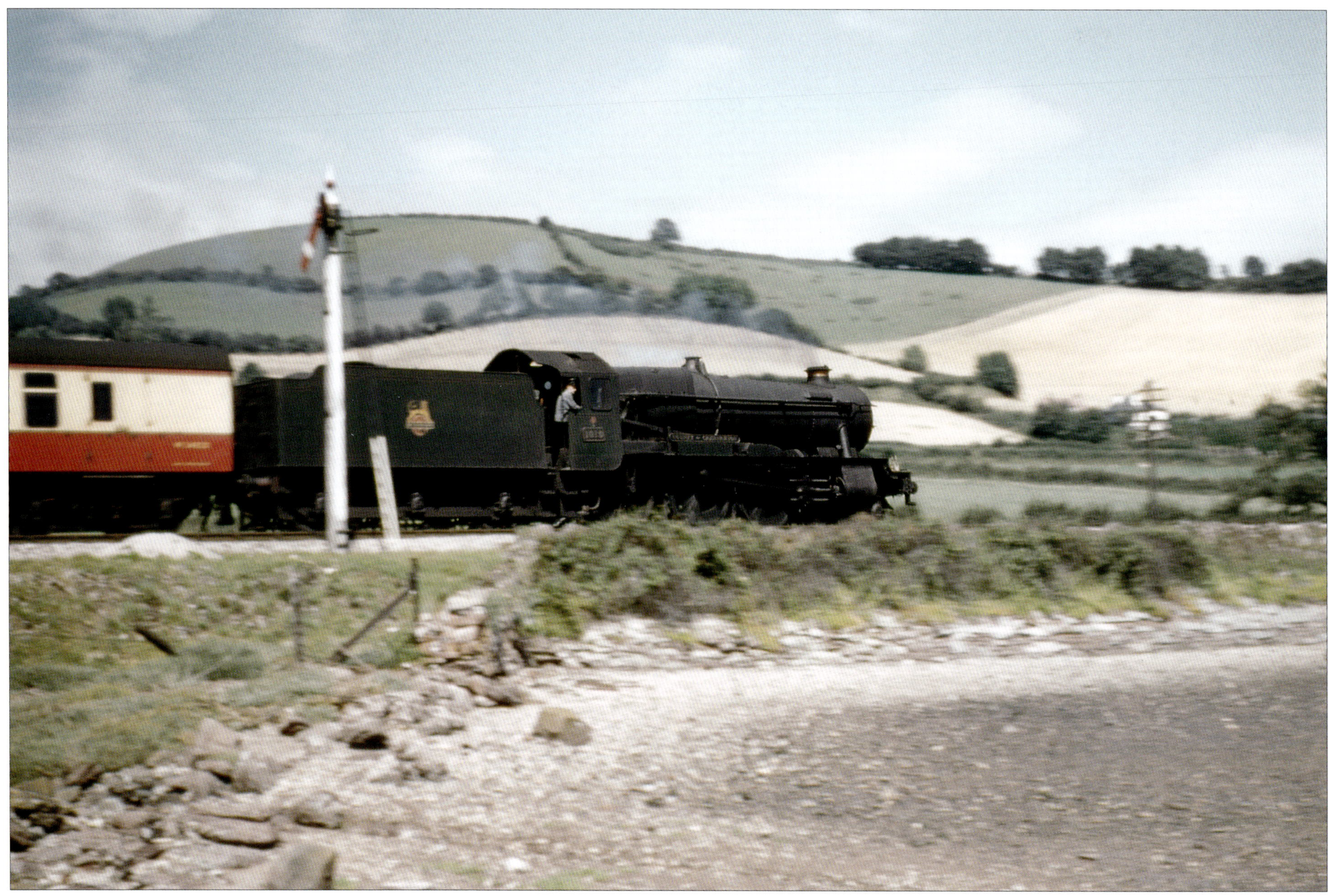

SLIDE 98 | Laira-based **1010 County of Caernarvon** on an unidentified up express heads east at low tide along the northern edge of the Teign Estuary near the village of Bishopsteignton with just over a mile to go before its next stop at Teignmouth. The driver has just shut off steam and the train has begun a slow deceleration, but Tom still has to pan his *Periflex* in order to freeze the action. Here, *1010* is seen still in possession of its original single chimney which would be replaced in January of the following year. Mistakenly named *County of Carnarvon* in 1947, almost two years after originally entering service unnamed, its name plates were altered accordingly in November 1951. One of the last of its class to be withdrawn from service in July 1964, *1010* was broken up by *Cashmore's* of Newport in December of the same year. *8/8/56 Periflex 1/125th F4.5 (Kodachrome)*

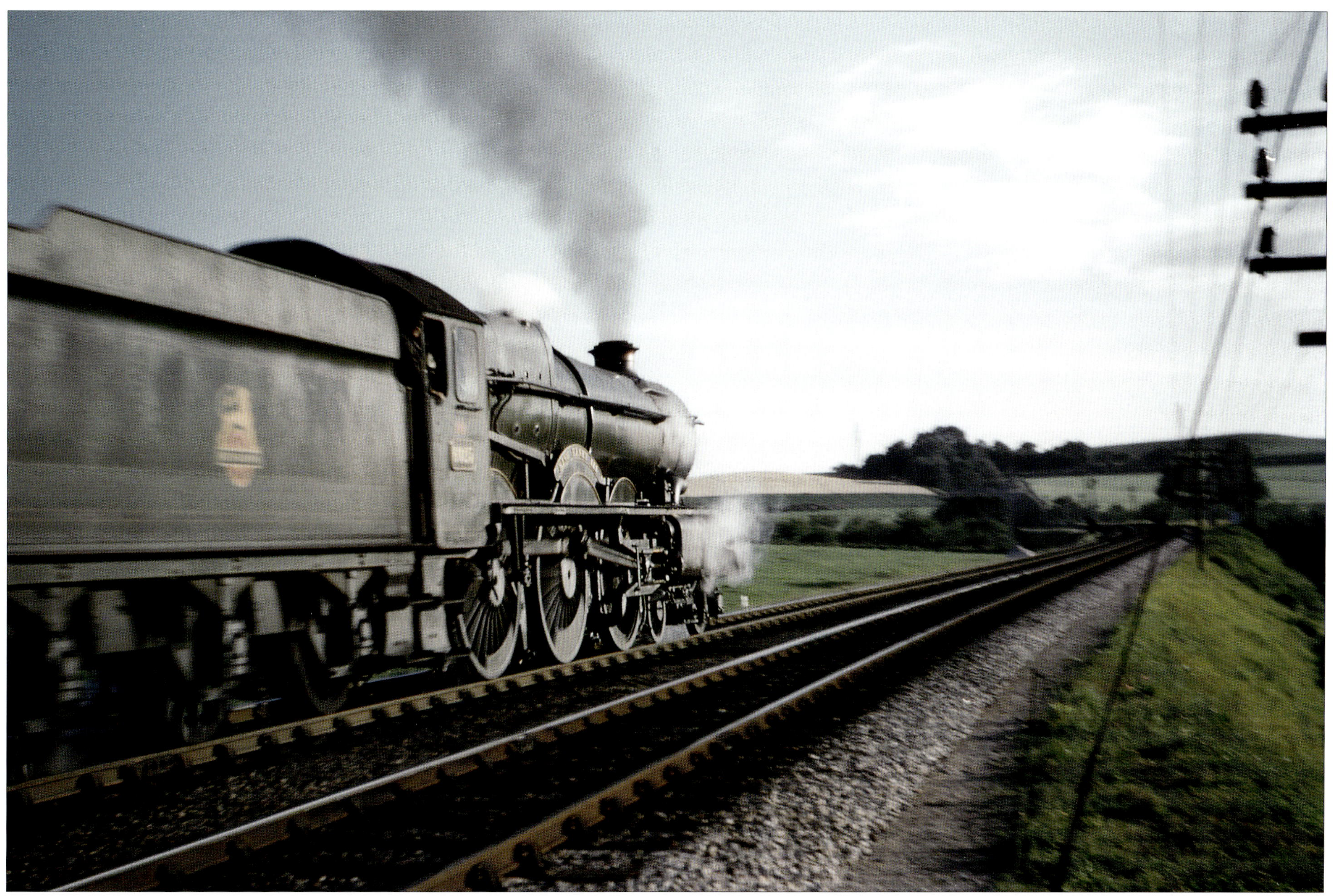

SLIDE 107 | Shooting into the evening sun with a desperately slow shutter speed, the photographer captures Laira-based **6025 King Henry III** hauling the 3.30pm Paddington to Penzance up the final 1 in 44 stretch of the climb to Dainton Tunnel's easterly portal which is just out of sight beyond the left-hand curve, hidden by trees. This photograph clearly shows the *BR*-sleeved single chimney and the mechanical lubrication assembly still in its original position, behind the outside steam pipe. It is also evident that, behind the halo of escaping steam, the boiler-side handrail has been distended: somehow pulled further out from the exhaust ejector than usual. Later photographs show that this anomaly would be rectified at some point during 1957. At the point of withdrawal in December 1962, it was noted that *6025* had achieving the second highest recorded mileage of its class (1,836,713) despite working two years less than **6013 King Henry VIII**, which had achieved an impressive mileage of 1,950,462 at the point of withdrawal six months previously. *8/8/56 Periflex 1/60th F3.5 (Kodachrome)*

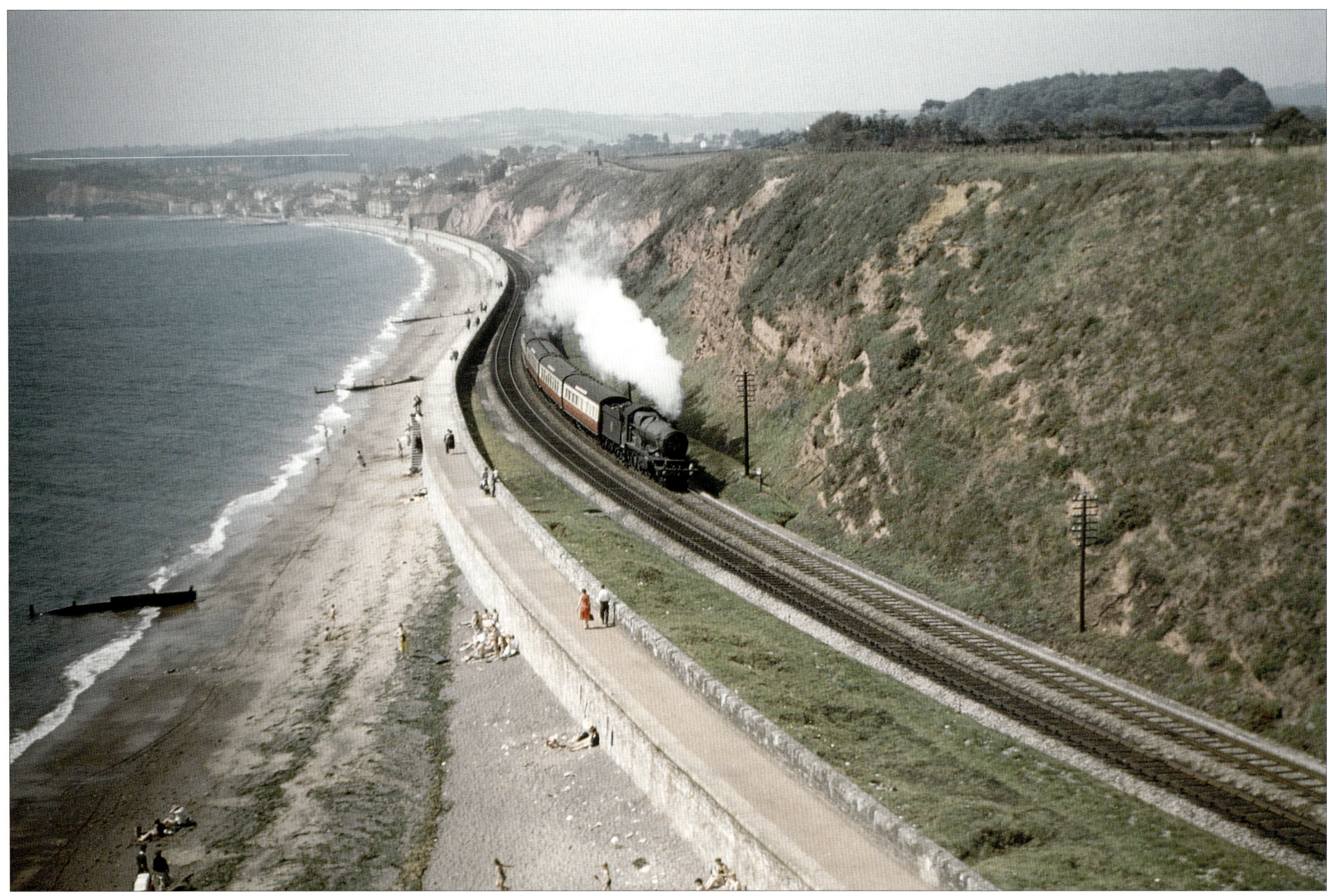

SLIDE 111 | Long-time Newton Abbot locomotive, **5028 Llantilio Castle** has just been reallocated to Laira and appears to be still awaiting its first clean of what would turn out to be an excessively busy Summer. It is captured here photographed from *Langstone Rock* with a fourteen-coach rake of *Great Western* stock, including restaurant car heading north-east towards Dawlish Warren with the inter-regional 7.30am Penzance to Liverpool (Lime Street) and Manchester (London Road). Dawlish East can just be identified through the morning Summer haze. Entering service in May 1934, *5028* was one of the first of its class to be withdrawn for scrapping, after a comparatively minor collision with a *D20/2* class diesel-hydraulic near Devonport Junction, Plymouth in December 1959. Its boiler was recycled; finding its way into **4085 Berkeley Castle** during overhaul. *9/8/56 Periflex 1/250th F3.5 (Kodachrome)*

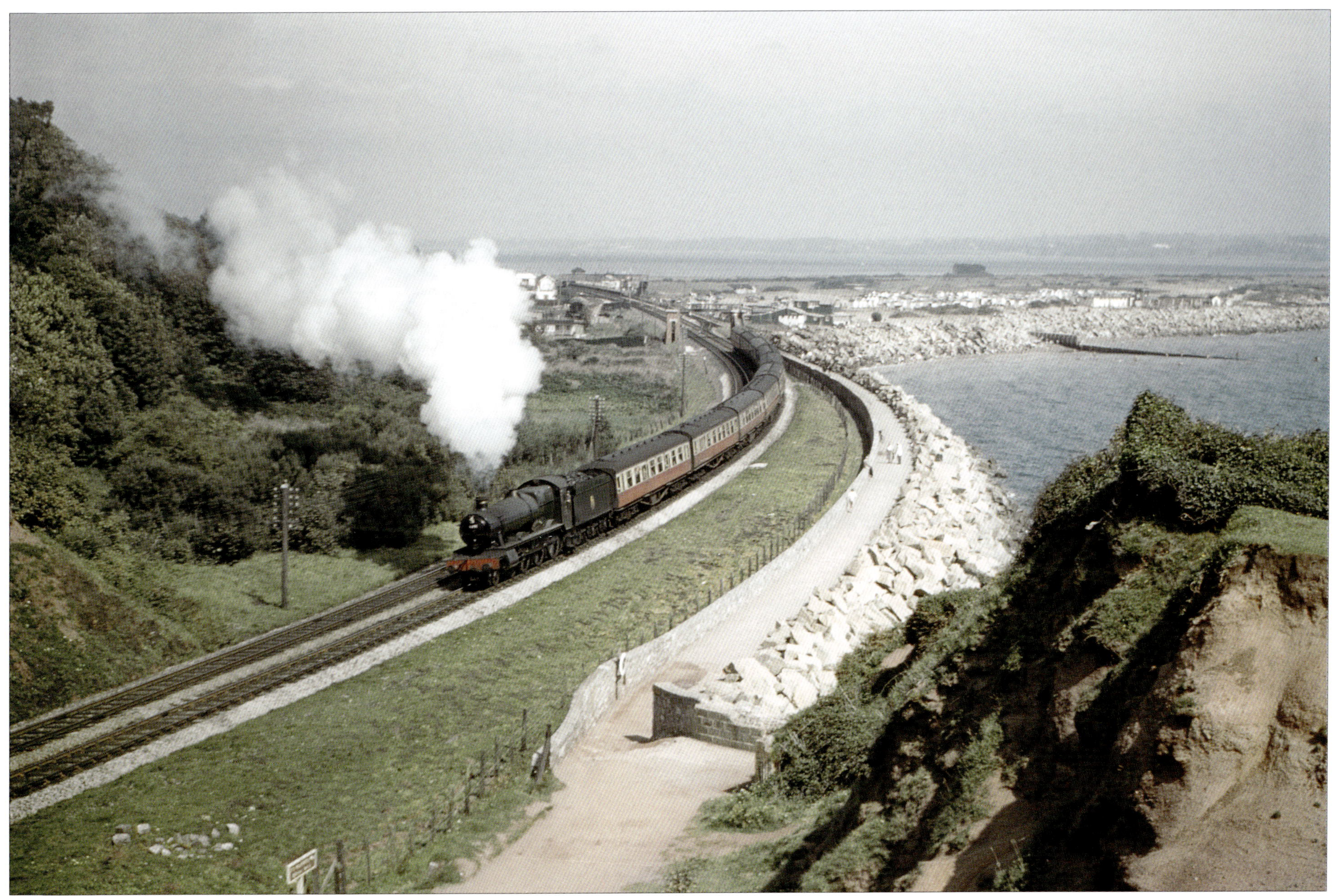

SLIDE 112 | The photographer turns around and points his camera in the opposite direction as Taunton's **4991 Cobham Hall** approaches from the north-east having just left Dawlish Warren Station with a morning stopping train to Kingswear. The scene at this location has barely changed since this photograph was taken, apart from the building of a small café at the foot of *Langstone Rock*, which had actually been a headland point continuous with the mainland, prior to the excavations necessary to facilitate the construction of the original broad-gauge railway by the *South Devon Railway Company*. The section, linking Exeter St. Davids to Teignmouth, was opened in May 1846, but by the end of the year had been extended to Newton Abbot. *4991* was to remain working out of Taunton for a further six years prior to reallocation to St. Philip's Marsh. *9/8/56 Periflex 1/250th F3.5 (Kodachrome)*

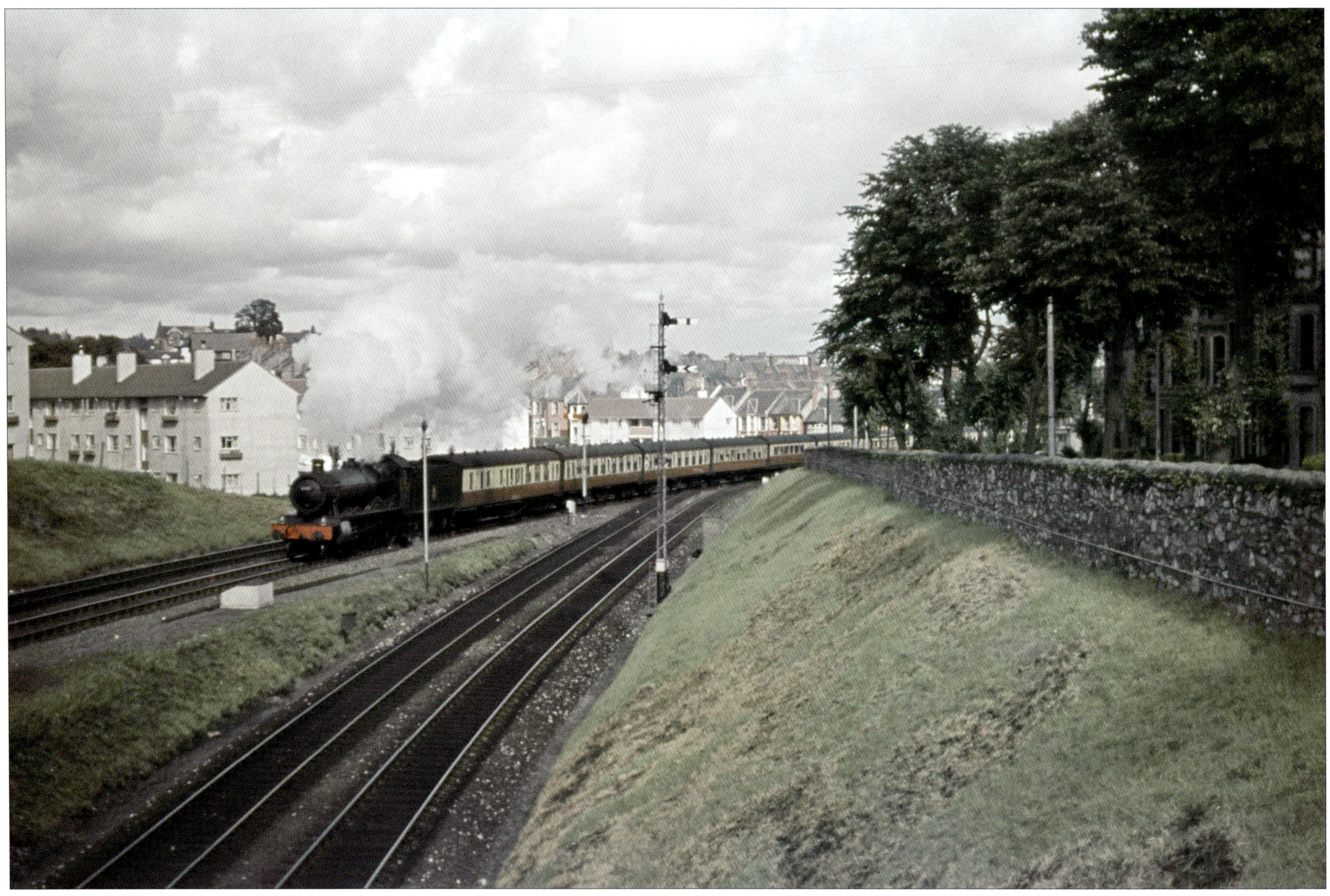

SLIDE 147 | Still sporting its 1949 black-lined livery, Truro's **6931 Aldborough Hall** heads west out of Plymouth with what we believe to be the down *Cornish Riviera*. This supposition is purely circumstantial as the surviving slides from this badly degraded film are not dated and not necessarily numbered chronologically, but what we believe to be the previous frame shows **6004 King George III** light engine at Plymouth North Road still sporting the *Riviera* headboard. Here the train is captured at Devonport Junction; the tracks in the foreground swinging south being the ex-*LSWR* line to Devonport (Kings Road) Station and the freight-only Ocean Quay terminus at Stonehouse Pool (which had lost its passenger services as early as 1910). Photograph taken from the *Wingfield Way* overbridge. *6931* was eventually withdrawn from Oxford during September of 1965 and broken up by *Bird's* of Risca, Newport early the following year. *5/8/56 Periflex (Gevacolor 26)*

38

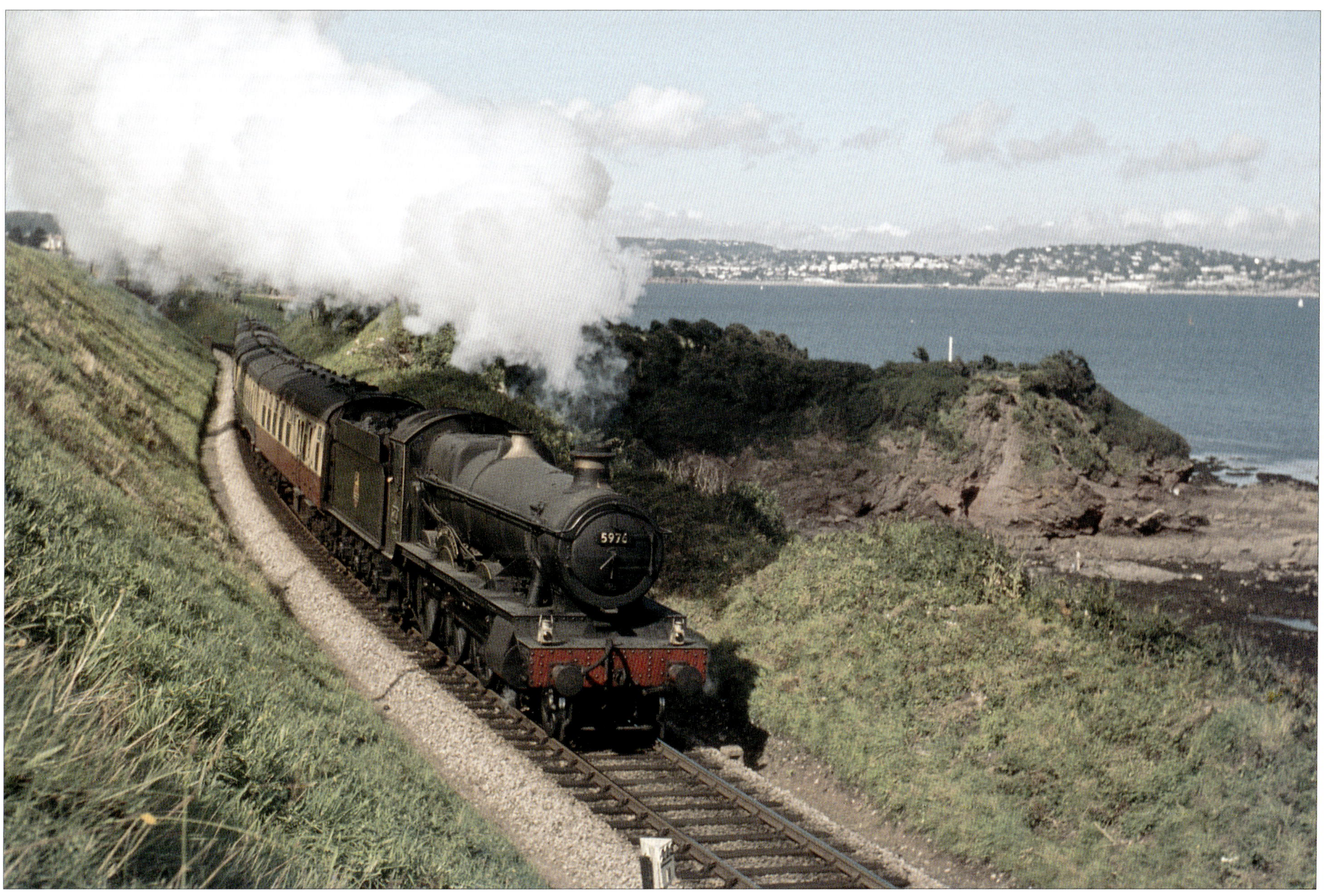

SLIDE 640 | With the sun-kissed buildings of Torquay illuminating the horizon and the red Devonian sandstone separating land from sea, Exeter's **5976 Ashwicke Hall** *(ex-oil burner 3951)* heads south past *milepost 223¼* along this unmistakable stretch of coastline at Saltern Cove, Goodrington on a Paddington to Kingswear train. This timeless scene will be well known to Heritage Railway enthusiasts; this section of line being bought by the *Dart Valley Railway Company Ltd.* in 1972 and currently running regular timetabled steam-hauled services between Paignton and Kingswear as the *Dartmouth Steam Railway* under the ownership of *Dart Valley Railway plc.* When this photograph was taken, *5976* was only a matter of months away from reallocation to Old Oak Common. *1/9/58 Leica IIIA 1/500th F4.5 (Agfacolor CT 18)*

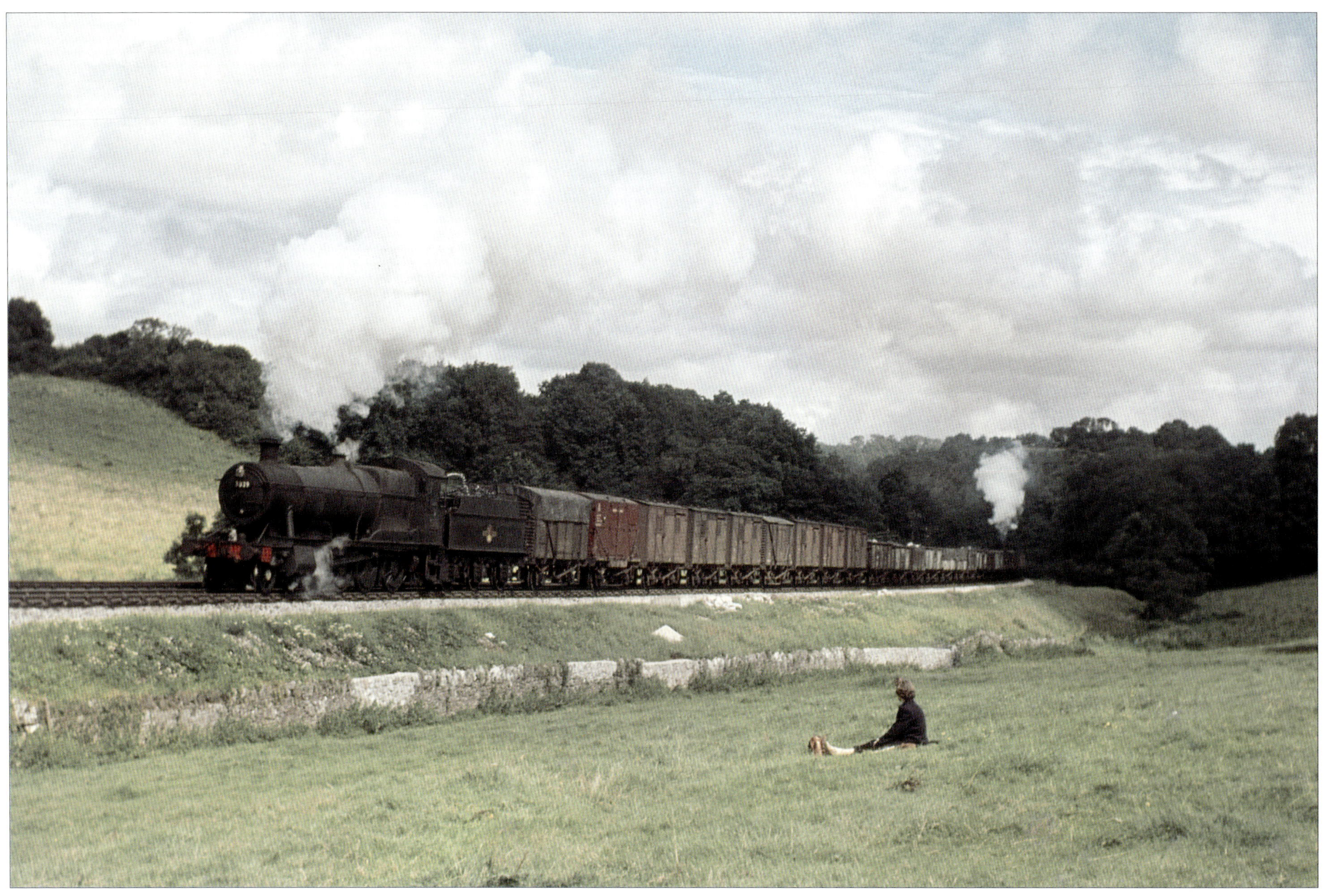

SLIDE 643 | Tyseley's *2884* class **3839** assisted in the rear by an unidentified *5101* class 2-6-2T makes steady headway up from the cutting separating Whiddon Copse and Dainton Hill on the 1 in 44 stretch of the approach to Dainton Tunnel with a heavy down mixed freight. Meanwhile, the photographer's wife sits patiently on the grass, pretending to be interested in the passing traffic! The banker will almost certainly detach when this train is halted at the summit to have its brakes pinned down, prior to a controlled south-westerly descent to Totnes. *3839* was an ex-oil burner; converted in May 1947 and renumbered to *4853*. As was the case with the rest of the thirty-six *GWR* locomotives so converted, the entire process had been reversed before the decade's end. What appears to be a pile of sand on the embankment close to the first wagon, possibly deposited for the purpose of providing a degree of extra traction for locomotives during slippy conditions, is more likely to be surplus material left over from the recent repairs to the boundary wall. *3/9/58 Leica IIIA (Agfacolor CT 18)*

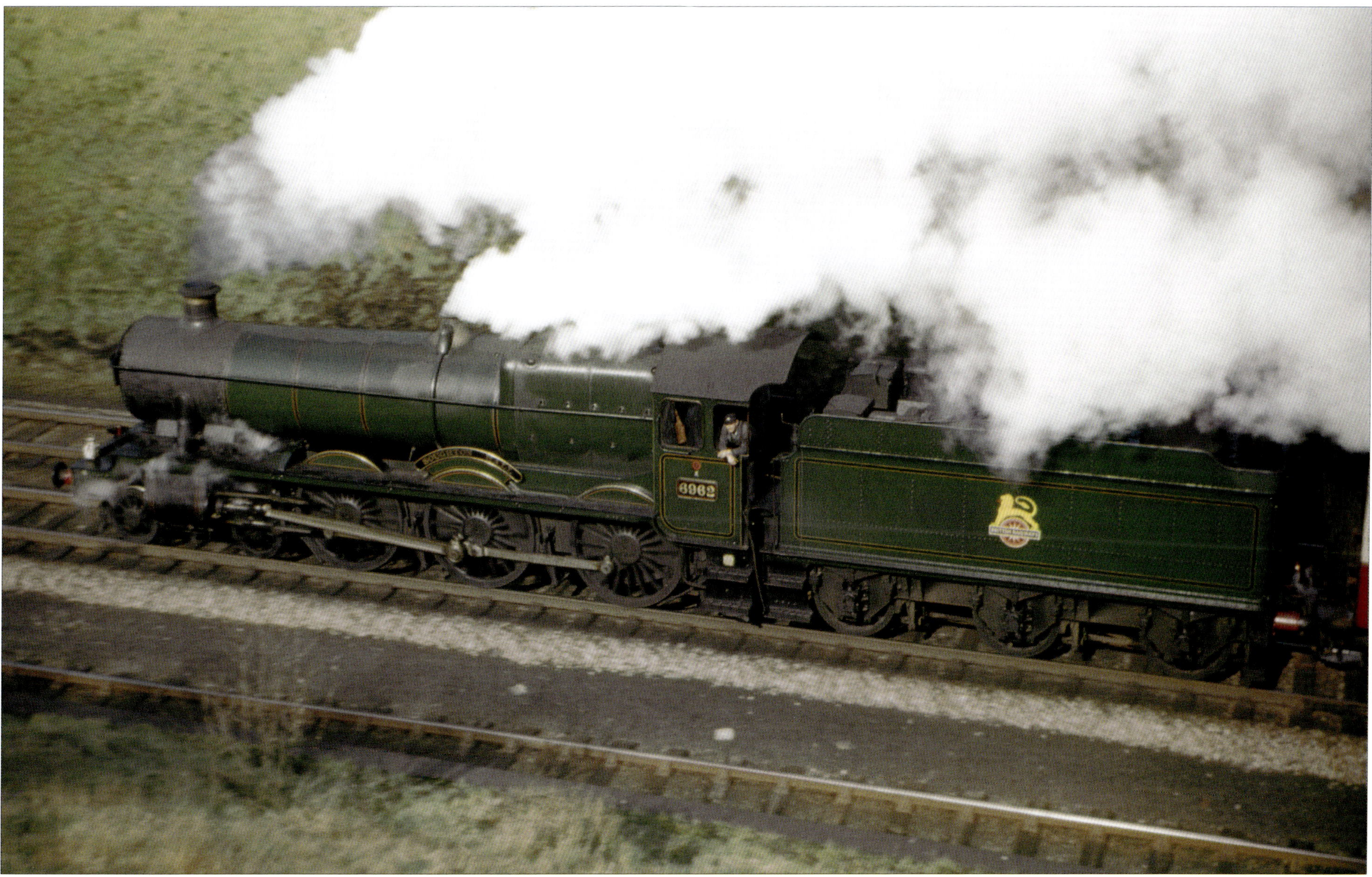

SLIDE 159 | Showing a full head of steam enhanced by the cold morning air of late Winter, Old Oak's *6959* class **6962 Soughton Hall** heads up the bank at Hatton, north-west of Warwick on a football special. Arsenal are playing West Bromwich Albion at The Hawthorns in an F.A. Cup 6th Round match. In the event, the match was to end a 2-2 draw, resulting in a replay at Highbury the following Tuesday, which *West Brom* were to win 2-1. Built in 1944; the fourth of the initial batch of twelve *Modified Halls* to come out of Swindon, *6962* like all *4900* and *6959* class locomotives built between 1941 and 1945, would enter service unnamed due primarily to the wartime shortage of brass. It spent all of its *BR* days working out of Old Oak Common, from where it was withdrawn for scrapping during January 1963; the first of its class to be taken out of service. *2/3/57 Periflex (Ilford 'D')*

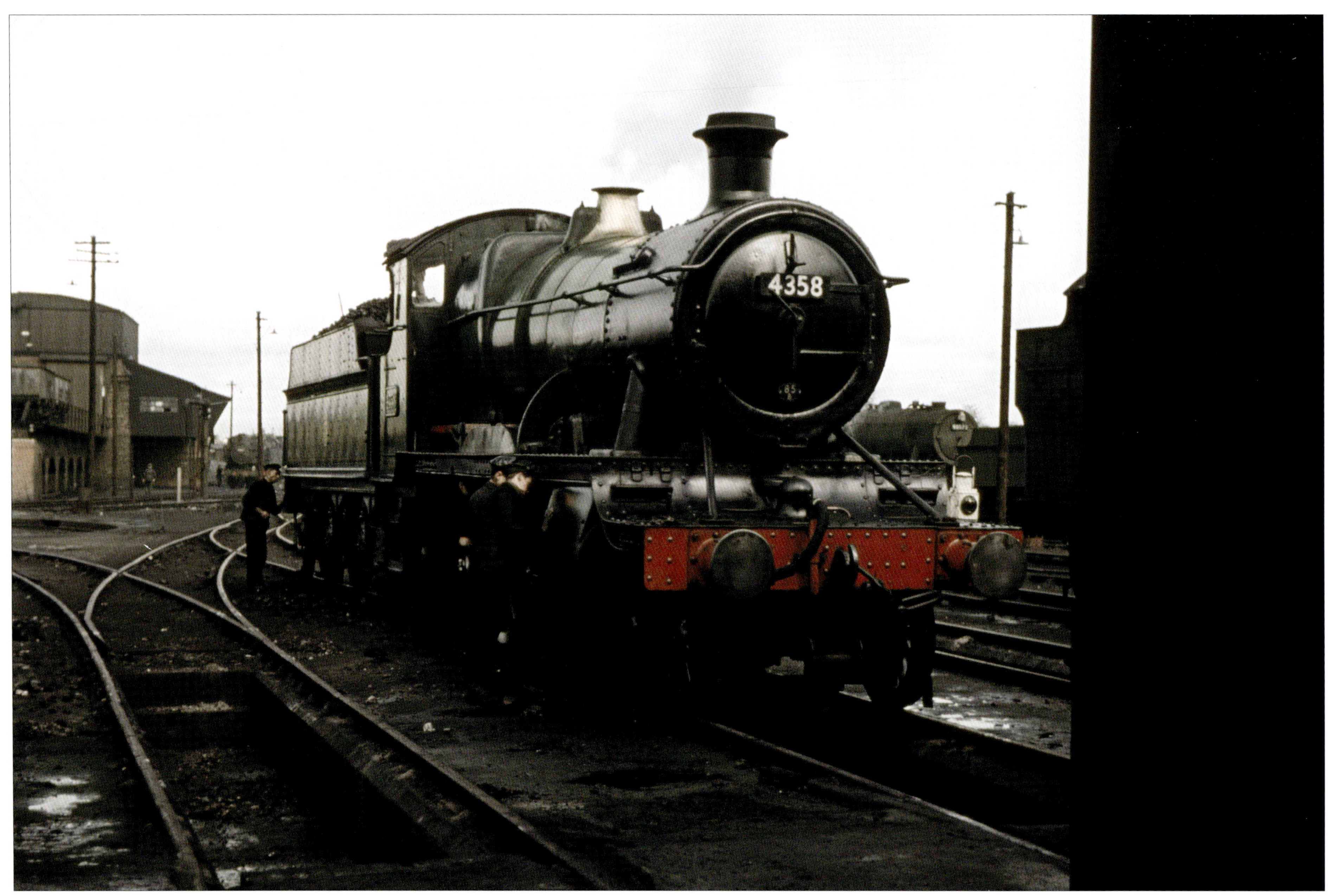

SLIDE 243 | On this cold and overcast Spring morning, Old Oak Common's **4090 Dorchester Castle** is en route from Paddington (via Standish Junction) with the first leg of the *Ian Allan 'Daffodil Express'* excursion. Meanwhile, the men at Gloucester Horton Road are readying *Churchward 43xx* class 2-6-0 **4358** to take the train forward to its second-leg destination at Neath, double-heading with the preserved *Churchward 4-4-0* **3440 City of Truro**. The 2-6-2T hidden behind the shed door is Horton Road stalwart *Churchward 3150* class **3171**, literally weeks away from withdrawal. Also just visible in the background is **90573**, one of Horton Road's allocation of *WD/8 Austerity* class locomotives. Note that in the above photograph, *4358* is sporting Caerphilly's signature red-painted reversing rod *(see also slide 493 on page 110)*. *18/5/57 Periflex (Gevacolor 26)*

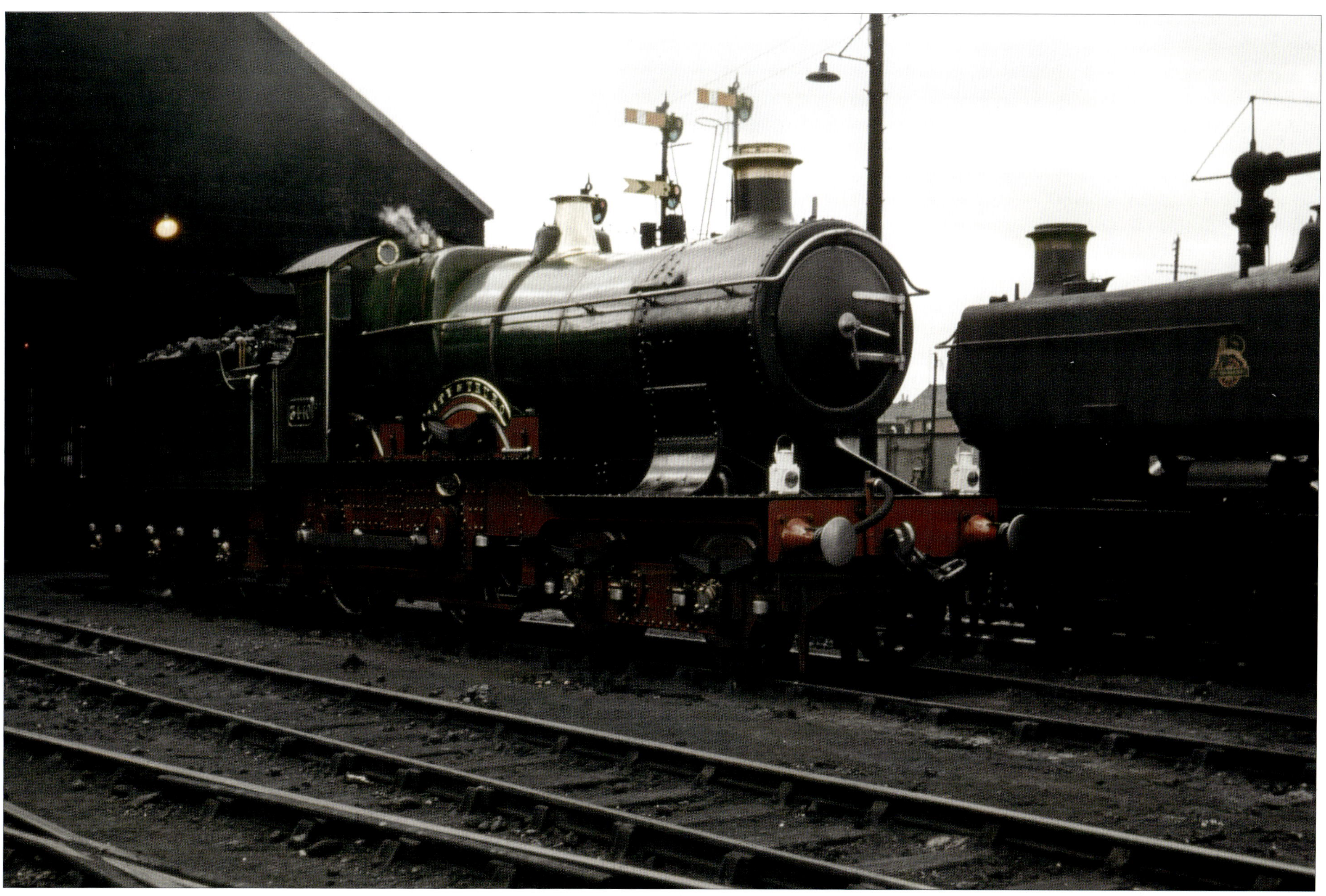

SLIDE 247 | **3440 City of Truro** has taken on water, been coaled-up and had a final 'bulling' from Horton Road shed staff, prior to being coupled as pilot to **4358** on the *'Daffodil Express'*. This train will set off at approximately 11.15am to its next stop at Grange Court and Tom, accompanied by Dick Blenkinsop and Brian England, will take off in advance of its departure in Dick's *Morris Minor* in the hope of photographing it at key locations along the route *(see slide 253 on the following page)*. Incidentally, the identity of the *Hawksworth 94xx* class 0-6-0PT on the right of this shot was not recorded by the photographer, but we believe it to be Horton Road's **9492**. *18/5/57 Periflex (Gevacolor 26)*

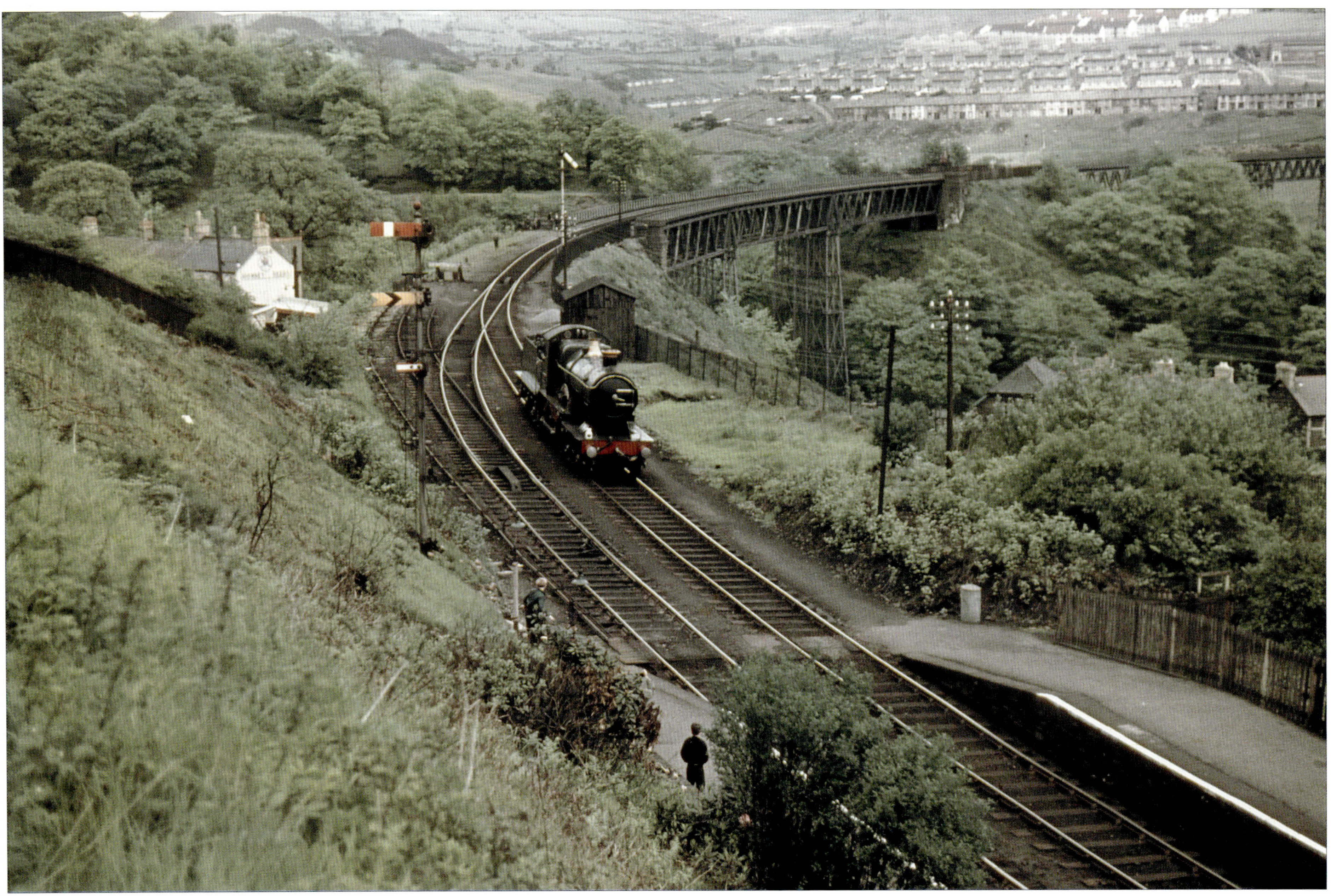

SLIDE 253 | Due to weight restrictions on the Crumlin Viaduct, **3440 City of Truro** is taken off the train and traverses this impressive structure (which incidentally was in its centenary year) at the regulation 8 mph. It is captured here approaching the platforms at Crumlin High Level Station. **4358** will follow shortly with its charge and *3440* will again act as pilot as far as Neath General. Both locomotives will be replaced here by *Churchward* 2-6-2T **8104**, taking the train via Landore to Swansea High Street, where *3440* and *4358* will reattach for the return journey to Neath and onwards to Newport. **4090** will then conclude the return journey to Paddington; this time via Severn Tunnel Junction and Westerleigh Junction. *18/5/57 Periflex (Gevacolor 26)*

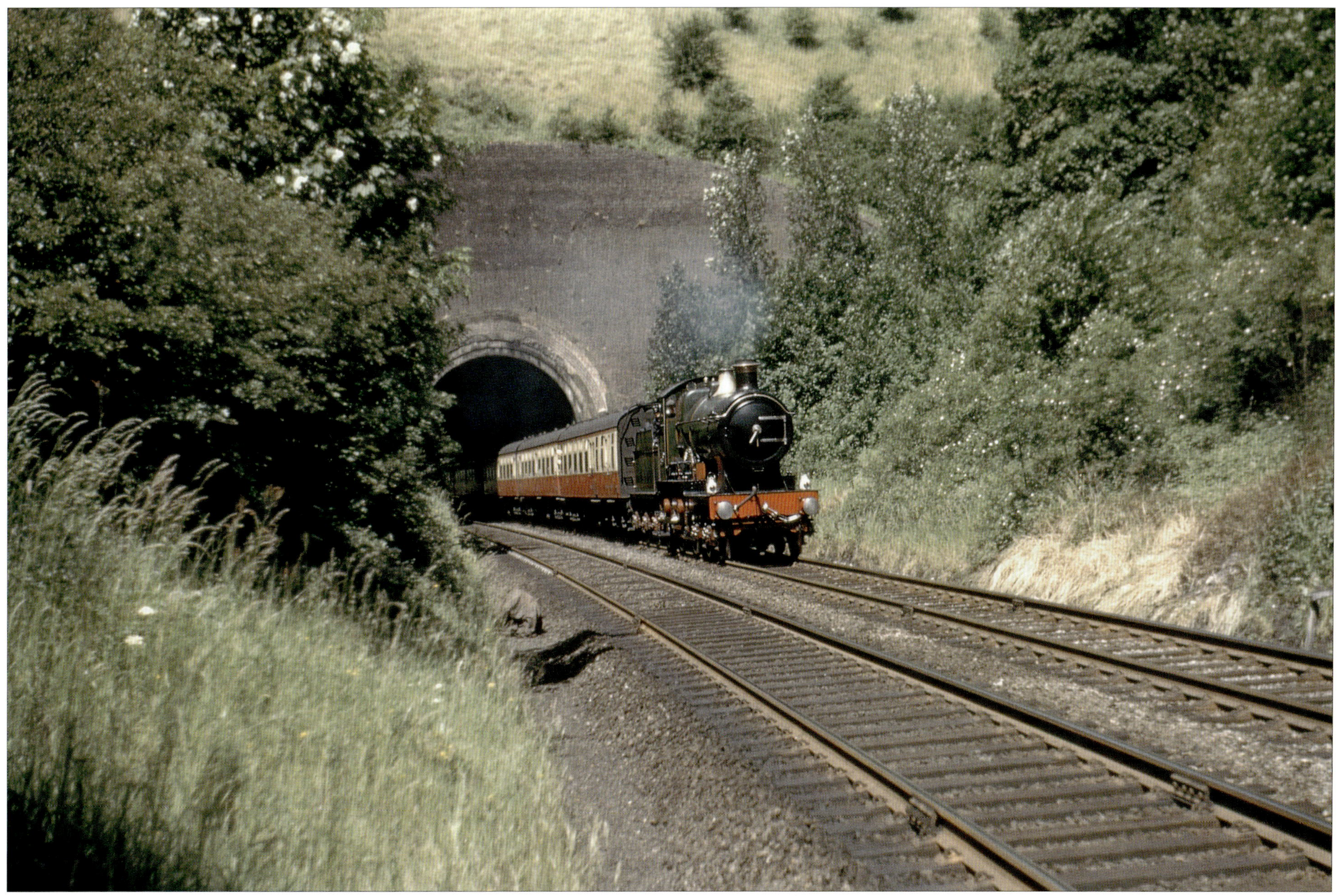

SLIDE 310 | At approximately 11.10am on this already sweltering Sunday morning, **3440 City of Truro** bursts out of Harbury Tunnel with the outward leg of a Wolverhampton (Low Level) to Swindon *SLS* special, which also included amongst its passengers, members of the *Wolverhampton Locomotive Club*. Running via Didcot's North and West Junctions and unusually carrying no headboard, this train reached its destination at approximately 1.10pm. Participants were then free to roam the Works at Swindon for around three-and-a-half hours. The return journey ran via the same route, with an unconfirmed report of 85mph being reached near the village of Bishop's Itchington approximately two miles from where the above photograph was taken *(see slide 333 on rear cover).* 16/6/57 *(Kodachrome)*

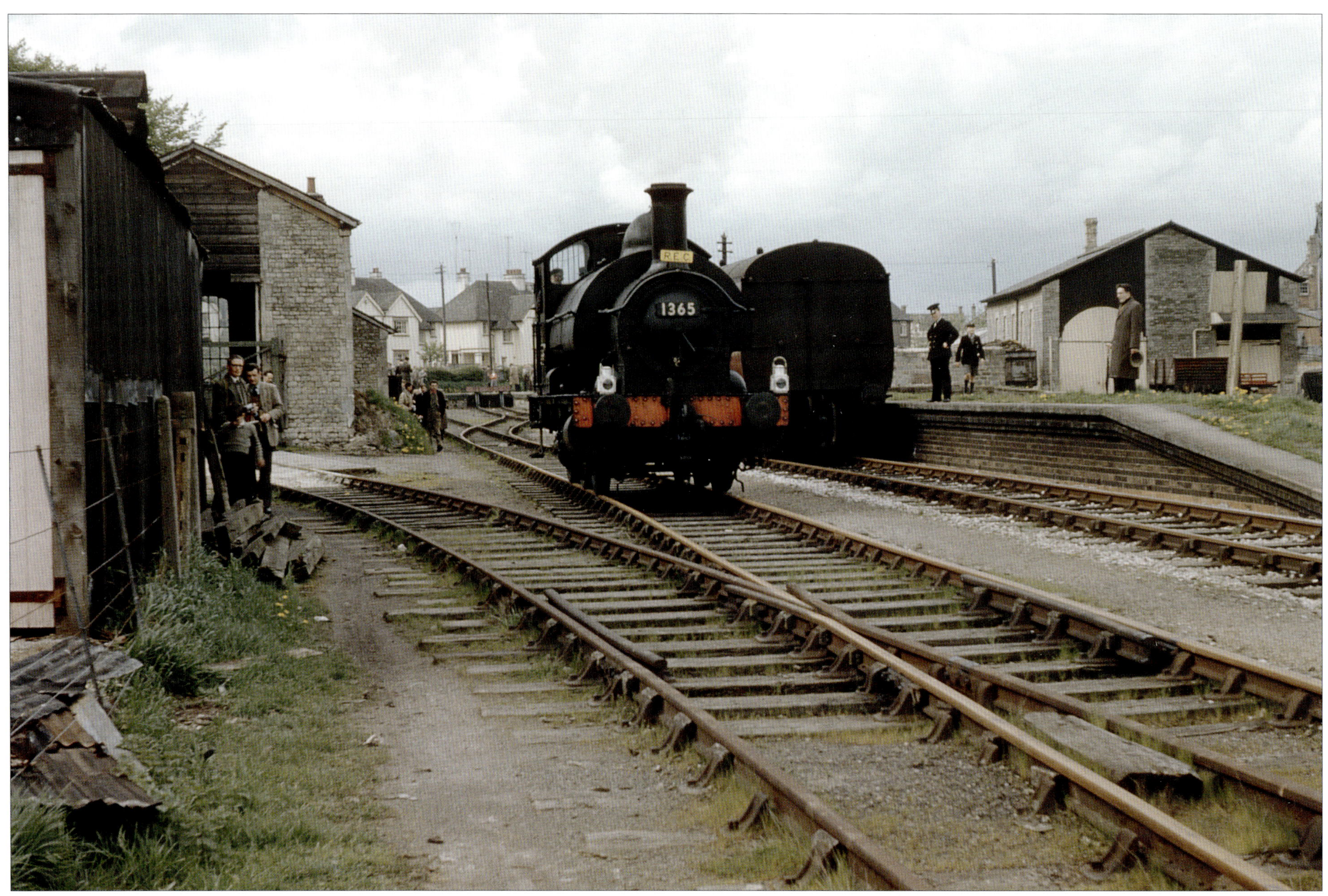

SLIDE 794 | In Spring 1959 the *Railway Enthusiasts' Club* organised a special over the short branch from Uffington Junction (between Didcot and Swindon) to Faringdon, on which passenger services had been terminated in 1951. The passengers for this trip were delivered via the 1.20pm Paddington to Cardiff, which made a special stop at Uffington where *Churchward 1361* class 0-6-0ST **1365** was waiting with its two-coach train. The 1910 vintage 'Humpy' is captured here at the branch terminus at Faringdon, running round its train in preparation for the return journey to Uffington and onwards to Challow, where the excursion would terminate. From here, passengers were delivered back to the capital on the regular 4.10pm Swindon to Paddington service. *26/4/59 Werra (Kodachrome)*

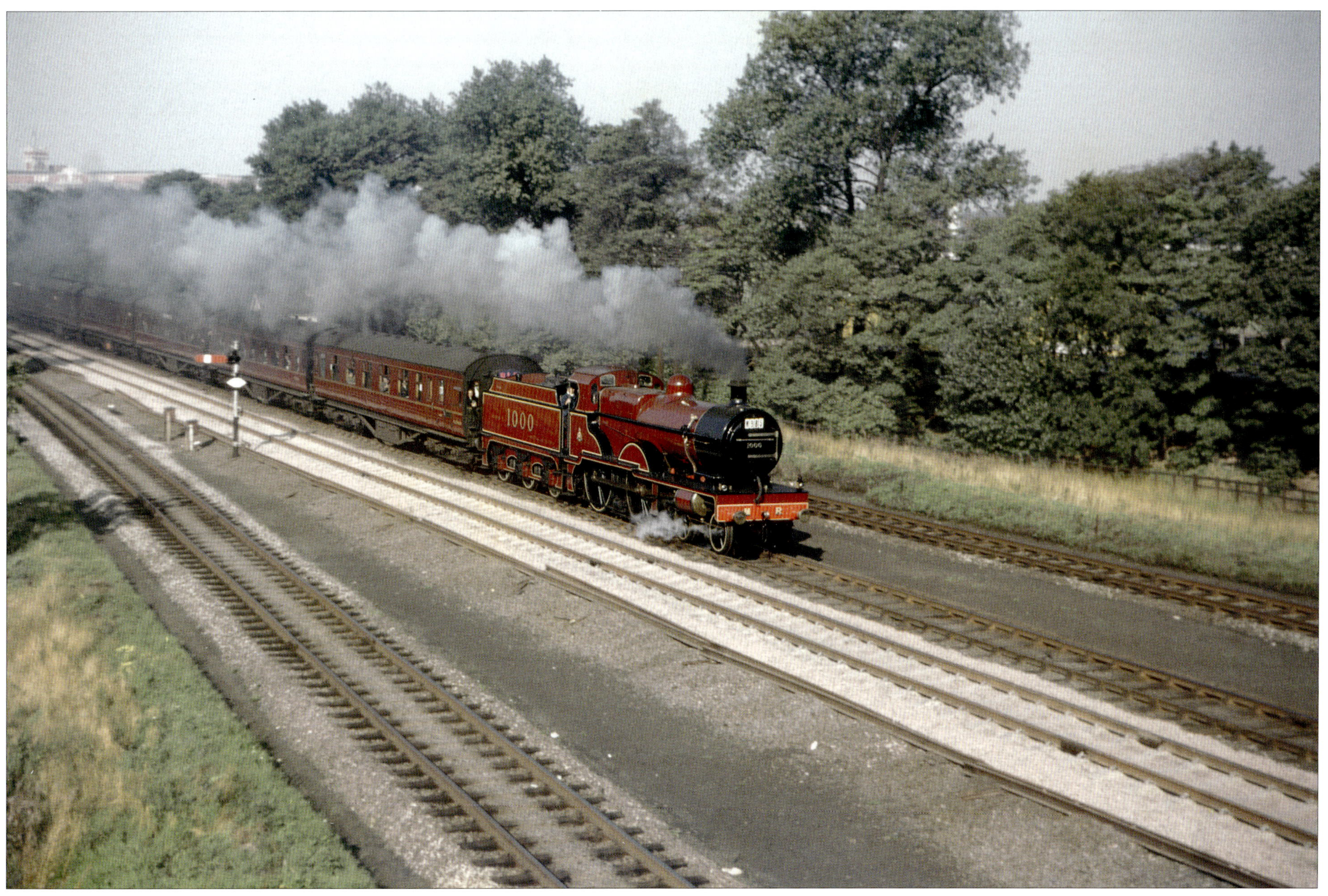

SLIDE 928 | On what is generally regarded as this locomotive's first true scheduled working after restoration, ex-*Midland Railway Compound* 4-4-0 **1000** heads north-east towards Castle Bromwich Station and Junction with an *SLS* special train for Doncaster and York. Originally built at Derby in 1902, the locomotive was rebuilt in 1914 and the restoration work carried out post-withdrawal reflected the latter incarnation. Photograph taken from the original *Chester Road* overbridge prior to the building of the 'new' bridge to accommodate a second carriageway. Note the *Fort Dunlop* factory buildings just visible in the background: at one time the largest factory in the world. *30/8/59 Leica IIIA (Ilford 'D')*

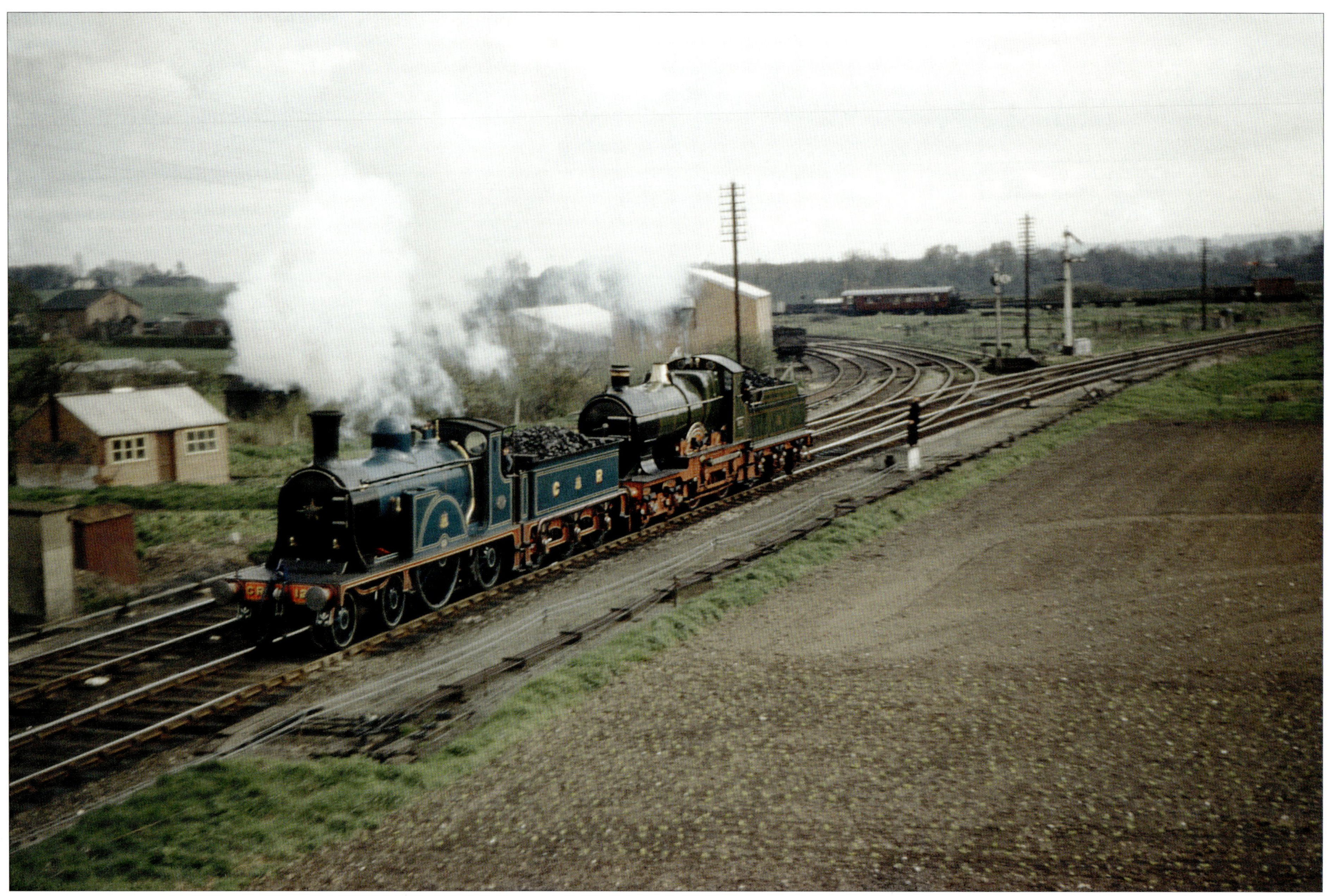

SLIDE 1002 | On this cold and dull Sunday afternoon, Tom has been tipped off that some 'special' traffic is due to head through his home-town and he quickly grabs his camera and endeavours to find a suitable vantage point. Preserved working locomotives, ex-*Caledonian Railway Neilson & Drummond* 4-2-2 **123** and ex-*GWR Churchward* 4-4-0 **3440 City of Truro** are hurrying light engine through Stratford-upon-Avon on their way to Tyseley in preparation for becoming temporary static exhibits at Birmingham Moor Street. Both locomotives have been serviced at Swindon and have worked their way north via the junctions at Honeybourne. This photograph is taken from the *Sanctus Road* bridge looking south towards the through-sidings linking the ex-*GW* line to the ex-*SMJ/LMS* station at Stratford's *Old Town*. *20/3/60 (Kodachrome)*

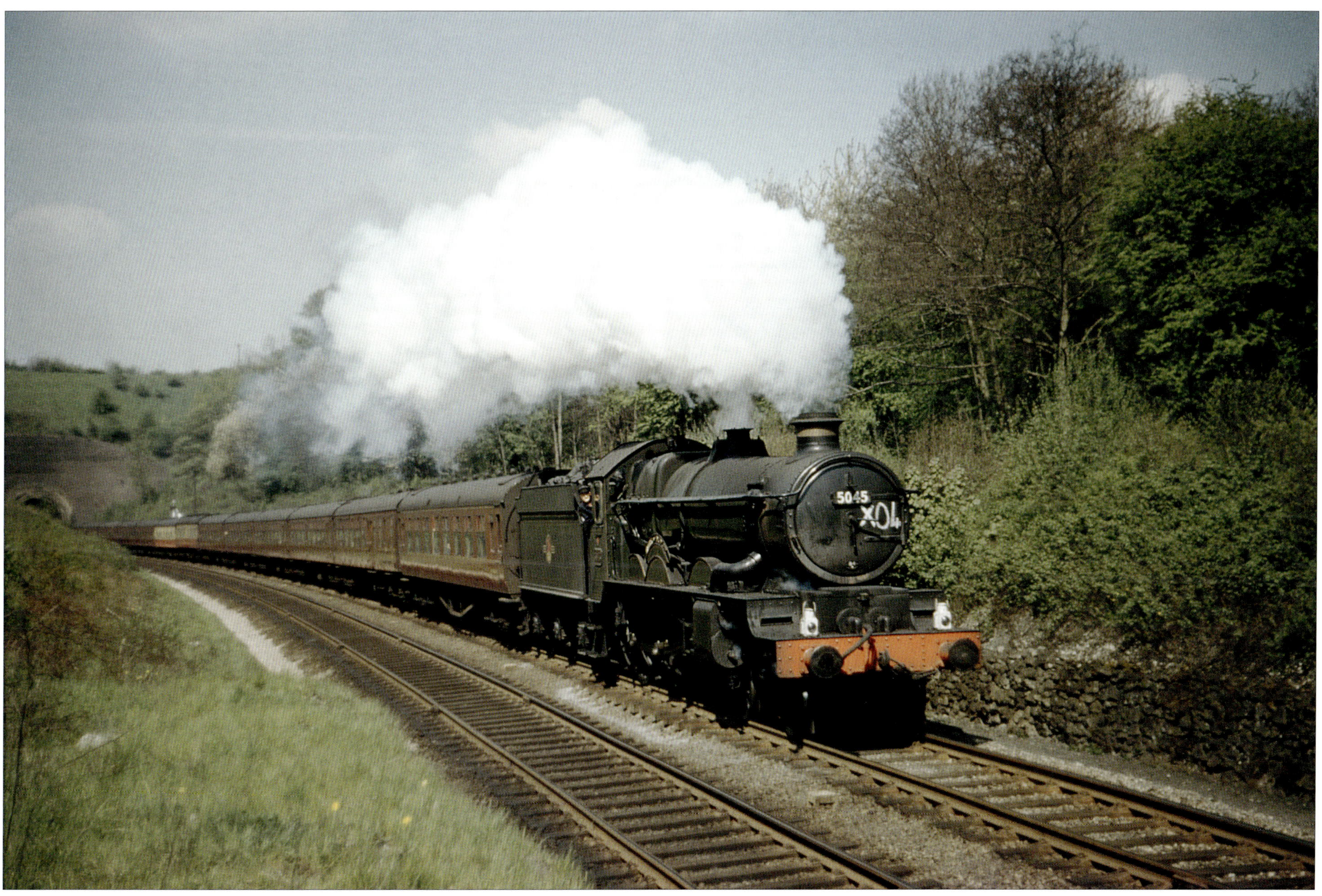

SLIDE 1017 | Wolverhampton Wanderers are playing Chelsea at Stamford Bridge on this glorious, but chilly Saturday and Stafford Road's *Castle* class **5045 Earl of Dudley** is full of hopeful *Wolves* supporters on their way to the match. The train is captured here passing the Southam & Harbury distant signal with Harbury Tunnel's distinctive south-easterly portal visible in the distance. In the event, Wolverhampton were to win 5-1, but were narrowly denied a third consecutive league title after Burnley finished one point ahead of them. They did however, win both the F.A. Cup as well as the F.A. Charity Shield and also managed to reach the quarter-final stage of the European Cup *(see also slide 1026 on page 50). 30/4/60 (Kodachrome)*

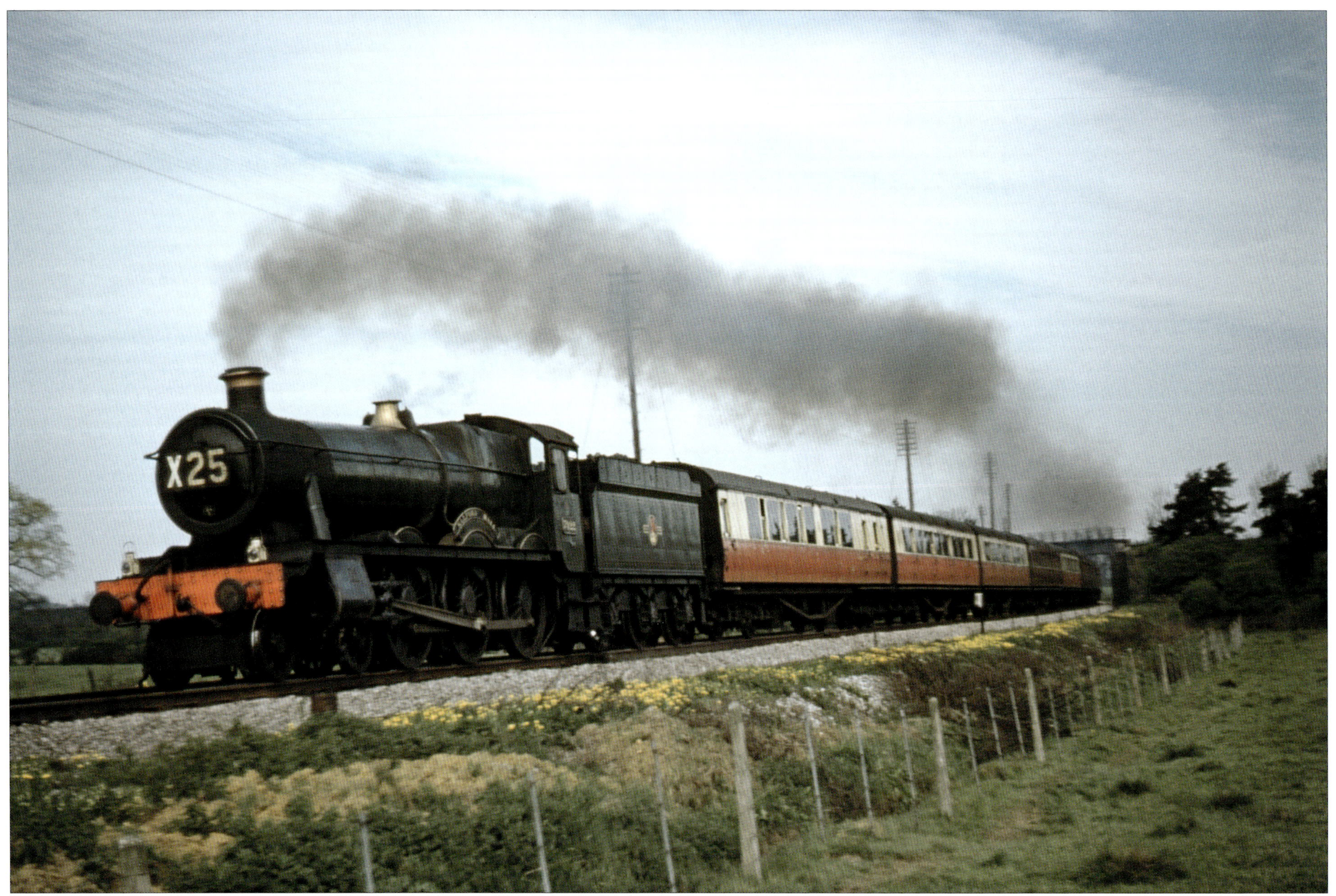

SLIDE 1026 | The following week, Shrewsbury-based **7922 Salford Hall** on another football special is captured near Fenny Compton where the Leamington to Banbury main line passes *Wormleighton Reservoir* and briefly runs parallel to the *Oxford Canal*. The bridge we see in the background carries the ex-*SMJ/LMS* line over the ex-*GW* line. The train is an F.A. Cup Final special crammed with *Wolves* supporters heading up to Wembley to face Blackburn Rovers. As it happens, Wolves were to lift the trophy for the fourth and most recent time, beating Blackburn 3-0. 1960 was to become the first year that the F.A. Cup winner would be given automatic entry into a European competition, in the newly-formed Cup Winners' Cup. *7/5/60 (Kodachrome)*

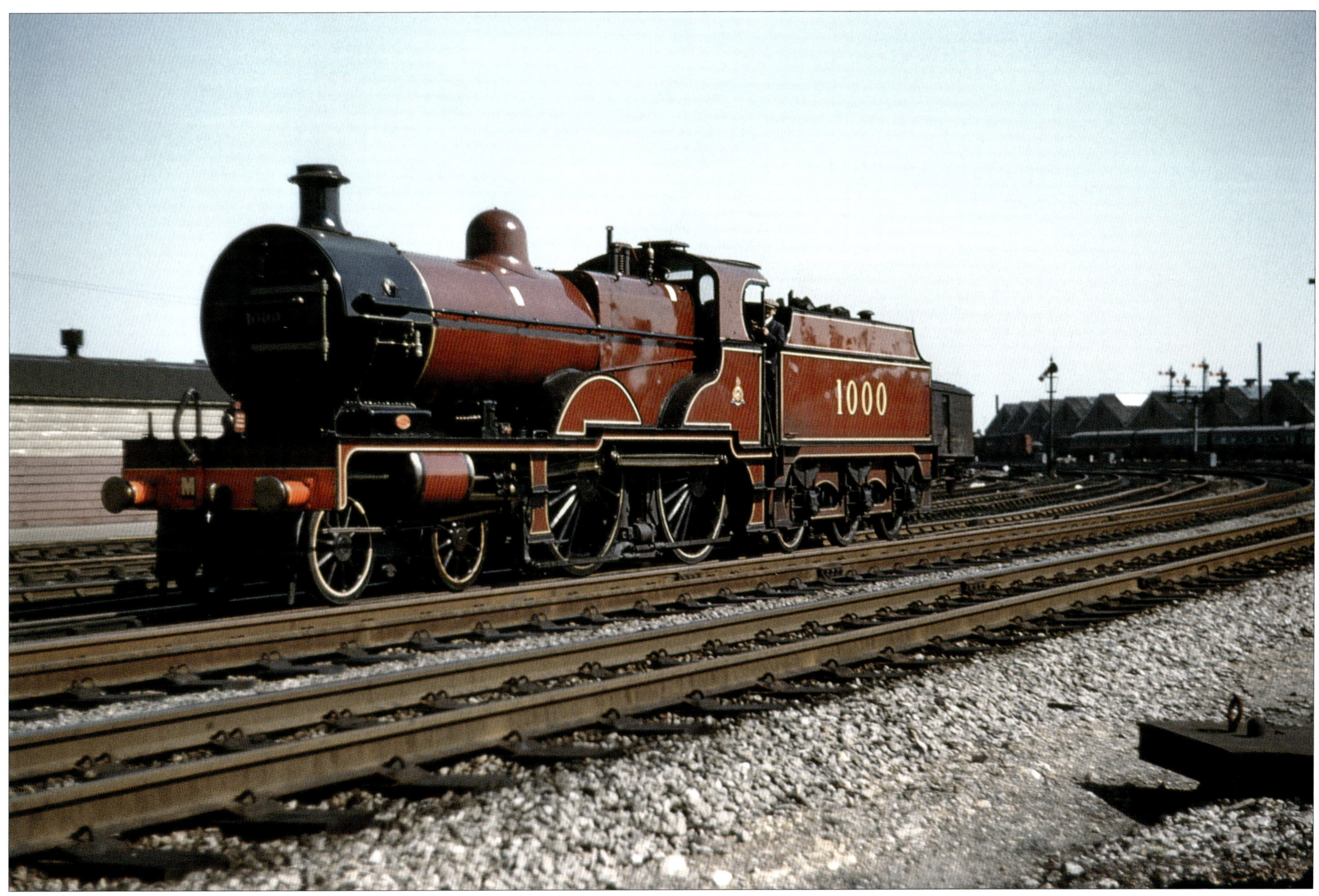

SLIDE 1129 | Ex-*MR/LMS Compound* **1000** runs into Swindon light engine after being taken off *RCTS* (East Midlands Branch) special train *The East Midlander No. 4 Rail Tour* at Oxford. This excursion originated from Nottingham Victoria with *1000* in charge initially and ran via Reading, Basingstoke and Eastleigh to Swindon. *Churchward 43xx* class **7317** took over at Oxford, taking the train forward via Didcot's North and East Junctions. *BR Standard* class 4 **76006** was also utilised on this journey, but only in order to allow *7317* to be watered and turned at Eastleigh (the *Compound* having taken water on Aynho Troughs, south of Banbury). The train returned to Nottingham Victoria with *1000* in charge *(see also slide 1138 on page 121). 11/9/60 Leica IIIA (Kodachrome)*

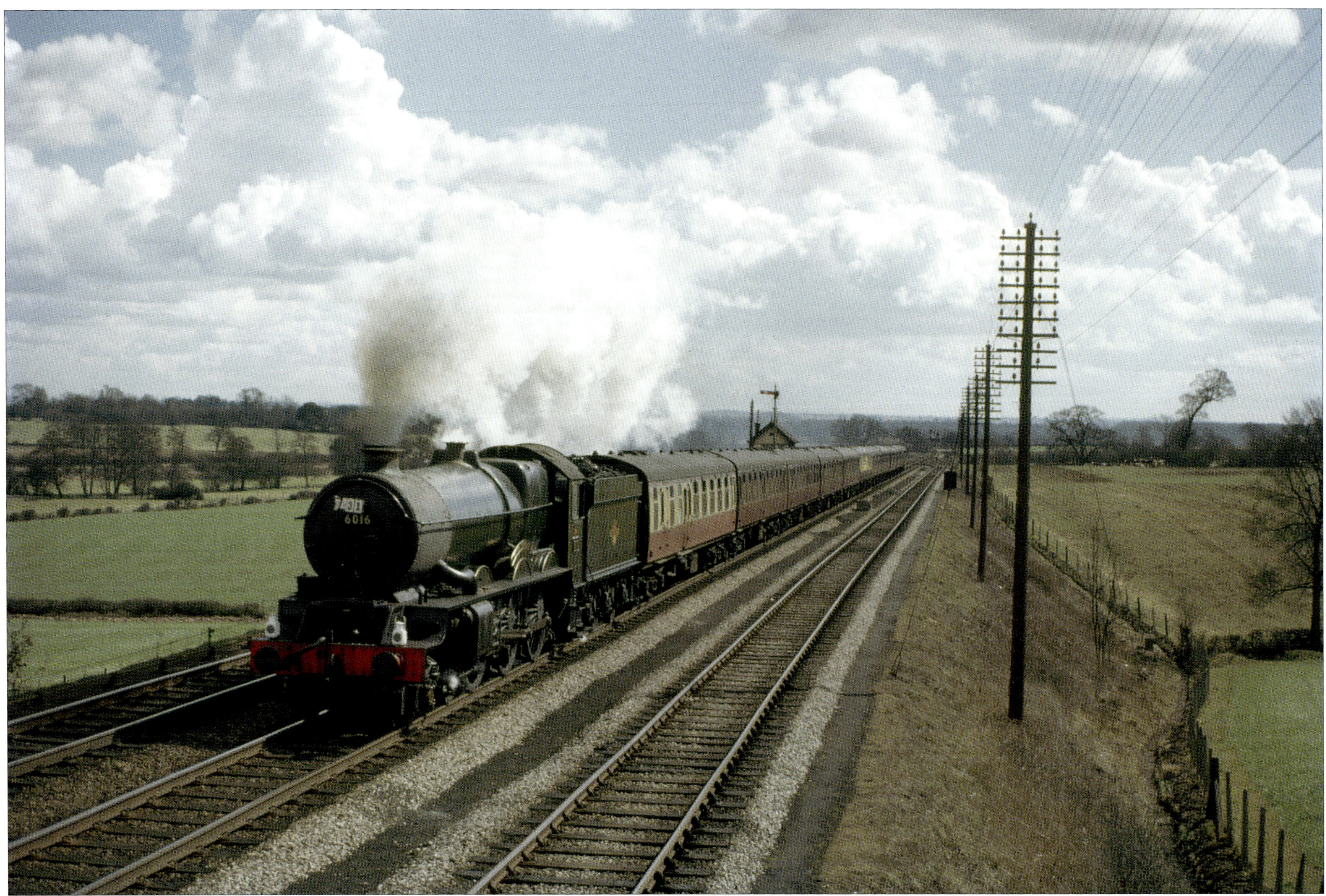

SLIDE 1204 | Considering Old Oak's **6016 King Edward V** was very much living on borrowed time when this photograph was taken, shed staff have done it proud with its polished brass reflecting handsomely in the mirror-like paintwork. It is seen here thundering past Budbrook Signal Box and down goods loop with a football special for Birmingham: Fulham are playing Burnley at Villa Park in the F.A. Cup semi-finals. This working was the last of five specials run from the capital: the others being *Castle*-hauled. In the event, the match was to end in a 1-1 draw, demanding a replay just over a week later (at Filbert Street, Leicester) which resulted in a 2-1 Burnley win. Several months after this photograph was taken, *6016* was transferred to Stafford Road where it spent its last three months prior to withdrawal. Photograph taken from the ladder of the down goods loop starting signal. Tom was well-known to Bill Rawlings, the Signalman at Budbrook and if 'given the nod', he would slow expresses down at the foot of the bank here; just enough to make them more camera-friendly! *31/3/62 (Kodachrome)*

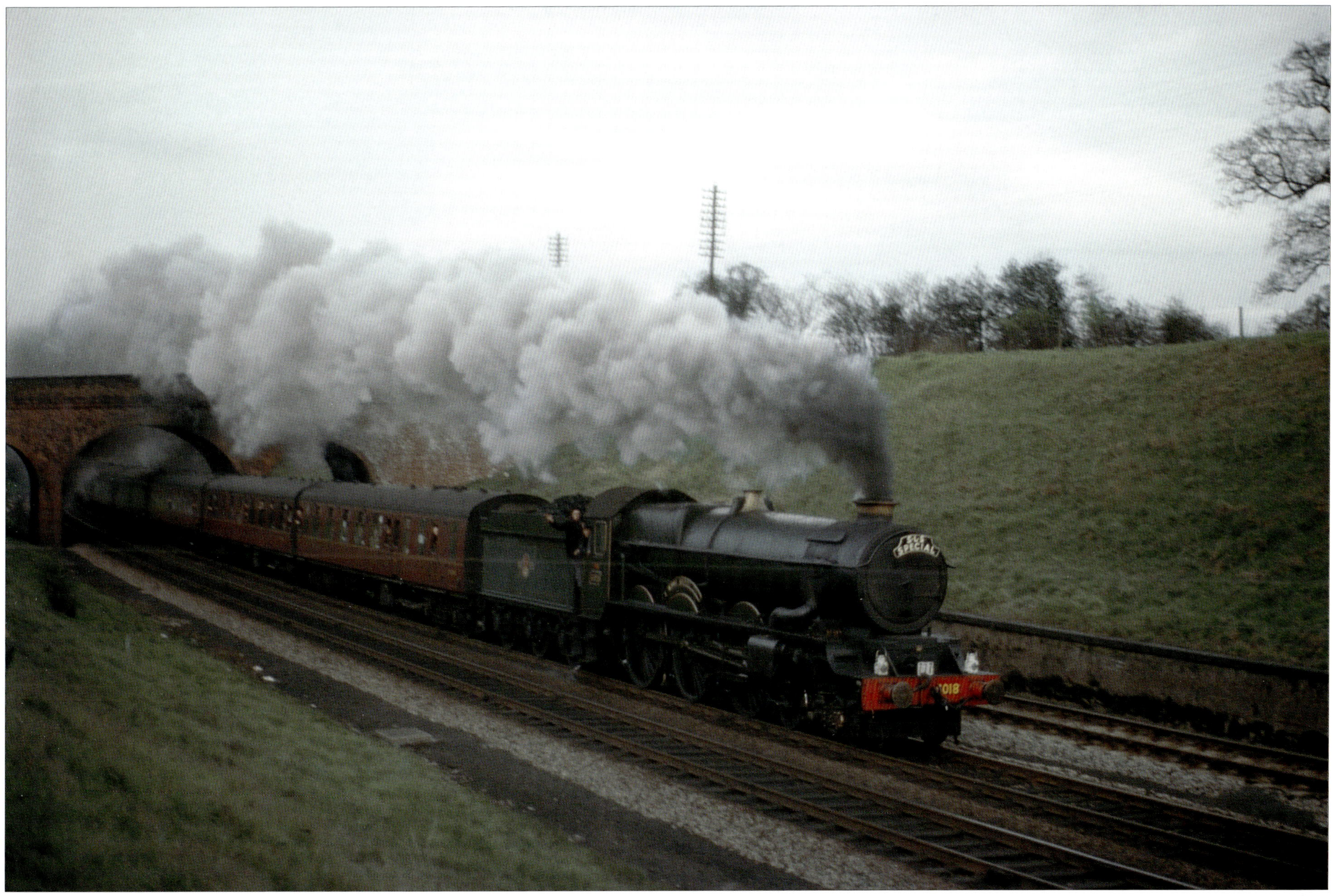

SLIDE 1603 | At around 7.15pm on this dull and intermittently wet Spring Sunday, **6018 King Henry VI** returns the *SLS Farewell to the Kings* special to Birmingham Snow Hill. This train ran from Birmingham to Swindon via Greenford and Southall, returning via Didcot and Oxford. With the light about to fail, it is captured here nearing the summit of Hatton Bank with around thirty minutes of the journey left to run. After withdrawal, *6018* had been specifically retained for working this special and during March 1963 underwent minor repairs at Tyseley Shed in preparation for its final duties prior to scrapping. During the final week of tests, culminating in a boiler washout and inspection on April 26th, this locomotive could be observed working Birmingham to Leamington Spa local trains *(see slide 1585 reproduced on page 27 of Volume 1)*. Rumours abound surrounding the last few months prior to 6018's final demise, but perhaps the most interesting relates to both Billy Butlin's and actor, Kenneth More's quest to purchase it. Sadly, neither man was able to stand in the way of the cutter's torch and the rest as they say, is history.
28/4/63 (Kodachrome)

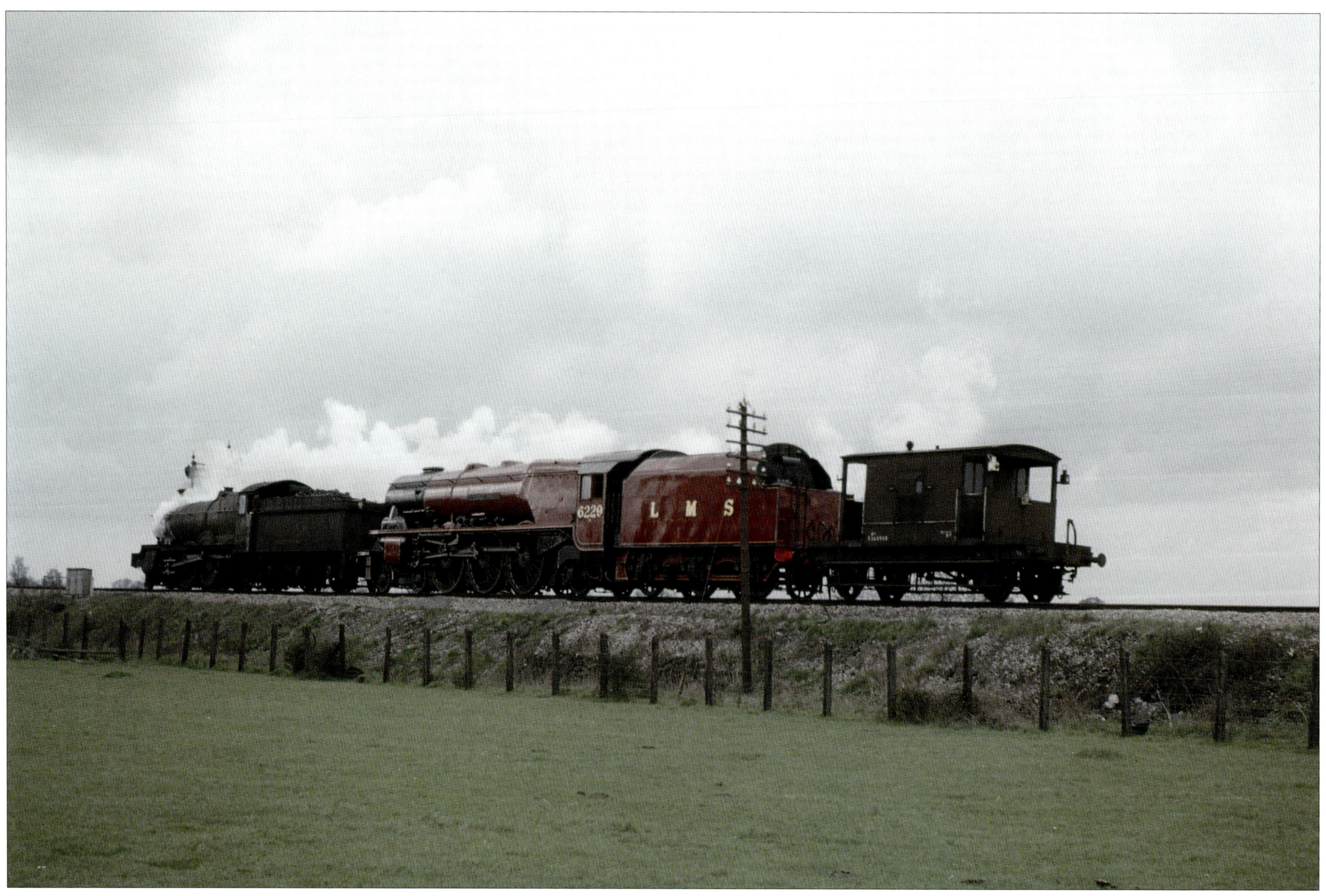

SLIDE 1714 | On this cold and dull Saturday morning, Reading's **6825 Llanvair Grange** looking tired and neglected, tows **(4)6229 Duchess of Hamilton** plus brake past Stratford-upon-Avon's derelict Racecourse Platforms (just out of frame on the right) bound for *Butlin's* holiday camp at Minehead. Note that *6229* still has its connecting rods attached, suggesting that the journey will be long, slow and tedious for the crew of *6825*! *46229* had been withdrawn from Edge Hill, Liverpool just two months previously and along with non-streamlined classmate **(4)6233 Duchess of Sutherland**, had been purchased by Sir Billy Butlin in his desire to place them as static playground exhibits at his holiday camps. *6229* eventually left Minehead in March 1975 on a twenty-year loan to the *Friends of the NRM* and the rest is history. Reunited with its 1938 streamlining at *Tyseley Locomotive Works* during the 2000s, *6229* currently resides in the *NRM*, York. *18/4/64 (Kodachrome)*

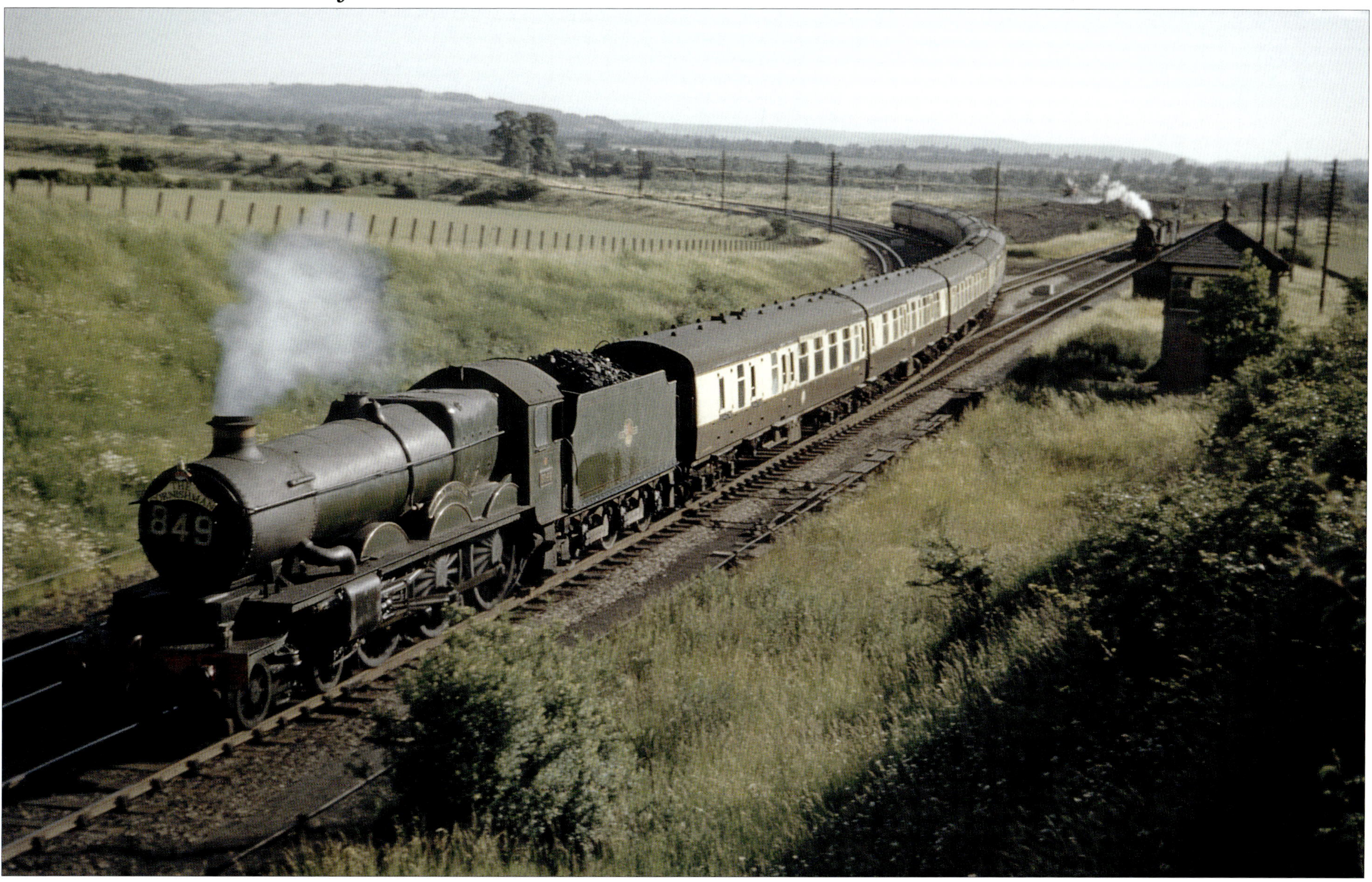

SLIDE 864 | On this glorious Tuesday evening, Stafford Road's *Castle* class **5046 Earl Cawdor** on the 10.30am SX Penzance to Wolverhampton *Cornishman* service heads north-east through the junctions at Honeybourne towards its next stop at Stratford-upon-Avon, whilst an unidentified *51xx* class 2-6-2T on a pick-up goods waits at signals. *5046* is just coming off the north loop and just below the horizon, overlooked by the northern edge of the *Cotswolds*, we can just make out the Worcester to Paddington main line running parallel to the skyline. The spire of *St Ecgwin's Church*, Honeybourne can also just be identified in the distance behind the North Box. *16/6/59 (Kodachrome)*

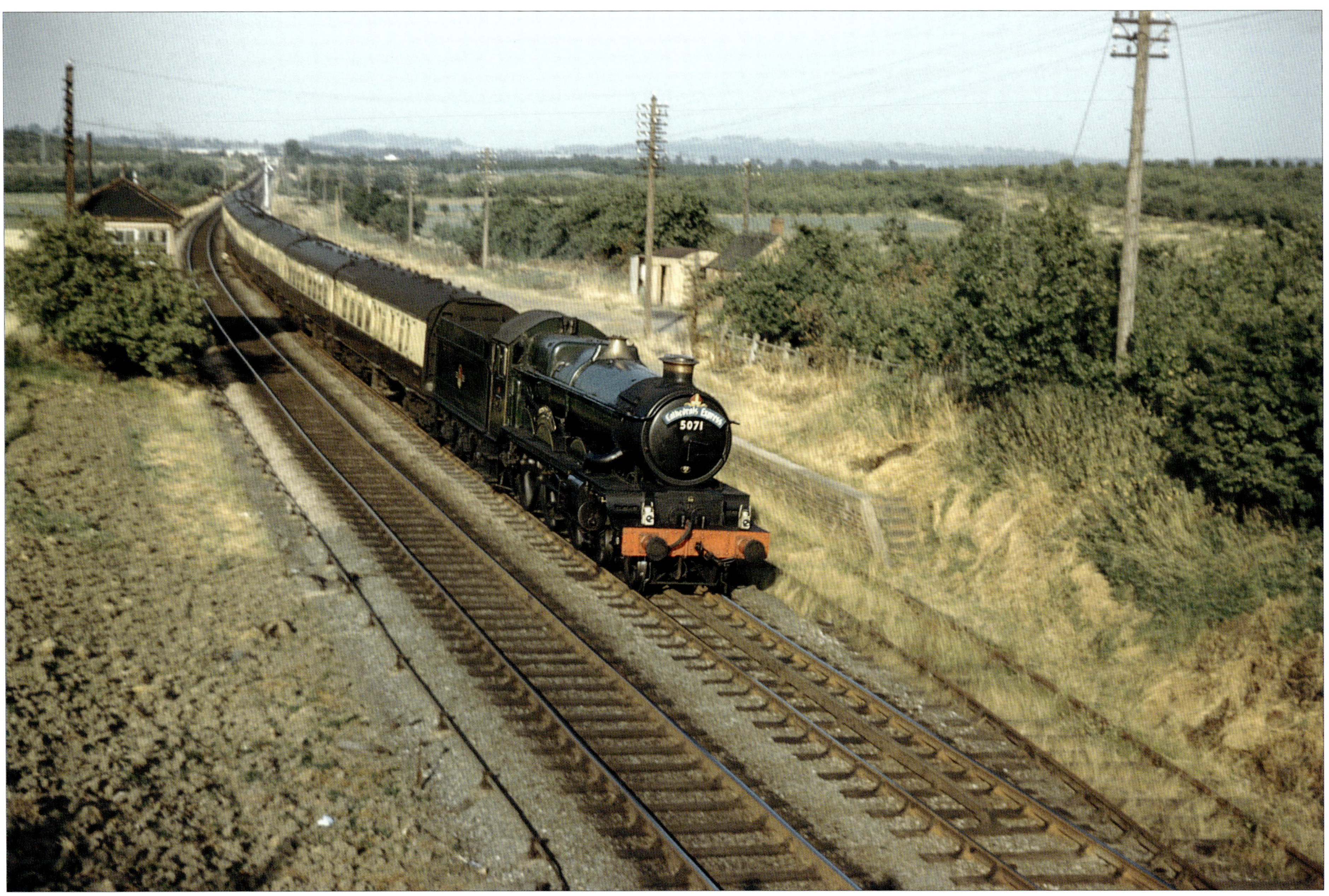

SLIDE 888 | Worcester's **5071 Spitfire** *(ex-Clifford Castle)* rolls along the *Avon Valley* into the evening sun with the down *Cathedrals Express*, seen here passing Aldington Signal Box and sidings between Honeybourne and Evesham. This location was busy only during the fruit and vegetable season; acting as a railhead for the *Vale of Evesham* farmers. The signal box was only active during these periods, being switched in and out by locum signalmen/shunters as requirements demanded; otherwise the section was Littleton & Badsey to Evesham. Photograph taken from the *B4510 Offenham Road* overbridge. Note the distinctive eastern horizon at this location: *Meon Hill* and *Larkstoke* straddling the border between Worcestershire and Warwickshire. *8/7/59 Leica IIIA (Kodachrome)*

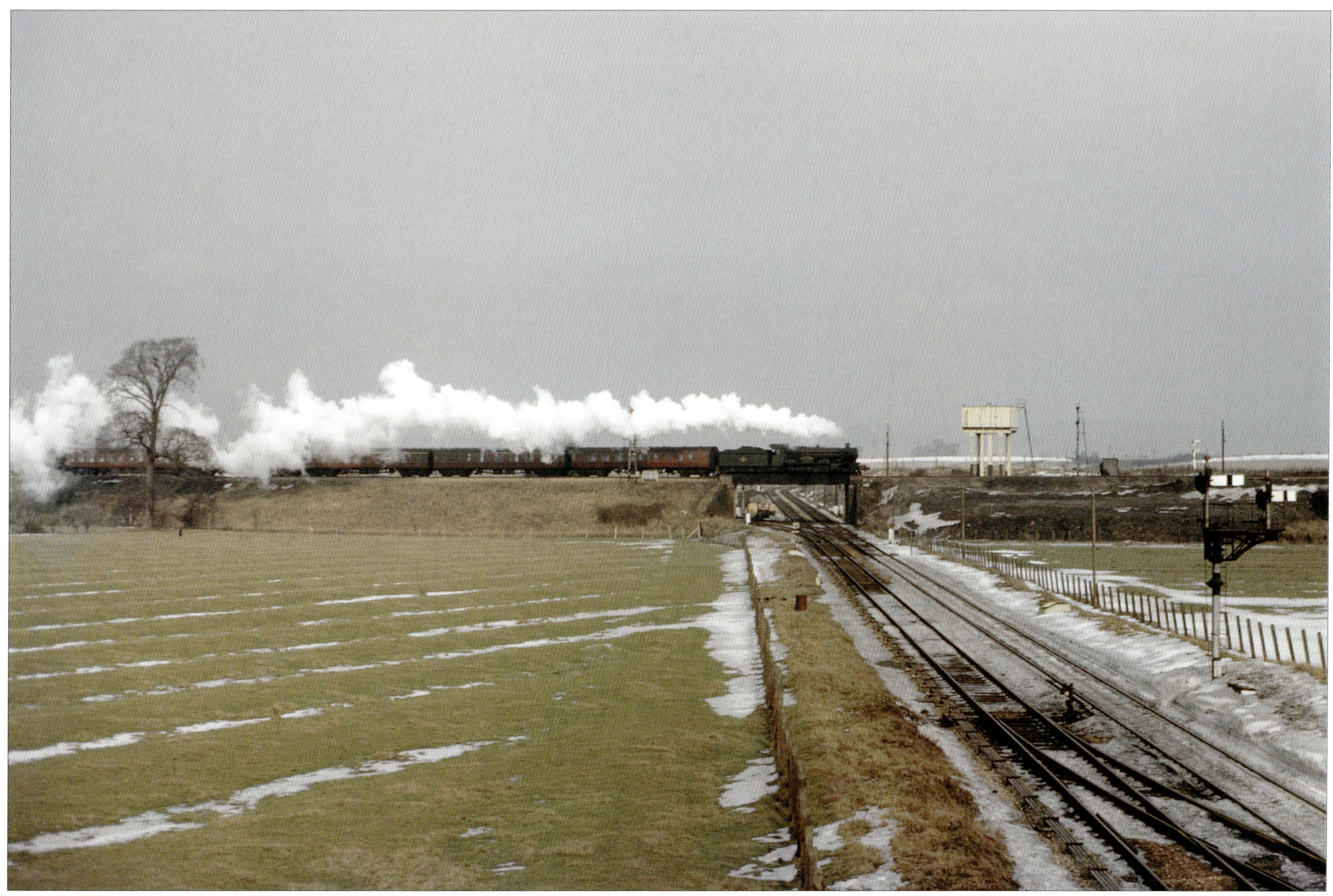

SLIDE 1564 | With the persistent snows of Winter 1963 continuing to remind us of the merciless temperatures that stretched almost into Spring, the photographer looks north-east from the *Mickleton Road* overbridge, just south of the Honeybourne 'triangle'. Here we see an unidentified *Castle* class on a Worcester to Paddington express: the lines in the foreground travelling to and from Cheltenham. This photograph is taken from almost exactly the same viewpoint as *slide 866* reproduced on page 98 of *Volume 3* and serves to illustrate how much this scene changed in just under four years. *?/3/63 (Kodachrome)*

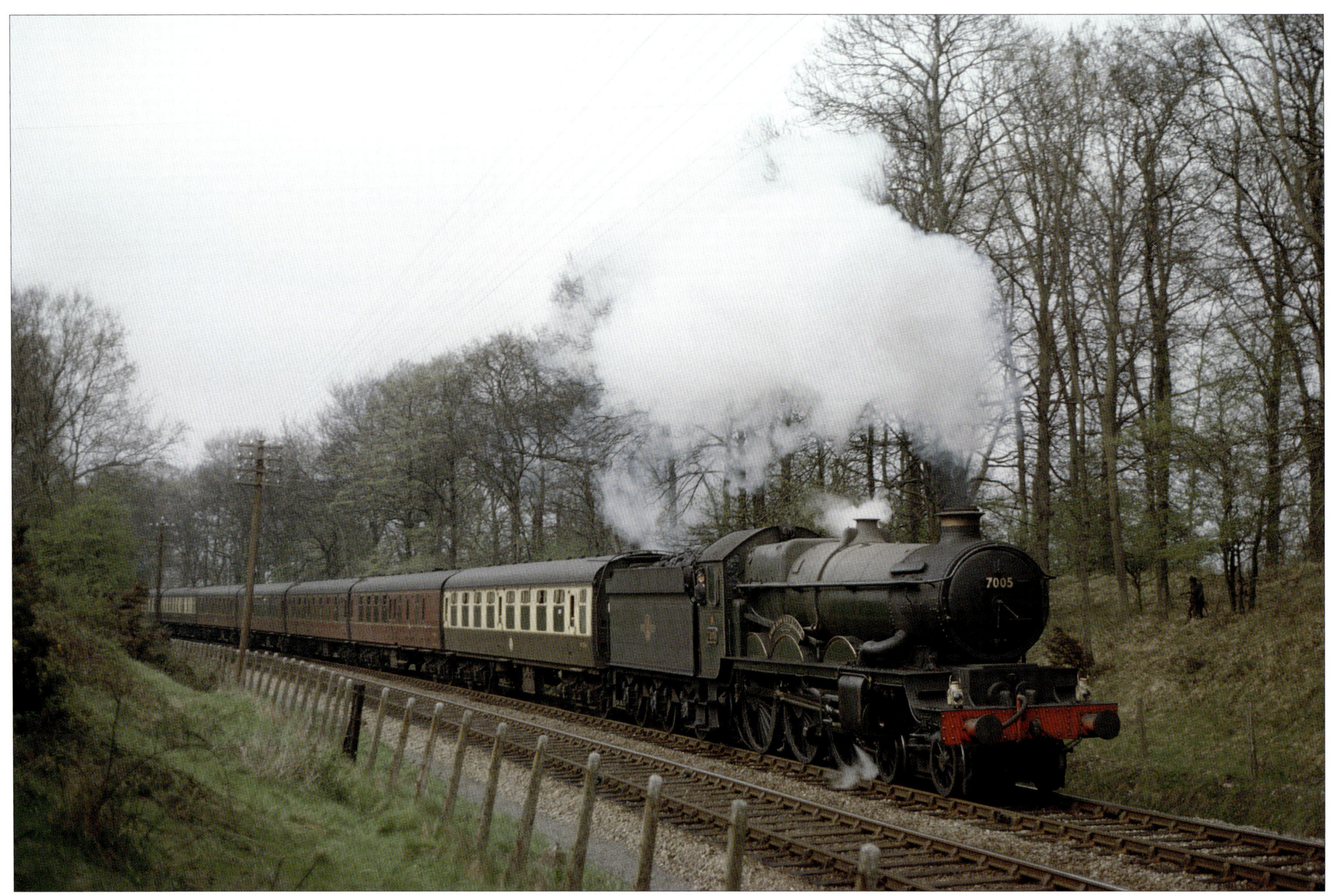

SLIDE 1600 | Coming towards the end of its short eighteen-year service life, but still looking far from being a spent force, Worcester stalwart, **7005 Sir Edward Elgar** on an unidentified afternoon Hereford to Paddington express, attacks the lower slopes of the 1 in 100 climb to Campden Tunnel. Despite its comparative youth: one of the last of the *Castle* class to be built by the *GWR*, this locomotive was at this stage on its ninth and final boiler and had already seen its last substantial visit to Swindon Works. After spending its entire life exactly where it should have been: working out of Worcester, *7005* was strangely reallocated to Southall shed for its final few weeks, from where it was withdrawn for scrapping in September 1964 *(see also slide 1100 on page 83)*. *27/4/63 (Kodachrome)*

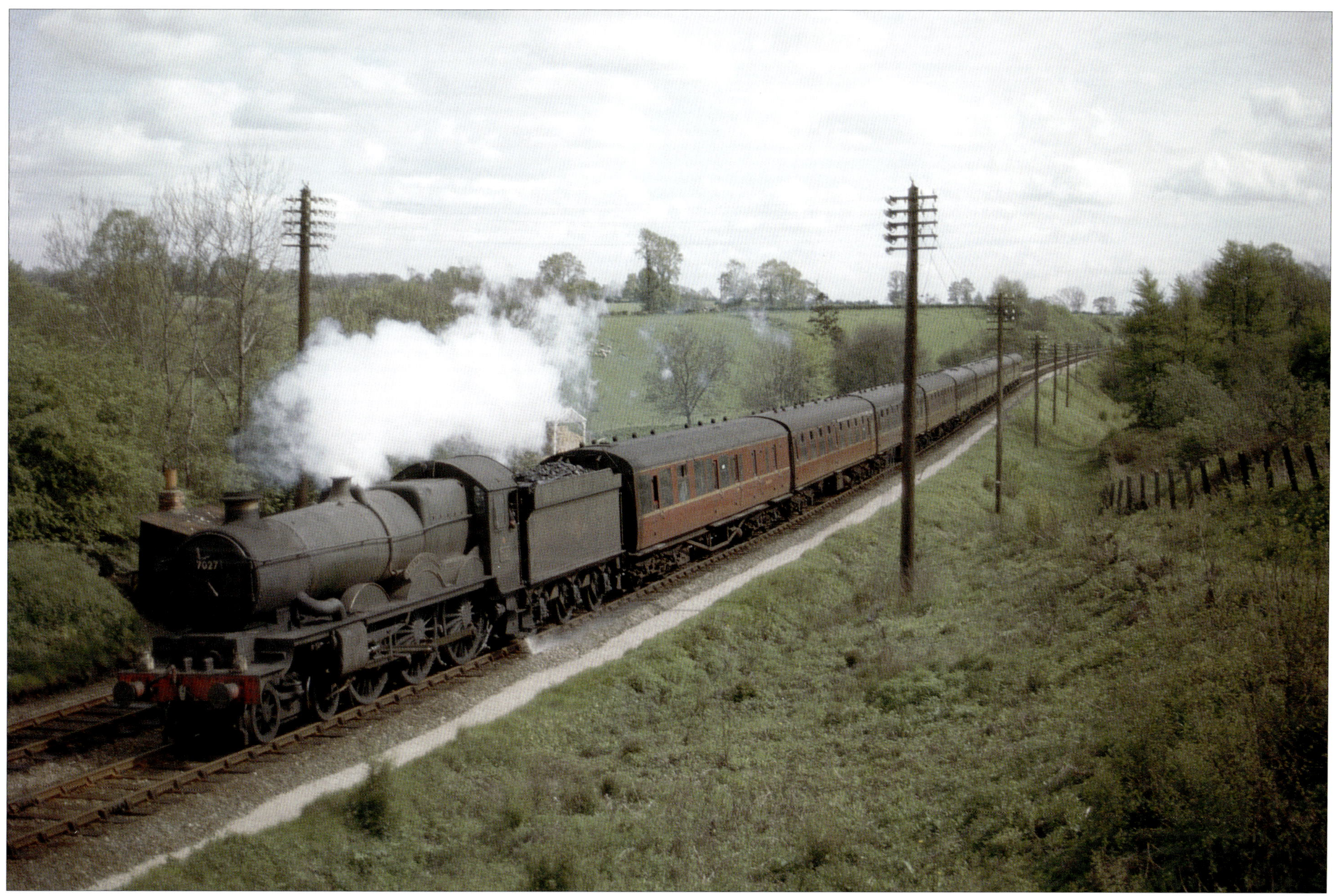

SLIDE 1612 | **7027 Thornbury Castle** with an unidentified Paddington to Worcester express approaches the village of Aston Magna, approximately two miles north of Moreton-in-Marsh, Gloucestershire. It is caught here about to pass the site of the *Batsford Estate Brick Works*, now long-gone, situated a hundred yards or so behind the photographer. The overbridge carrying the works access road (where the photographer is standing) was dismantled in 1965. Today, only the partial remains of the bridge abutments are still identifiable beneath dense vegetation. Having been a Worcester locomotive since April 1960, *7027* was only three months away from reallocation to Reading shed when this photograph was taken. *10/5/63 (Kodachrome)*

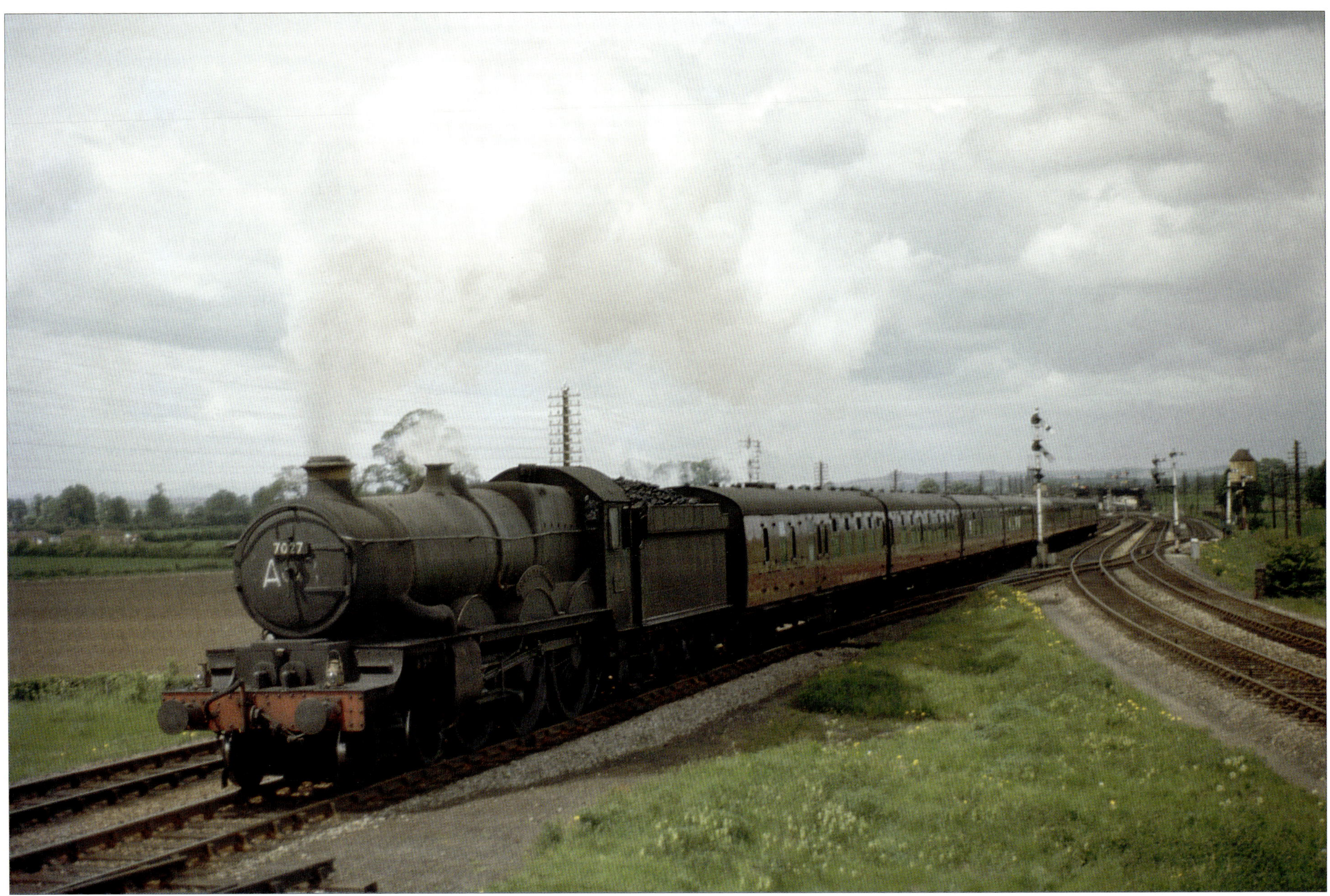

SLIDE 1617 | The following week, **7027 Thornbury Castle** is captured again running at speed through Honeybourne on the Worcester to Paddington main line with an unidentified up express ready to attack the climb up through the northern edge of the *Cotswolds* and into Gloucestershire. The remains of a chalked reporting number probably refers to a working from the previous day. The tracks we see curving off to the right head to Stratford-upon-Avon and Birmingham and in the distance, one can just make out the steel span of the *Buckle Street* overbridge with the station complex beyond. *7027* was withdrawn from Reading just over six months after this photograph was taken and sold to *Woodham's* at Barry. Purchased by what was the *Birmingham Railway Museum* in 1972 and passing through several well-intentioned owners, it is currently under restoration by the *Great Central Railway*, Loughborough. *18/5/63 (Kodachrome)*

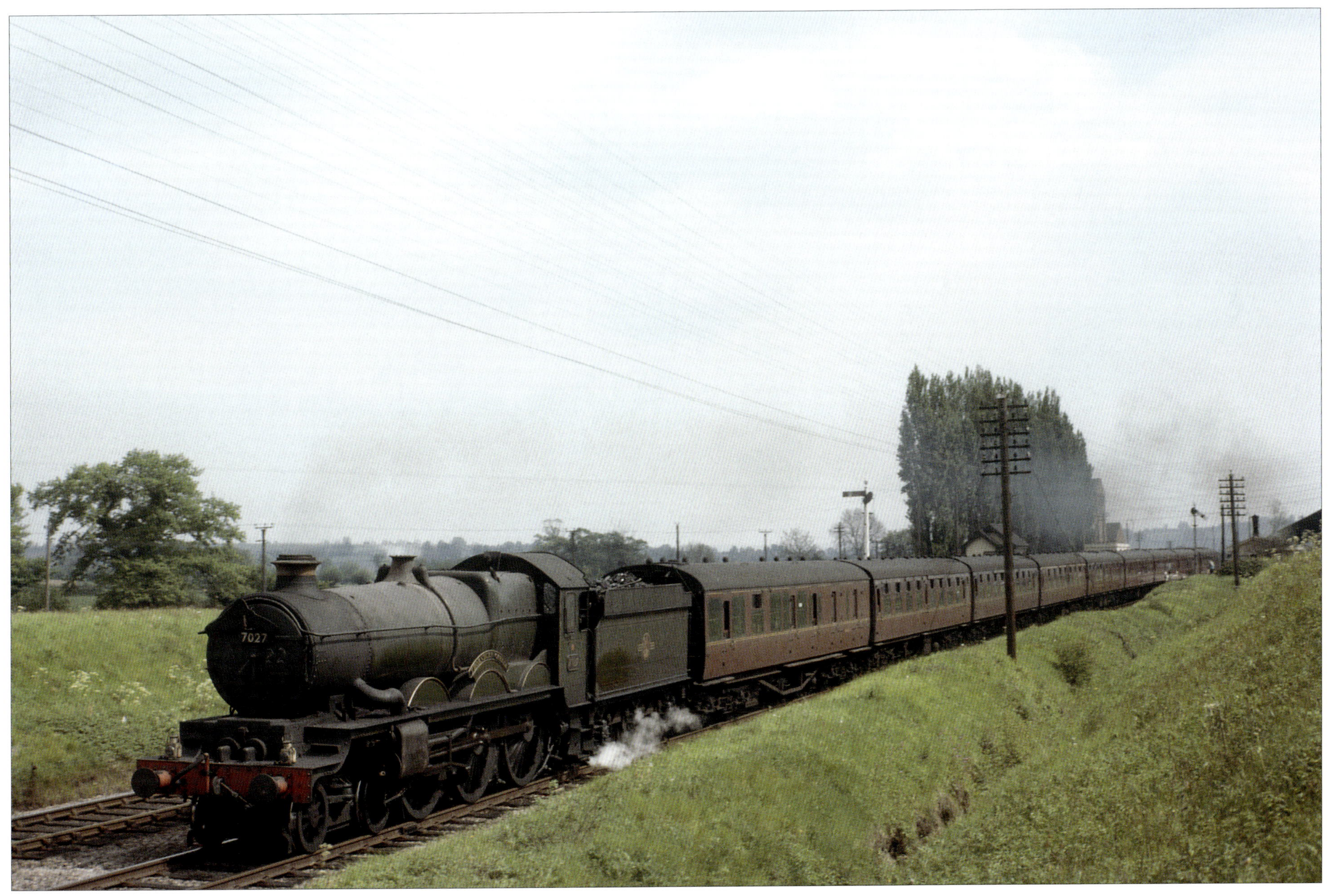

SLIDE 1621 | A week or so later, but on an unspecified date, **7027 Thornbury Castle** is this time caught running downhill through Chipping Campden Station and level crossing with an afternoon Paddington to Hereford express. Note that *7027* appears to be returning the reversed *Cathedrals Express* headboard to Hereford ready for the following day's service. When the station at Chipping Campden was first opened by the *Oxford, Worcester & Wolverhampton Railway Company* in 1853, it was originally named after the other nearby village of Mickleton, but was later renamed simply Campden. It wasn't until 1952 that it acquired the full title of Chipping Campden, though this would be short-lived. The station was closed almost exactly fourteen years later, with very little evidence now that it ever existed. The level crossing still remains, albeit remotely controlled. *?/5/63 (Kodachrome)*

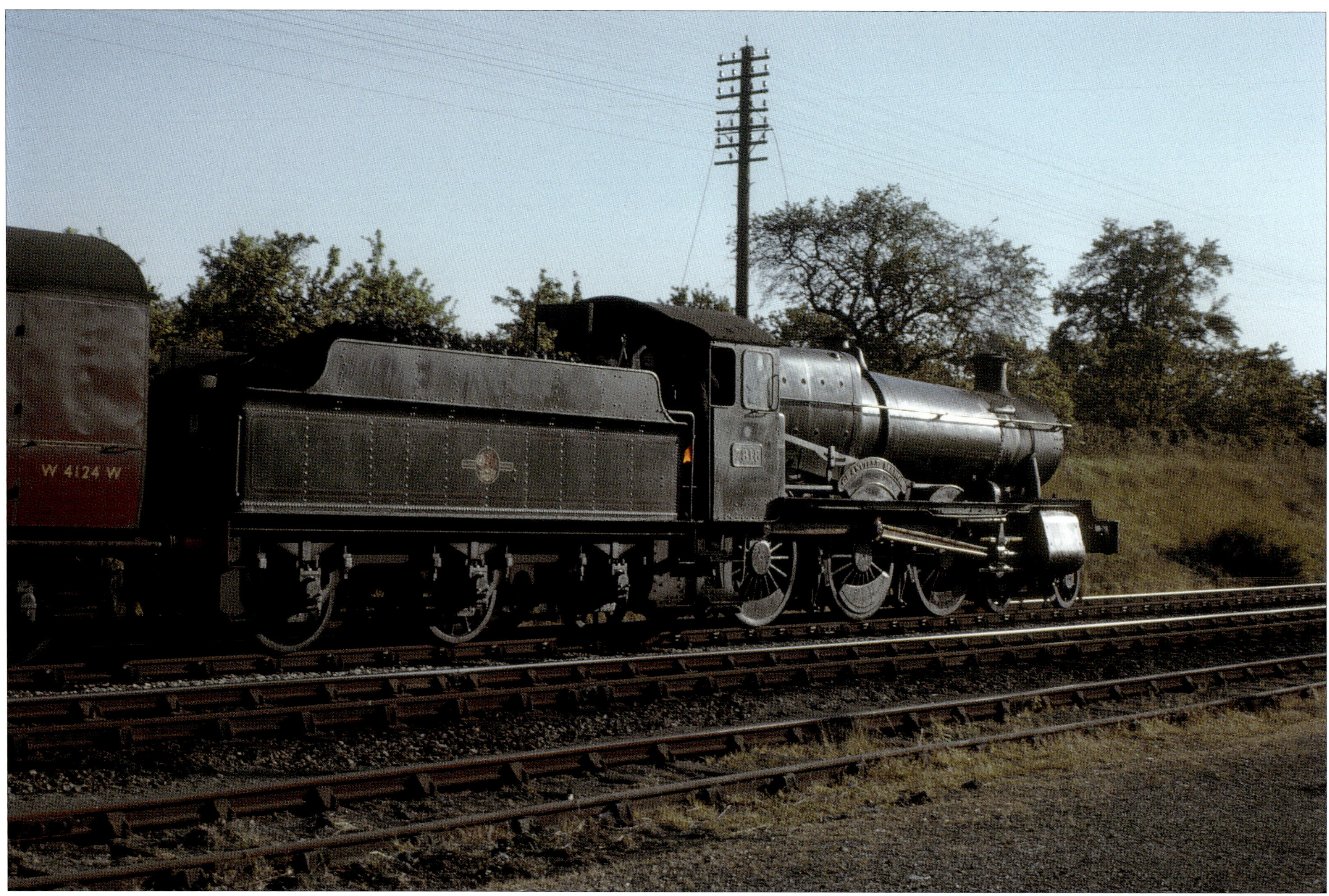

SLIDE 1650 | We published the accompanying 'approach' shot of this train in *Volume 1*, but felt that the skill and artistry demonstrated in capturing this image was too important to ignore. **7818 Granville Manor** pulls away from Littleton & Badsey with an Oxford to Worcester semi-fast working in the perfect light of a cloudless Summer's evening. There appears to be a plethora of misinformation surrounding this locomotive's movements during its twilight years and as a result, we previous stated that at this time it was working out of Machynlleth. Evidence has since come to light that it may actually have been shedded at Tyseley. Either way, its withdrawal and disposal details seem unambiguous. It was taken out of service in January 1965 and became one of six of its class to be broken up by *Cashmore's* of Great Bridge just three months later. *?/6/63 (Kodachrome)*

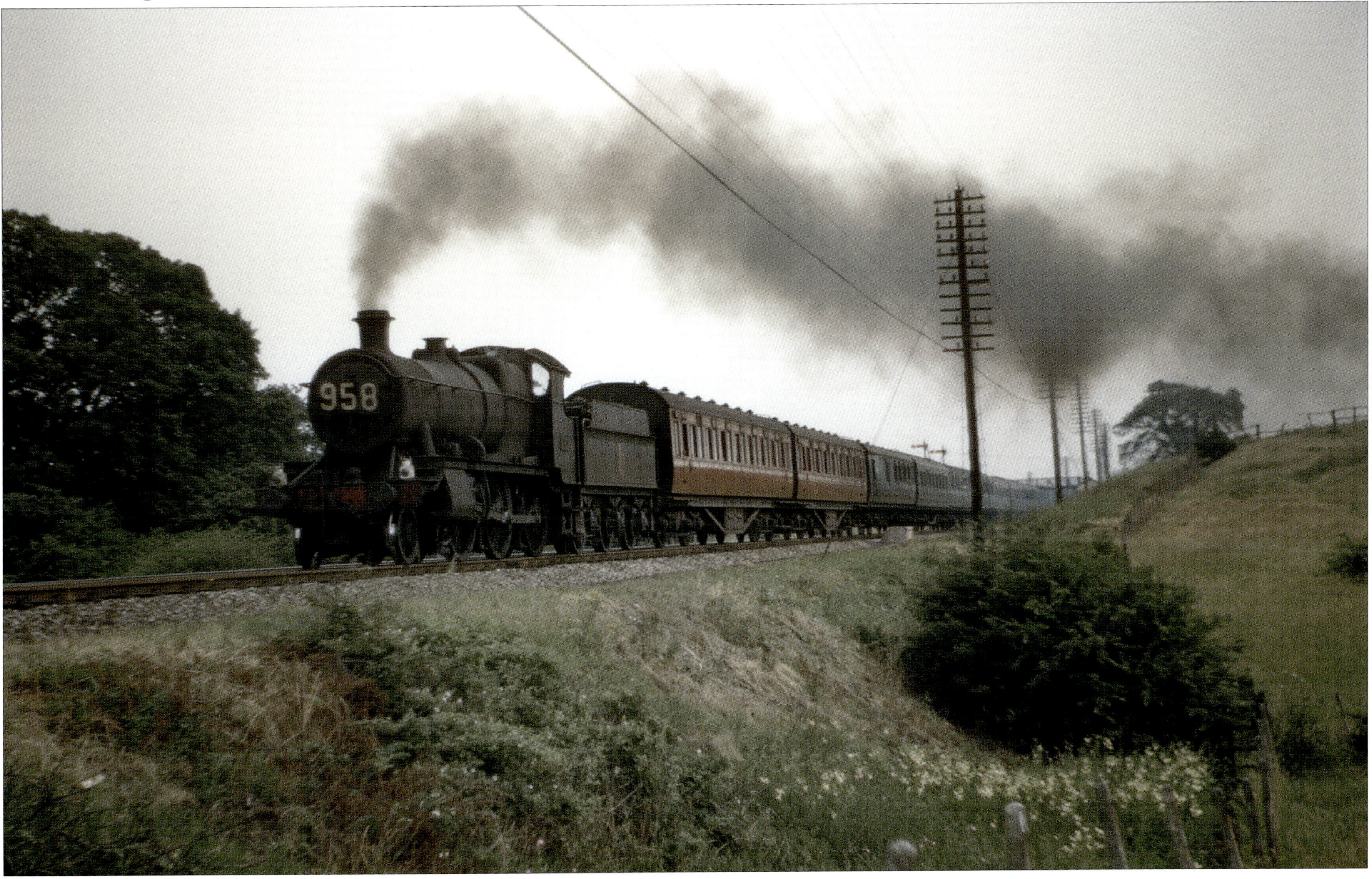

SLIDE 364 | The fireman of grubby Oxley-based *Churchward 43xx* class *Mogul* **7305** has had a job on his hands as his charge hauls the heavily-loaded 8.55am SO Margate to Birmingham up the bank and through Hatton North Junction (signal box and footbridge just visible in the distance). It was relatively common to observe filthy *43xx* class locomotives on express duties during this period of the 1950s; many of them pressed into service at comparatively short notice to help out with the volume of Summer Saturday holiday relief workings, to and from the south and south-east. *7305* spent approximately three years at Oxley before being reallocated to Banbury shed in May 1958. Its last two years of service were spent at Taunton, from where it was withdrawn for scrapping in September 1962. *6/7/57 (Kodachrome)*

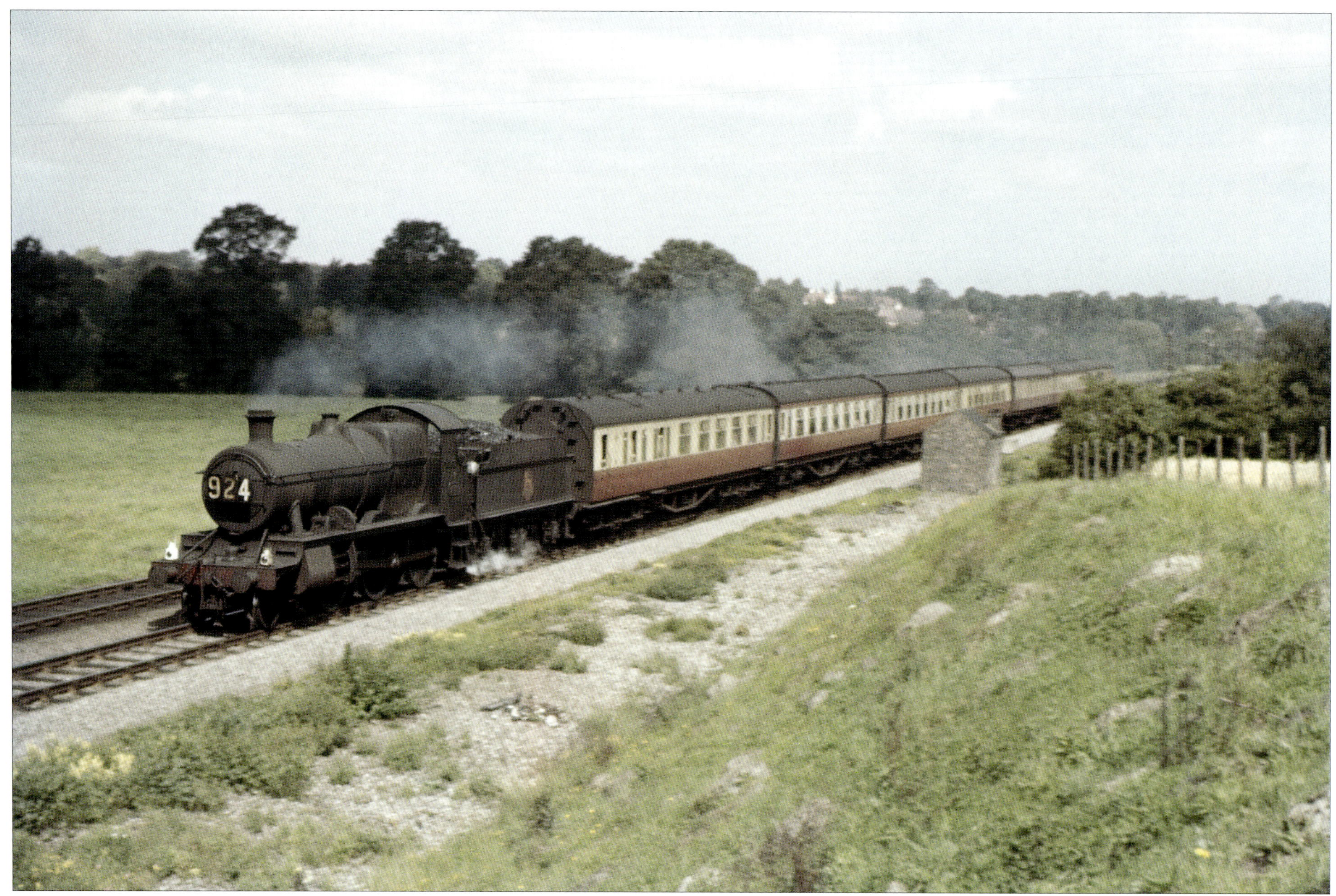

SLIDE 389 | Reading-based *Churchward 43xx* class *Mogul* **6366** is captured on an unidentified holiday express just south of Lapworth Station (the train is possibly a Birkenhead to Margate/Ramsgate relief working). The untidy and overly-wide nature of the cutting slope on which the photographer is standing, is a result of historic work carried out in preparation for the planned quadrupling of the line here, which ultimately never came to fruition. Despite being originally ordered in 1922 as a part of *Lot 216* (a batch of twenty-eight locomotives) *6366* wasn't actually built and delivered until late 1925 as a part of *Lot 230*. This was down to Swindon Works being overloaded with a backlog of orders for new locomotives, compounded by the need to keep step with regular overhauls and repairs on existing ones. *6366* was eventually withdrawn from Cardiff Canton in September 1962 and broken up by *Cashmore's* of Newport in January of the following year. *3/8/57 (Kodak Ektachrome)*

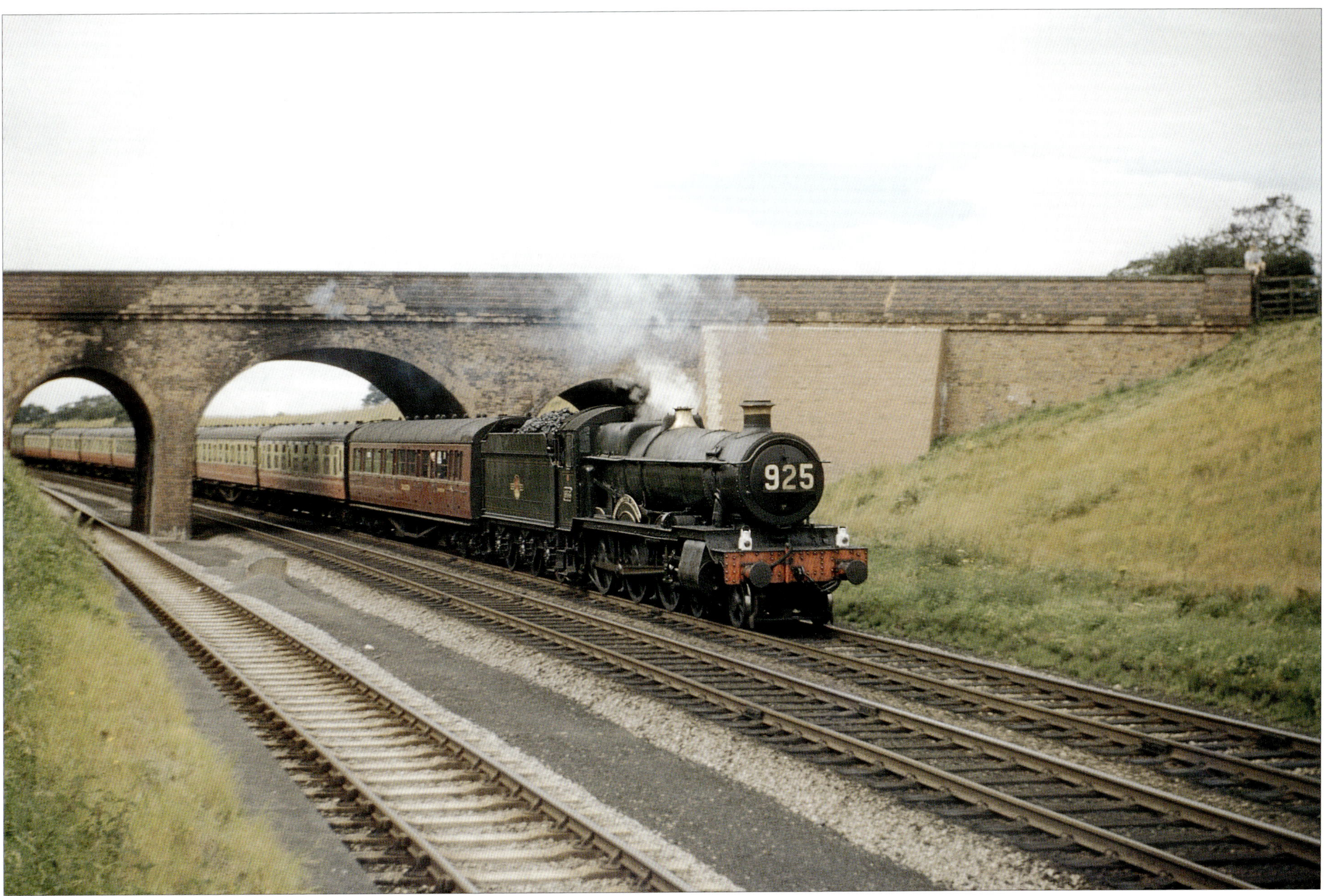

SLIDE 602 | Tyseley stalwart **6853 Morehampton Grange** descends Hatton Bank with the 12.10pm SO Birmingham to Bournemouth Central. *6853* was one of the many locomotives *almost* saved from the cutter's torch by either localised campaigning, or shed staff pooling their resources. In this case, when it became known to Tyseley men that *6853* was due for withdrawal (and it was understood to have been still in good working order) a local railwayman put in an offer for its purchase. Unfortunately, soon after a figure of £1,200 had been agreed, *6853* blew a steam manifold valve. As the Shed Master at Tyseley had previously been given a directive that no repairs were to be carried out on steam locomotives, even though spare components were still abundant, he refused to go against orders and as a consequence, the purchaser had little choice but to let the locomotive go to scrap. *6853* became one of nine *Granges* sold to *Cohen's* of Cransley, Kettering in late 1965, being broken up in March of the following year. *16/8/58 Leica IIIA 1/200th F2.5 (Kodachrome)*

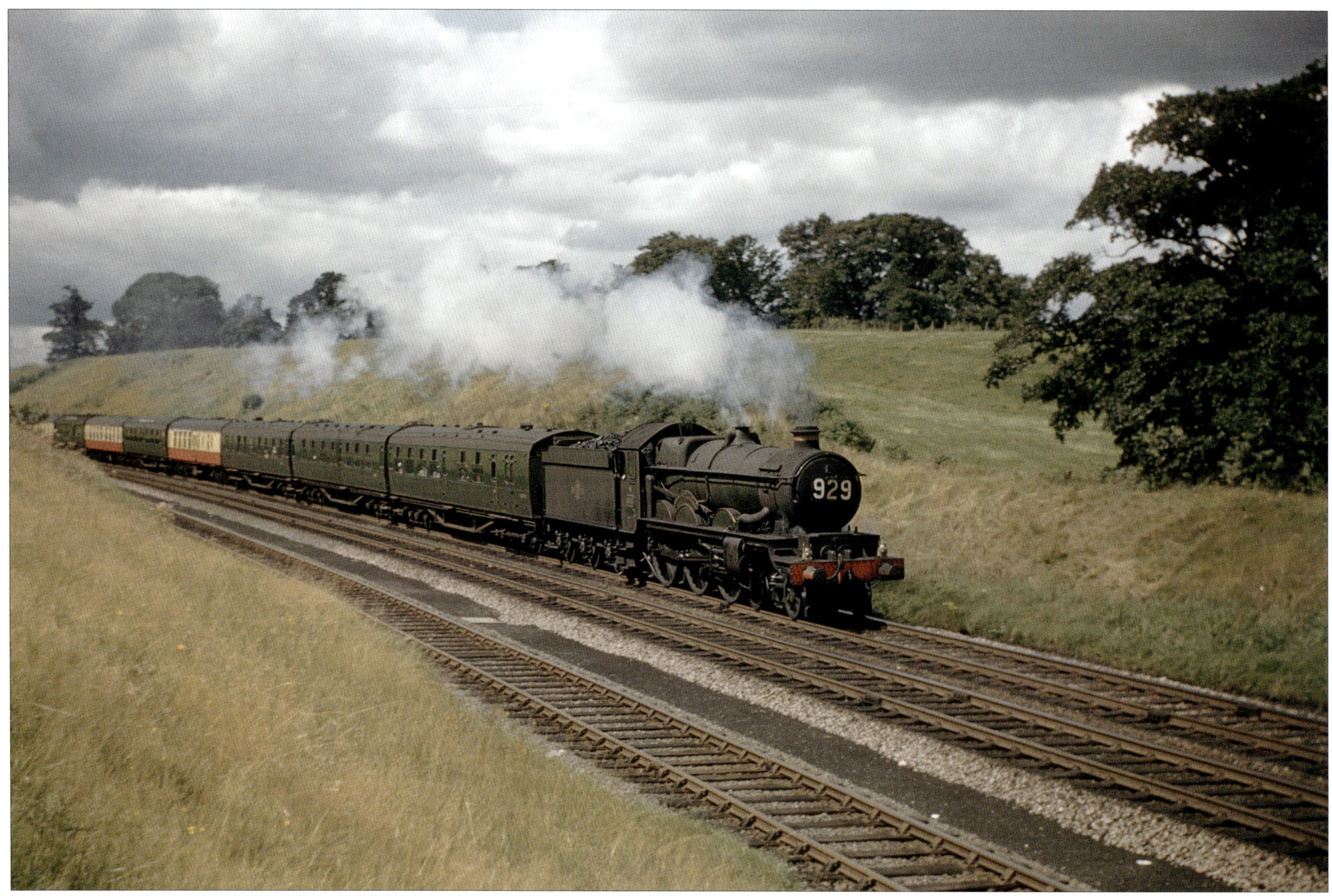

SLIDE 614 | We have paired these two photographs together for obvious reasons and they don't just represent consecutive frames on a film! Oxford-based **5033 Broughton Castle** begins the descent of Hatton Bank with the 9.30am SO Birkenhead to Bournemouth West. When this photograph was taken, *5033* had just been reallocated to Oxford Shed after spending more than a decade at Chester West and its appearance suggests that a clean was due prior to this transfer. Still in possession of its single chimney, *5033* acquired a new double chimney relatively late in the day: between August and November 1960 during a heavy general overhaul. During the same Swindon visit, the locomotive was also fitted with a new boiler and replacement *Collett* 4,000 gallon tender, only to be withdrawn from service less that two years later. *23/8/58 Leica IIIA 1/200th F2.5 (Kodachrome)*

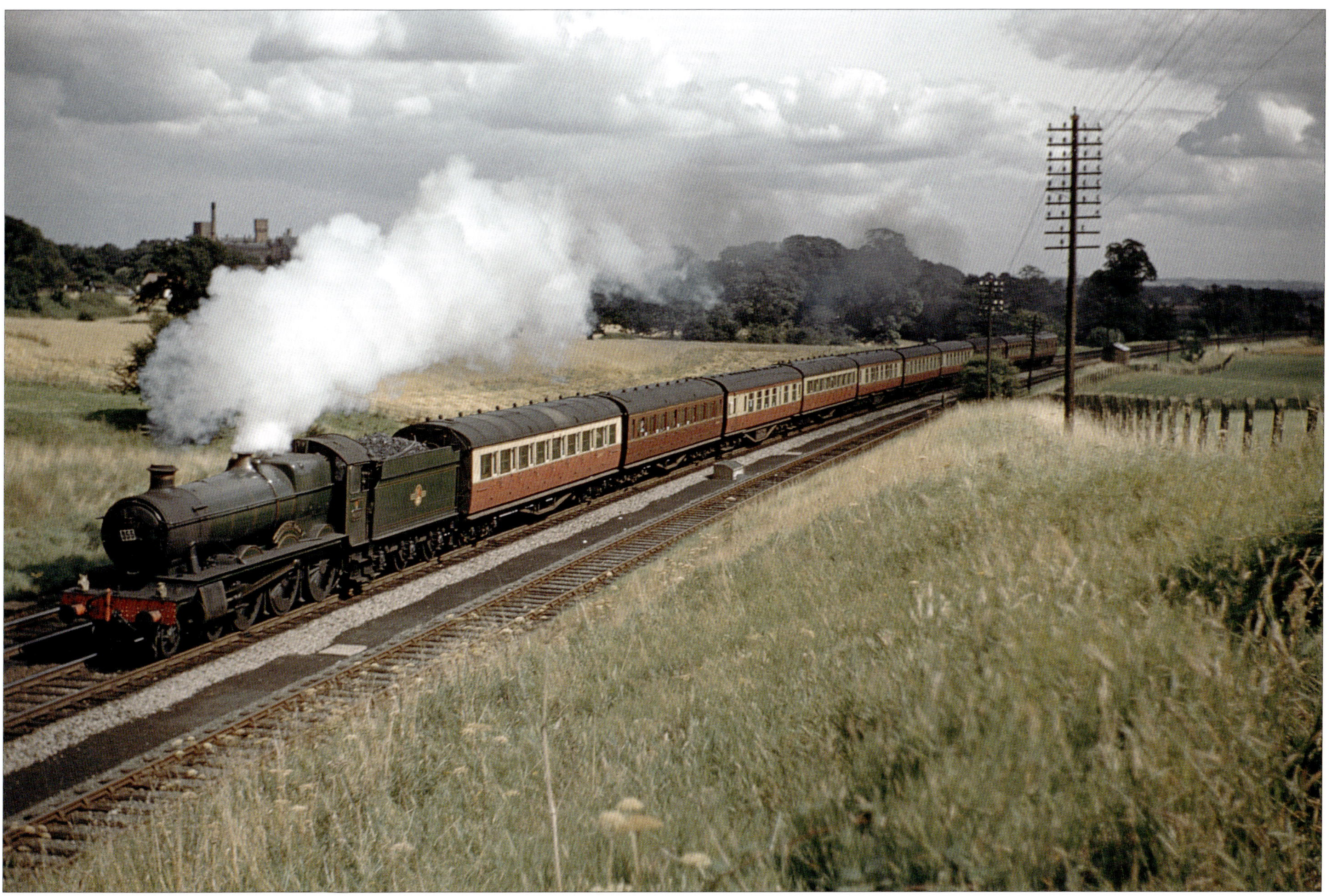

SLIDE 615 | Within a minute or so of capturing the previous image, Tom is alerted by the sound of a train approaching in the down direction and his elevated position gives him prior warning as to whether the train is worthy of a frame of colour film. It is Southall's **4907 Broughton Hall** *(ex-3903 oil burner)* on the SO 9.11am Portsmouth Harbour to Wolverhampton, showing a good head of steam and displaying a far better turn-out than **5033**. During its time as an oil burner (1947-1950) this locomotive was working out of Old Oak Common, but on reconversion and renumbering (the last of its class to go through the process) it was reallocated to St. Philip's Marsh. The rest of *4907's* service life was quite nomadic; undergoing no less than four shed reallocations during 1953 alone. It was eventually withdrawn from Hereford in August 1963. *23/8/58 Leica IIIA 1/200th F2.5 (Kodachrome)*

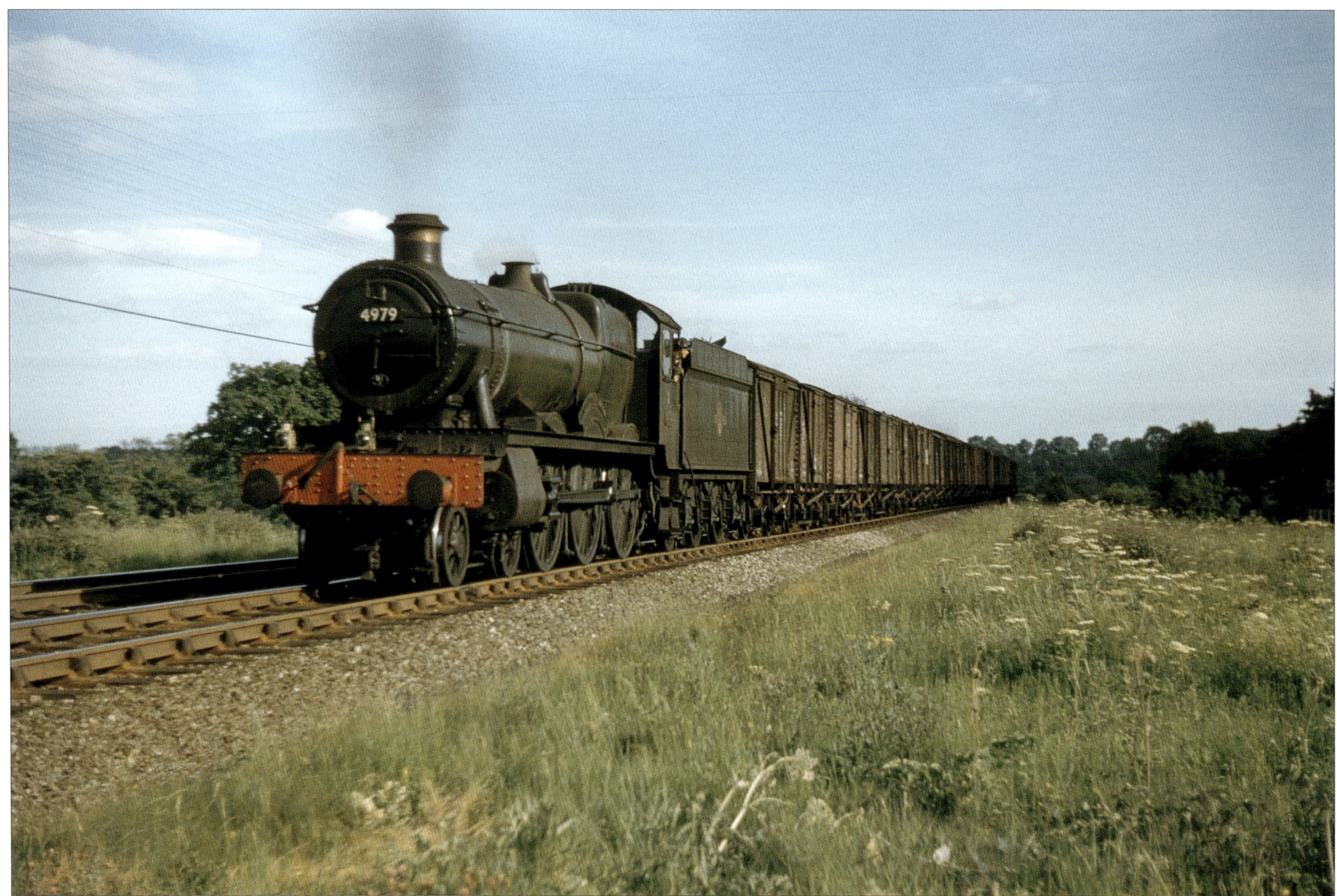

SLIDE 843 | At around 6.30pm on this glorious Tuesday evening, Oxford-based **4979 Wootton Hall** on a train stocked largely with vegetables and fruit from the *Southern Region*, hauls its charge into patch of sunlight on the approach to Lapworth as it heads north-west towards Birmingham. The plateau-like embankment at this location, as in the case of the cutting we see in *slide 389* reproduced on page 64 (approximately 500 yards north of this location) was created to accommodate the two extra tracks which were never actually laid. Withdrawn from service in December 1963, *4979* became the one hundred and seventy-ninth departure from *Woodham's Yard* at Barry in October 1986 and although very little actual remedial work was carried out over the following two decades, there are now strong indications that there is light at the end of the tunnel regarding restoring the locomotive to steam in the not-too-distant future. This work will be carried out under the auspices of the *Furness Railway Trust* at the *Ribble Steam Railway*, Lancashire. *2/6/59 Leica IIIA (Kodachrome)*

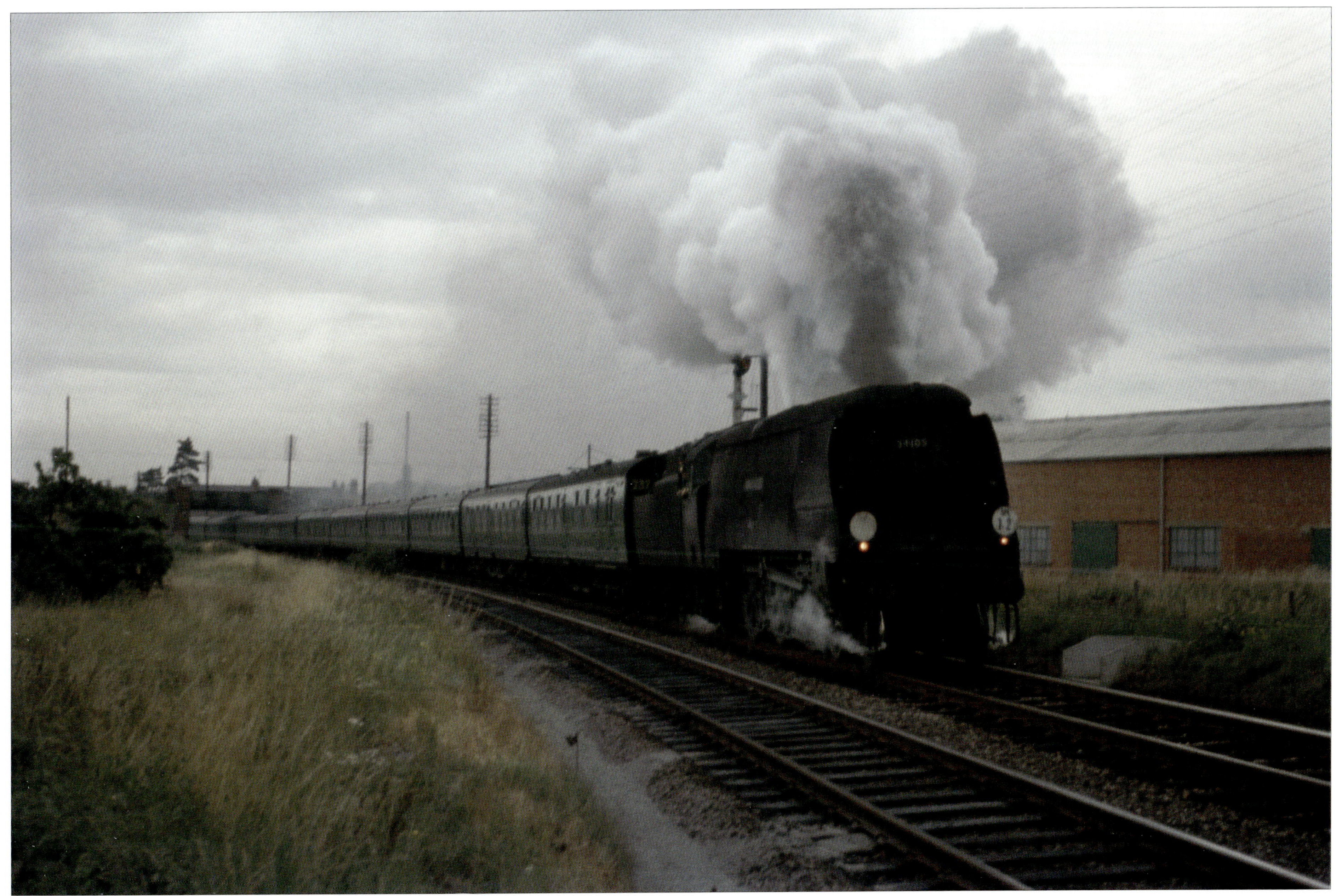

SLIDE 1661 | A rare visitor to the region, *Bulleid West Country/Battle of Britain* class **34105 Swanage** is heading a returning excursion train to the south. It is captured here heading out of Stratford-upon-Avon along what is now the northern arm of *Seven Meadows Road*. The passengers on this train have travelled from the *Southern Region* to see a matinee performance at the *Shakespeare Memorial Theatre* (probably Peter Hall and John Barton's adaptation, *The Wars of the Roses*). The standard route for these specials was ordinarily via Reading, Oxford and Leamington Spa, but at this time the Paddington to Birmingham route was overloaded with traffic diverted from the Euston to Crewe line, due to ongoing electrification work. Thus, trains were sent via the Worcester line, swinging north at Honeybourne. *34105* was based at Bournemouth at this time and was withdrawn for scrapping just over a year after this image was captured. After languishing for many years at *Woodham's*, it was eventually purchased for preservation. Although not currently operational, it forms part of the *Mid Hants Railway 'Watercress Line'* fleet. *?/7/63 (Ansco)*

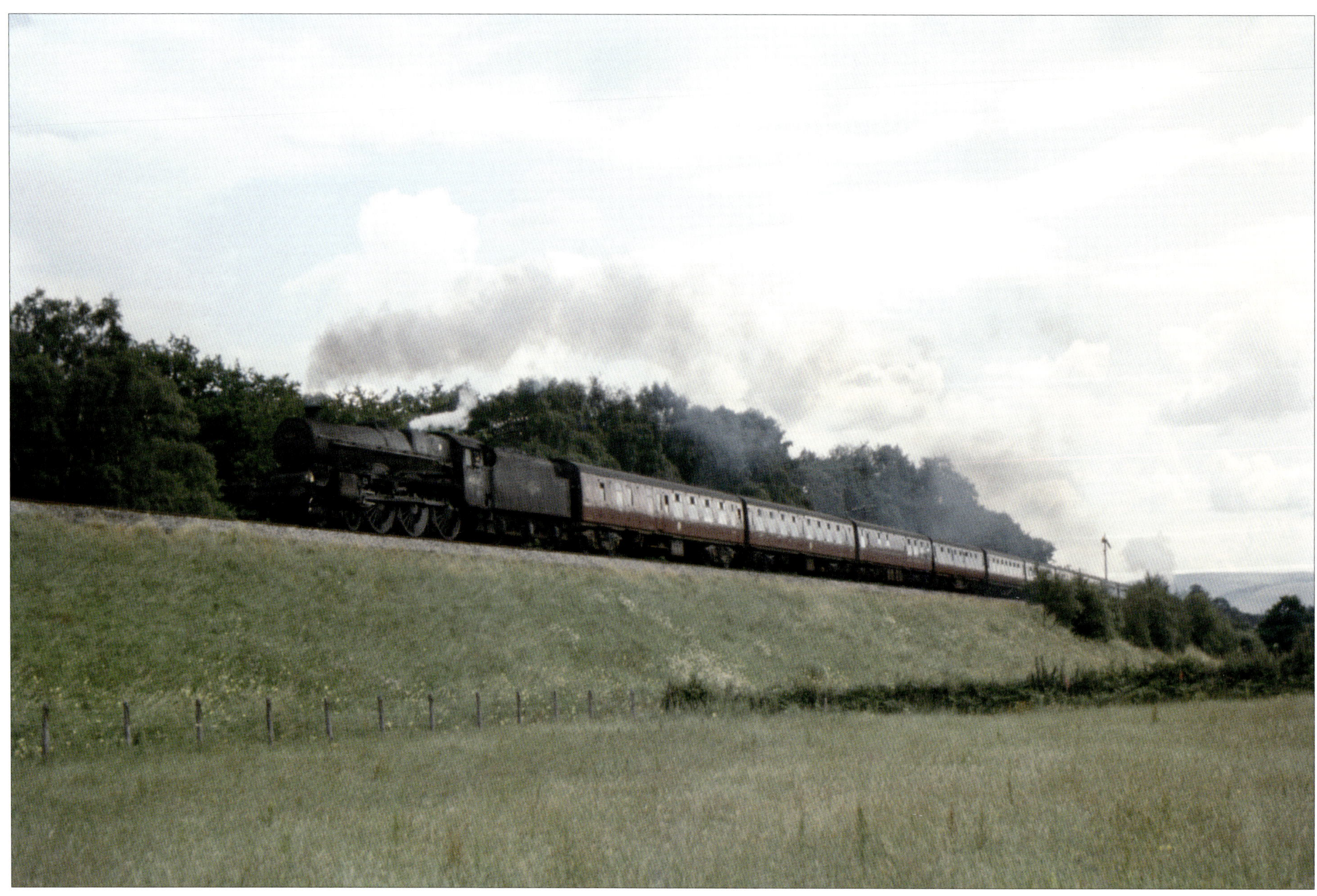

SLIDE 1667 | A shabby-looking *Stanier Jubilee* class **45567 South Australia** *(ex-LMS 5567)* climbs the bank approximately half-a-mile south of Llanvihangel, Monmouthshire with a heavily loaded north-bound holiday relief train (twelve coaches). At this location the main line briefly runs parallel to the *Hereford Road* and the track bed of the long-defunct *Lanfoist to Llanvihangel Tramway*. The photographer is facing south-east: the area locally known as *Blaen-Gavenny Wood* occupying the expanse of ground on the far side of the embankment. We don't know the destination of this train, but *45567* was based at Crewe North at the time *(see slide 1666 on opposite page)*. *13/7/63 (Ansco)*

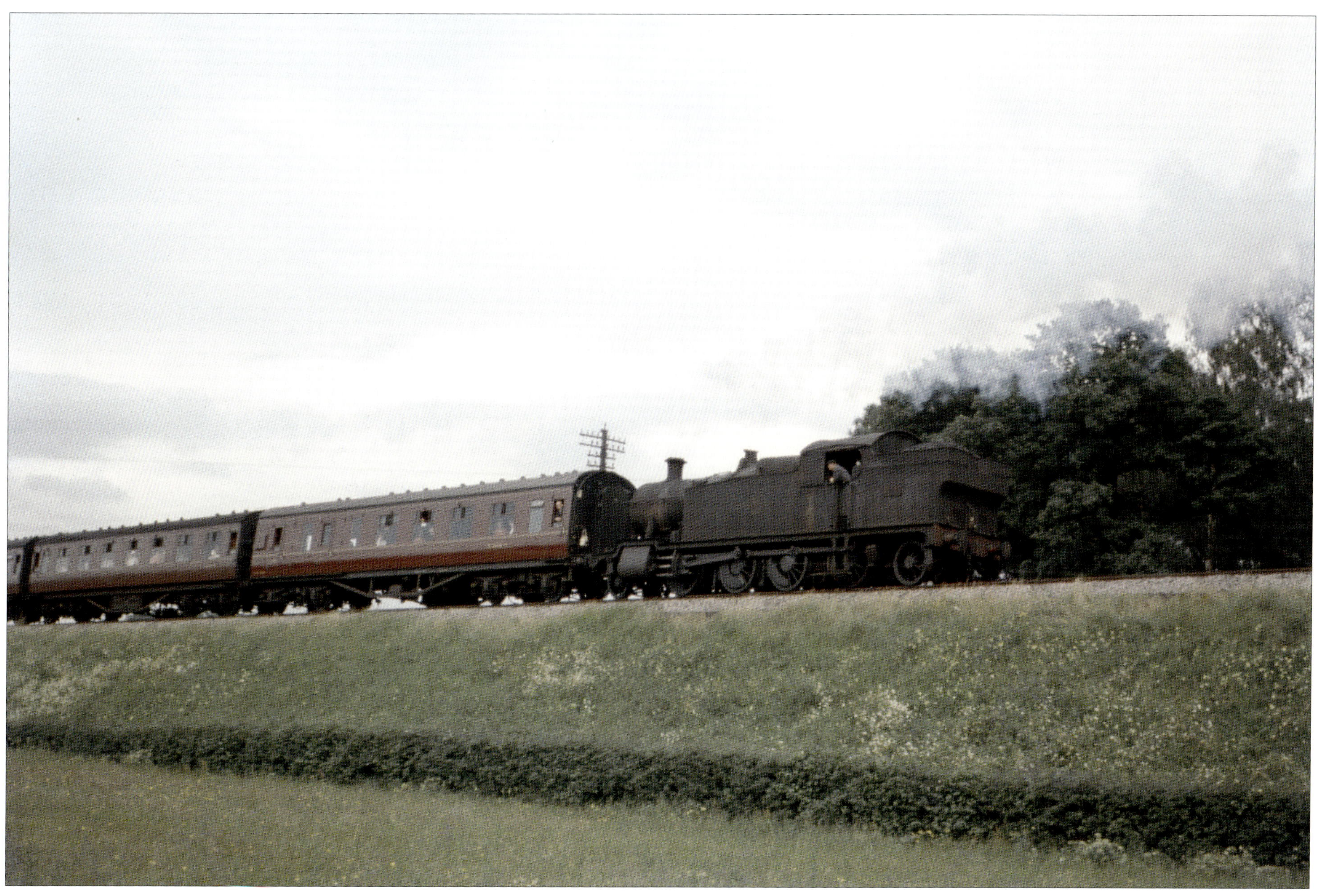

SLIDE 1666 | Even with a very high resolution scan and enhancing software, we are still not able to identify this *Collett 72xx* class beyond all doubt, but it is almost certainly Pontypool Road's **7246**; 1938 rebuild of *Churchward 42xx* class *4234*. It is banking the north-bound holiday relief train (uncoupled) behind **45567 South Australia** captured in the previous image. Note that *7246* is still sporting the early 'tall' style of safety valve bonnet (which appears to be damaged). We have paired these two photographs together in chronological order for reasons of continuity, but note that the photographer's numbering is non-sequential: probably just an oversight. *13/7/63 (Ansco)*

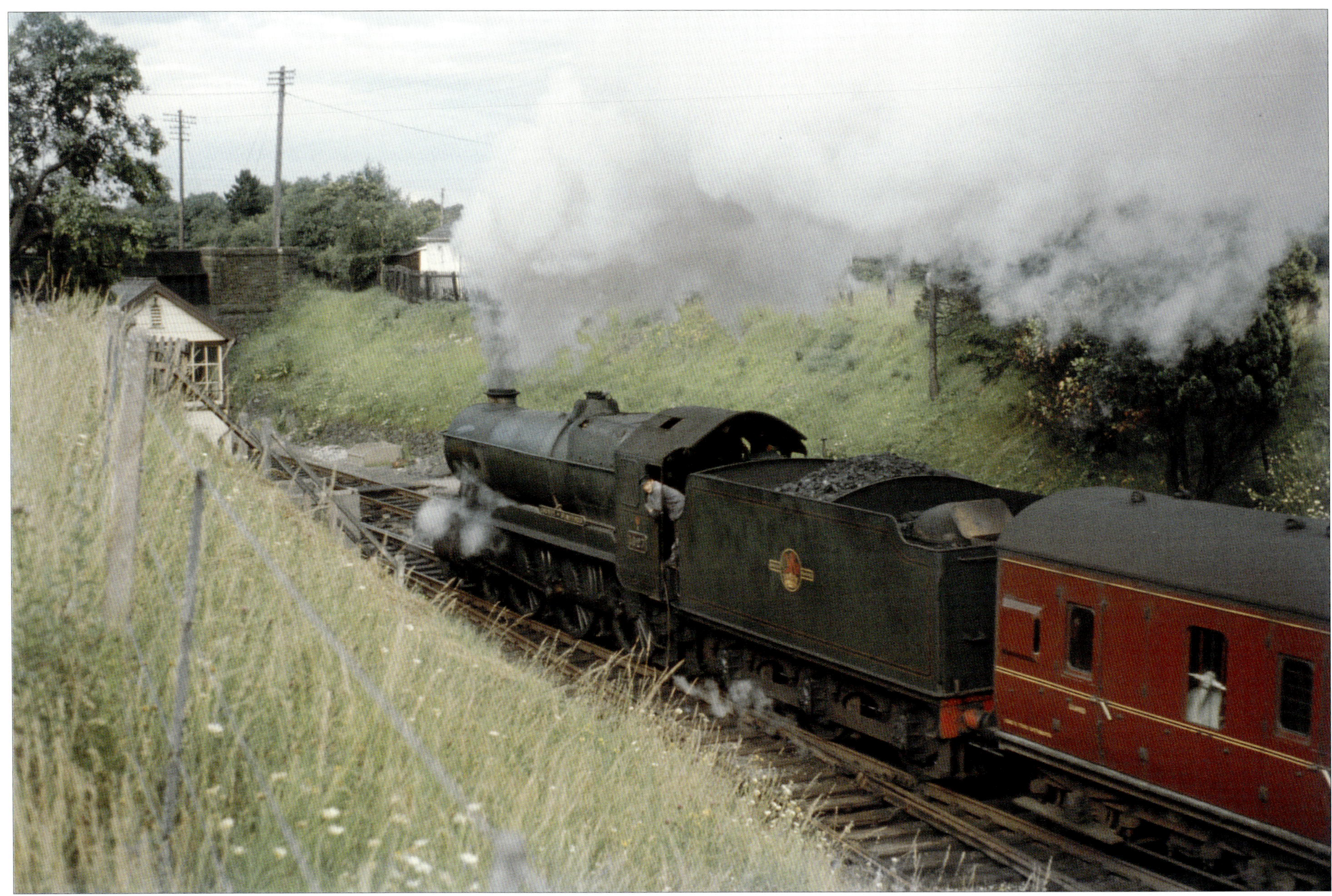

SLIDE 1671 | The Fireman of Shrewsbury-based **1027 County of Stafford** on a Kingswear to Manchester *(LMR)* express can afford a breather as the summit of the 1 in 82 north-easterly climb from Abergavenny is in sight. The photograph is taken from the access road to the disused goods sidings at Llanvihangel, where the *Hereford Road* crosses the Newport to Hereford main line. Further down the bank on which the photographer is standing and only really identifiable in Winter when the vegetation had died back, lay the track bed of a section of the long-defunct *Grwyne Fawr Reservoir Railway*, which in common with so many other such purpose-built railways, was constructed purely to facilitate reservoir construction traffic and abandoned once its task was complete. The tracks were lifted in 1928. Note the signal box here that had become all but redundant by this time. *13/7/63 (Ansco)*

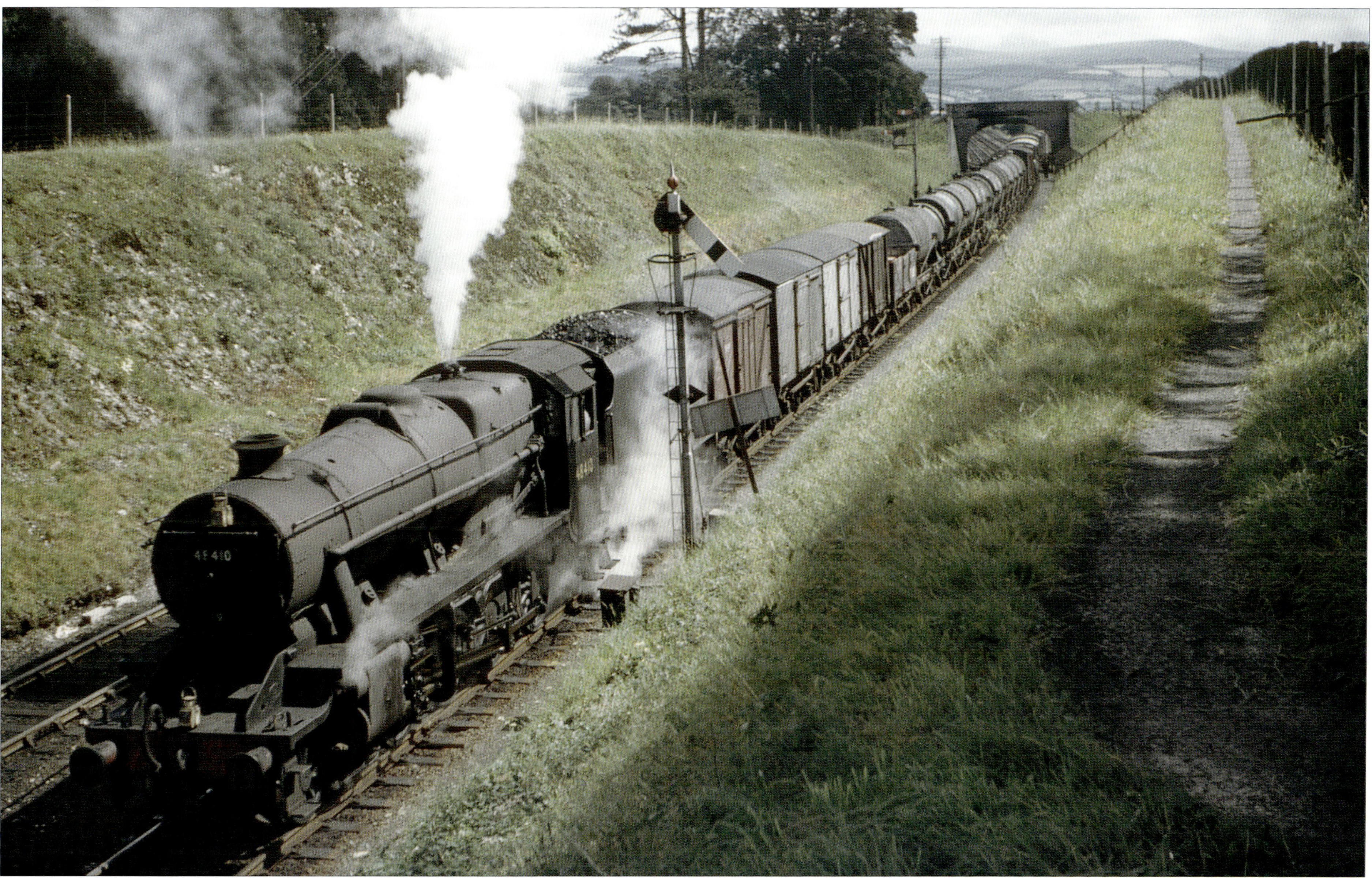

SLIDE 85 | Looking east from *Sparkwell Bridge*, Hemerdon, we see one of the eighty Swindon-built *Stanier* 8F's, **48410** at the head of a heavy Bristol to Plymouth mixed freight that is moving off after having had its brakes pinned down whilst straddling the summit. In the distance, under the arch of *Moor Bridge*, one can just make out the figure of the Guard who is about to jump aboard his van as it passes by. The orientation of the rear end of this train indicates that it has been held in the down goods loop; almost certainly to allow a passenger express to pass. Shedded at St. Philip's Marsh when this photograph was taken, *48410* was eventually withdrawn from Rose Grove, Burnley in August 1968 and broken up at an unknown location during January of the following year. Photograph taken approximately 100 yards from the location of *slide 87* reproduced on page 32.
5/8/56 Periflex 1/125th F4.5 (Kodachrome)

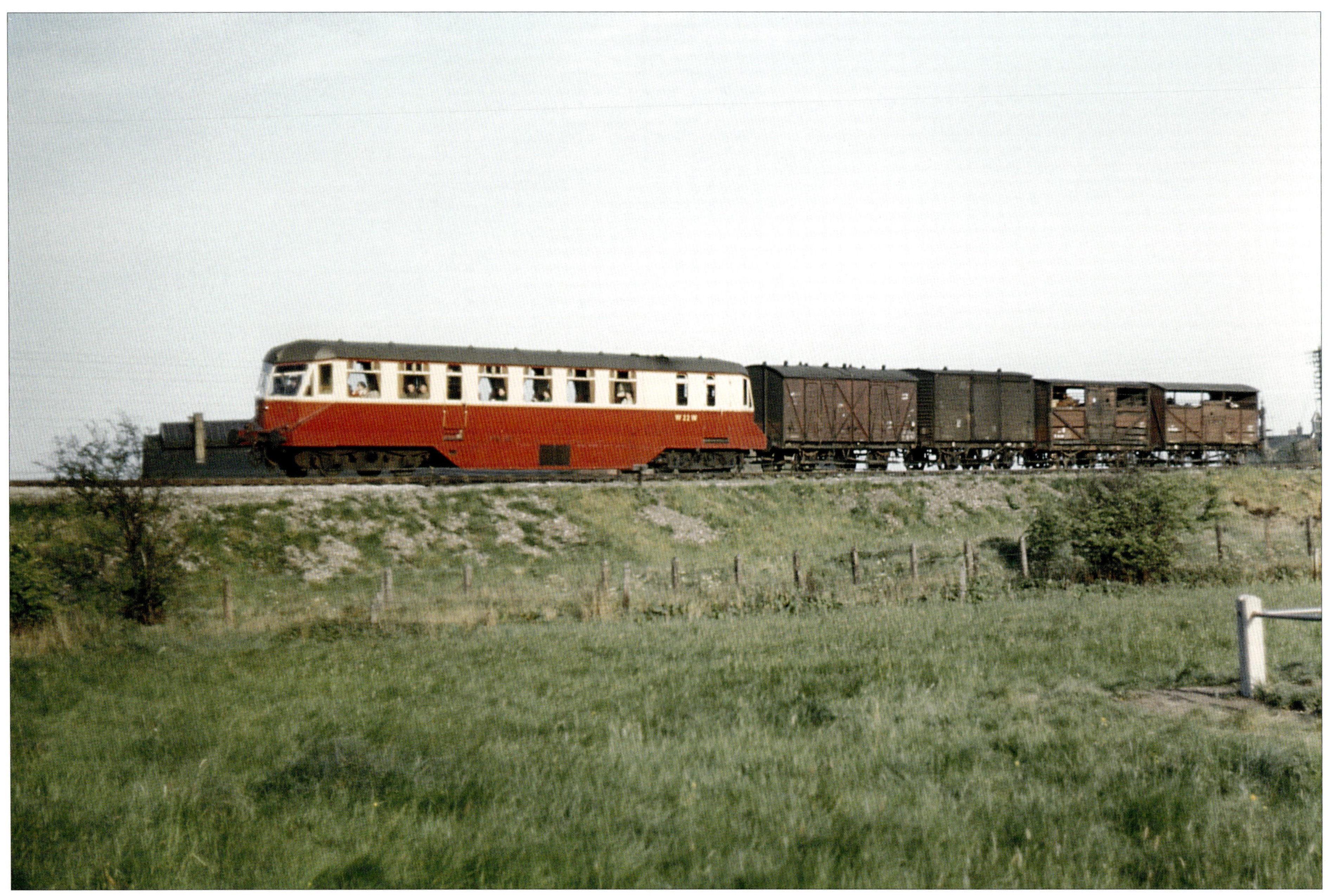

SLIDE 221 | It has been Cattle Market day at Stratford-upon-Avon and the evening sun sees Leamington's *AEC* Railcar **W22W** loaded close to regulation limits heading north past the Masons Road *Stratford Town Football Club* pitch on the 6.50pm Stratford to Leamington. As far as we can ascertain, this combination was a unique working never to be repeated. It is fair to say that on this occasion, the ride up the bank to Wilmcote will not be a breeze! *W22W* was one of three railcars working out of Leamington Spa at this time, generally deployed to passenger duties alone, but could occasionally be observed hauling a single mail van from Stratford. The other two Leamington-based Railcars were **W26W** and **W29W**. Another, **W17W** was a dedicated parcels version *(see also slide 1197 on page 122). 30/4/57 (Kodachrome)*

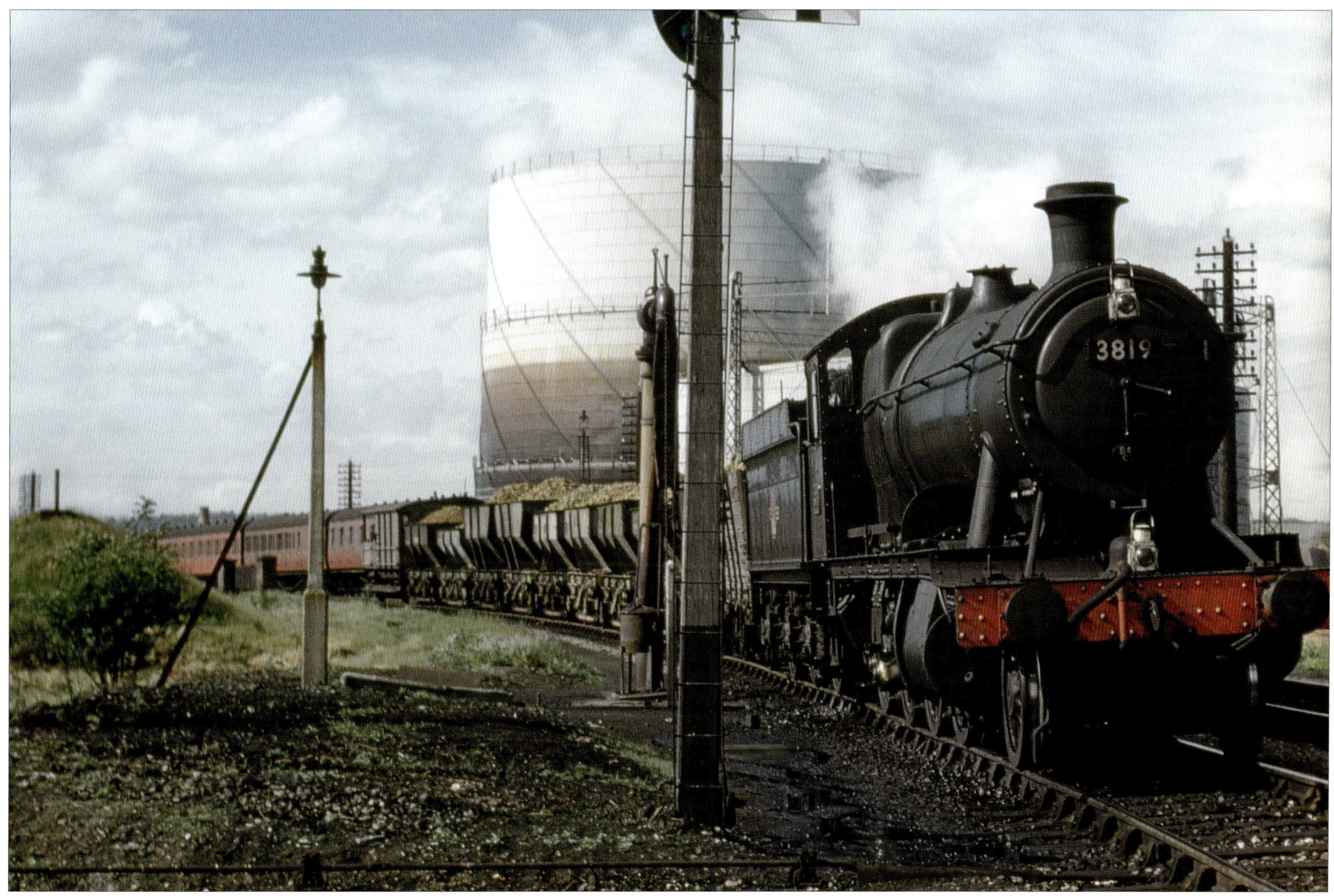

SLIDE 238 | On this bright but fresh Spring Saturday, Banbury-based *Churchward/Collett 2884* class **3819** with an ironstone train bound for South Wales waits at signals on the down goods loop at Stratford-upon-Avon. This image contains plenty of detail for the modeller: note the water column which has its own illumination, allowing through-freights to take on water day and night without needing to access the station platforms; potentially delaying passenger services. This class of locomotive proved so popular among ex-*Great Western* crews that, post-Nationalisation, the *Western Region* operating authorities asked that more be built. However, this request was turned down in favour of the 'new' *BR Standard* 9F. *3819* didn't remain at Banbury Shed for much longer; being transferred to Westbury, Wiltshire just over a year after this photograph was taken. *11/5/57 (Kodachrome)*

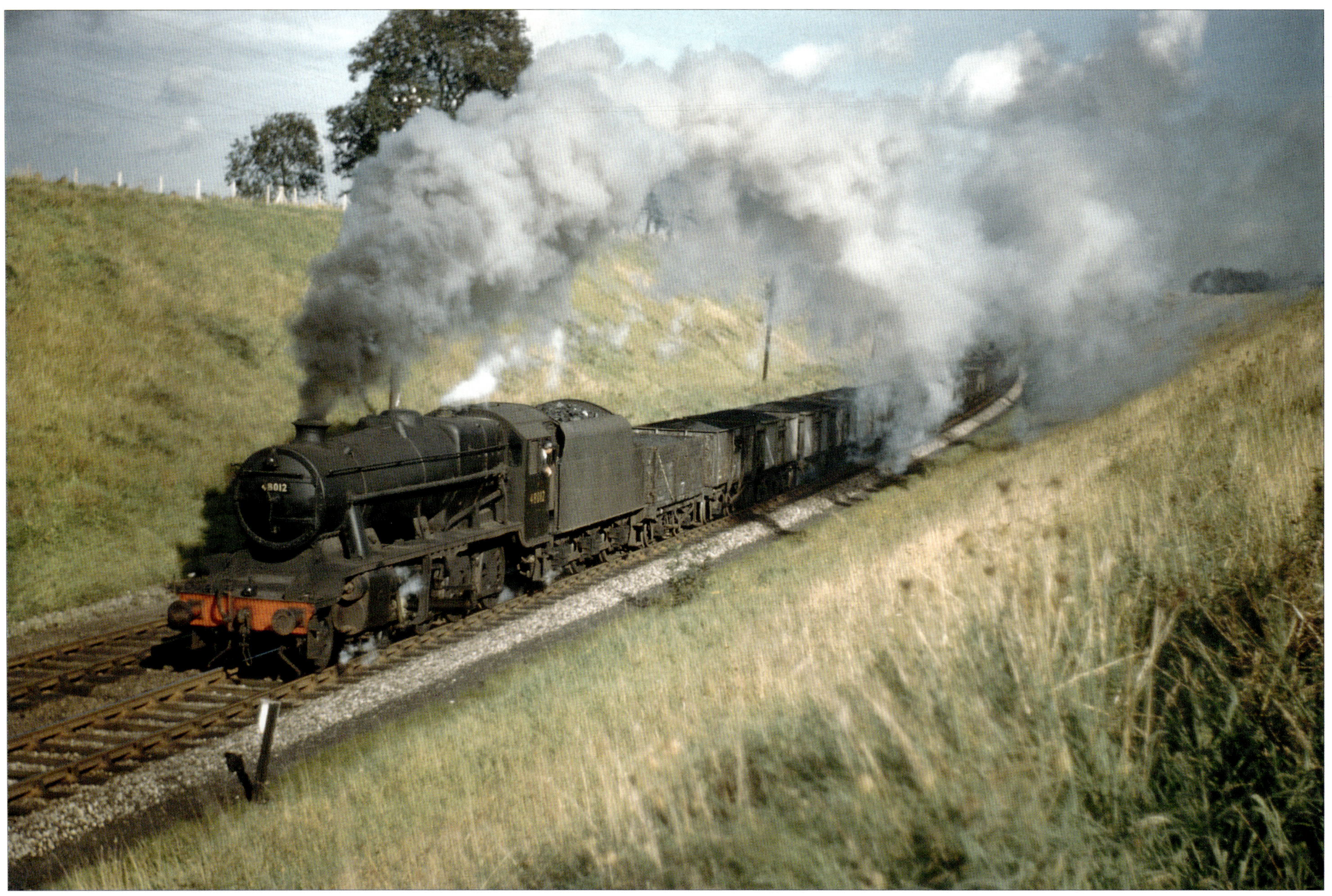

SLIDE 686 | Photographed from the bridge just east of St. Margaret's Church, Whitnash, Warwick (Milverton)-based *Stanier* 8F **48012** *(ex-LMS 8012)* is captured on the climb through the cutting approximately a mile south of Leamington Spa with a heavy coal train (about to pass *milepost 104¾*). This locomotive was one of thirteen of the first batch of its class built at Crewe and requisitioned by the War Department *(renumbered 70577)* in 1941 and in December 1949, became one of the first ten of its class to be purchased by *BR*. When the above photograph was taken, *48012* was only a matter of weeks away from reallocation to Northampton Shed. It was eventually withdrawn from Edge Hill, Liverpool in March 1968, although details of its disposal remain unclear. *17/9/58 (Kodachrome)*

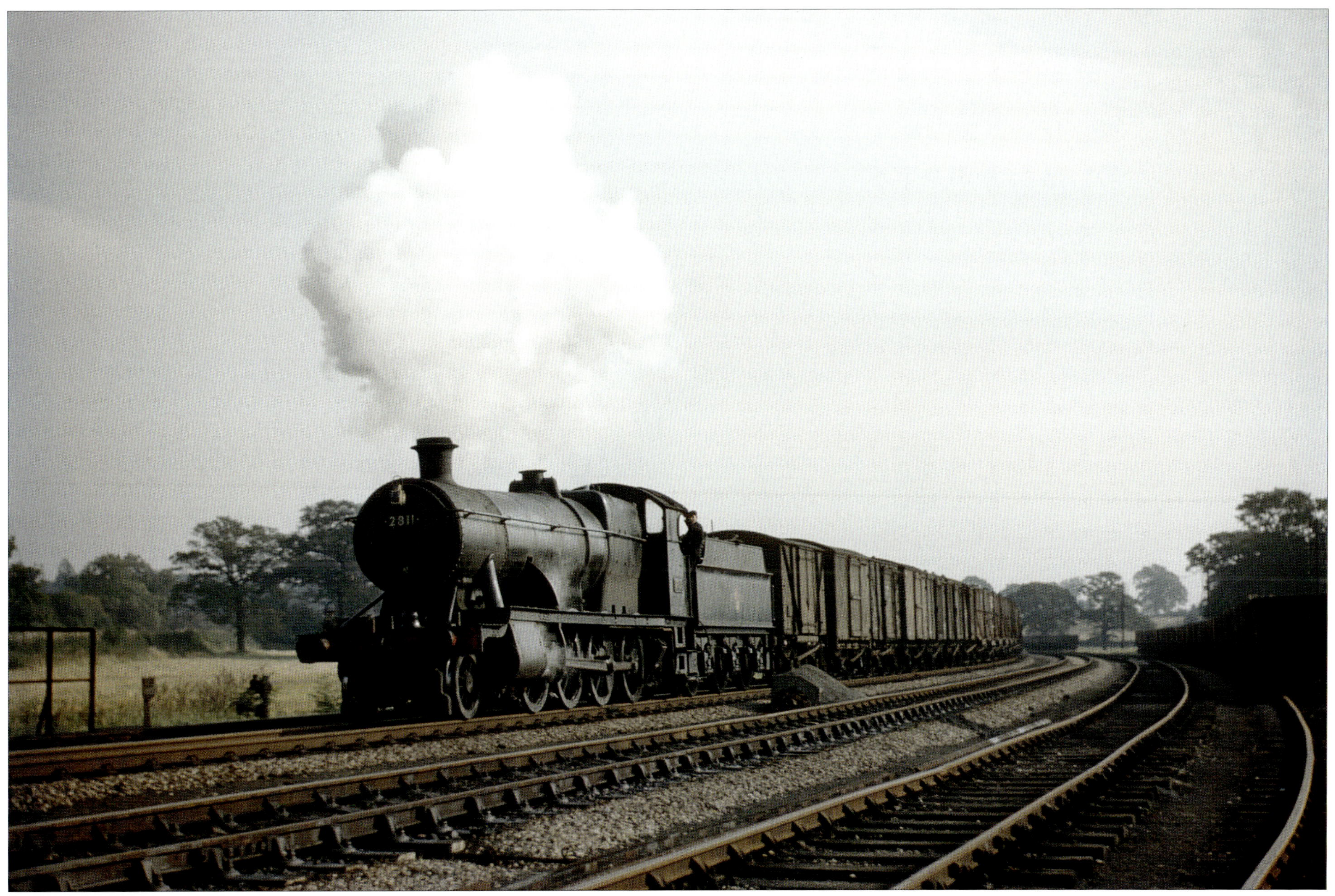

SLIDE 696 | Westbury-based *Churchward* 2-8-0 **2811** on a down freight is routed on the main line at Hatton and it passes *milepost 112* on its approach to the station and junctions. The destination of this train is not known, but its routing on the main line, rather than the goods loop suggests that it is unlikely to be swinging south towards Stratford-upon-Avon, but rather heading north-west to Birmingham or the *Black Country* beyond. When this photograph was taken, *2811* was only a year away from withdrawal. Entering service in November 1905 and receiving its outside steam pipes in early 1943, this locomotive became one of only twenty sold to *Round Oak Steelworks*, Brierly Hill, where it would be broken up during March 1960. *27/9/58 Leica IIIA (Kodachrome)*

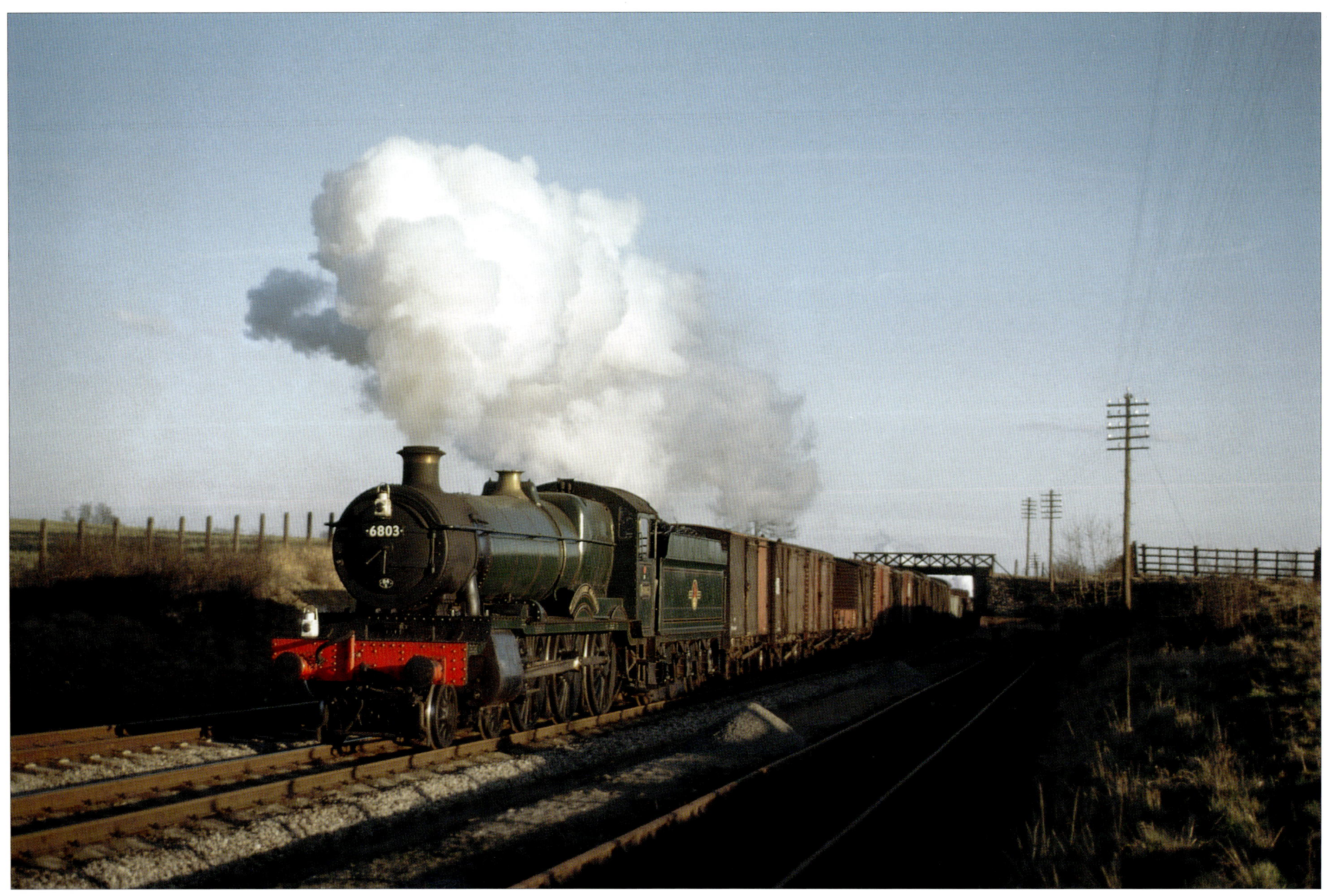

SLIDE 1201 | Fortunately, the clocks have just gone forward allowing Tom to capture the sun's dying rays illuminating Tyseley's freshly-cleaned **6803 Bucklebury Grange** as it nears the summit of the 1 in 75 climb from Stratford-upon-Avon to Wilmcote with a partially fitted mixed freight train from Honeybourne, bound for Bordesley Green. It has been banked from Stratford by an unidentified *Collett 2251* class: its exhaust just visible in the distance beyond the span of *Canada Bridge*. *6803* didn't remain very long at Tyseley; being reallocated to Oxley Shed just a few months after this photograph was taken. In common with **6854 Roundhill Grange**, it became one of only six of its class to be broken up locally, at *Bird's* of Long Marston approximately eight miles from this location *(see also slide 1534 on page 116)*. *30/3/62 (Kodachrome)*

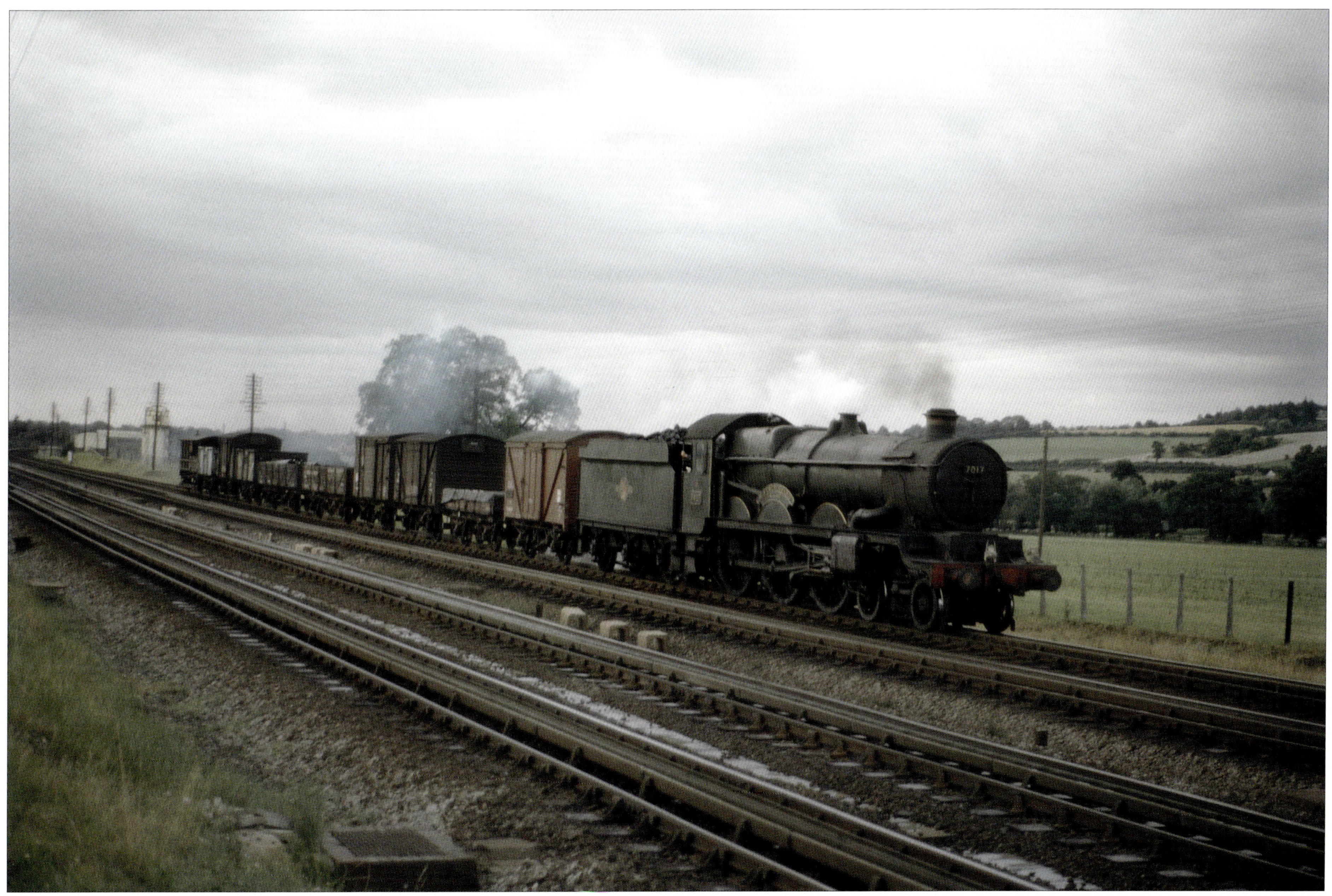

SLIDE 1502 | Looking tired, neglected and living on borrowed time Old Oak's **7017 G.J. Churchward** on an embarrassingly light goods working takes water on Goring Troughs as it heads south-east at approximately 6.30pm; the light just beginning to fail. Approximately three months after this photograph was taken, *7017* would be put into storage at Old Oak Common, never to return to main line duties. It was officially withdrawn for scrapping in February 1963 and sold to *King & Sons* of Wymondham, Norfolk, where it was broken up a year later. Although over one hundred other steam locomotives, notably five of the nine *47xx* class, met their fate there, Archie King's breakers yard was better known for the disposal of military equipment and condemned rolling stock; the latter generally being effected by the burning-off of all combustibles, leaving only the metallic components for reclamation. Indeed, they were responsible for the destruction of the *Royal Mail* van at the centre of the notorious, so-called *Great Train Robbery* of 1963; this action apparently sanctioned by *BR* top brass. *4/8/62 (Kodachrome)*

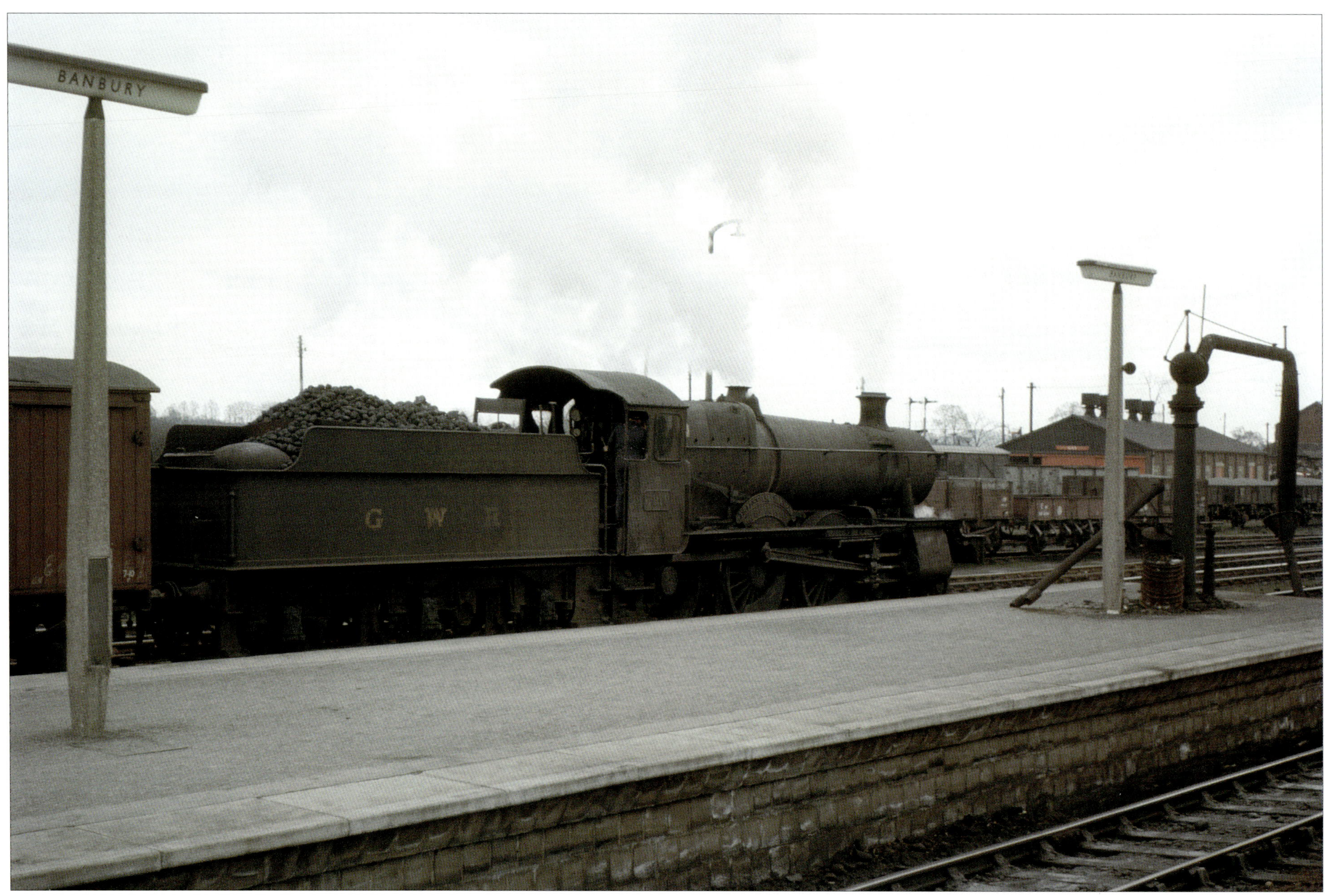

SLIDE 1707 | Pictured here at Banbury in charge of an up freight, Reading's **7816 Frilsham Manor** shows very little evidence of having been shown a caring hand for quite some time. Incredibly for this period in the 1960s, the flush-riveted *Churchward* 3,500 gallon tender that *7816* has been paired with (dating from 1914) still retains its *GWR* transfers that would have been applied circa 1947, but this is most likely a result of the avulsion of subsequent paint layers by the elements; not that there would have been many! Eagle-eyed readers will also spot that this vintage tender has received various visible modifications throughout its history, including the fitting of *Collett* cast brake hangers and flanged plate supports on the spring hangers. *7816* would remain working out of Reading Shed for a further four months, prior to reallocation to Swindon. *11/4/64 (Kodachrome)*

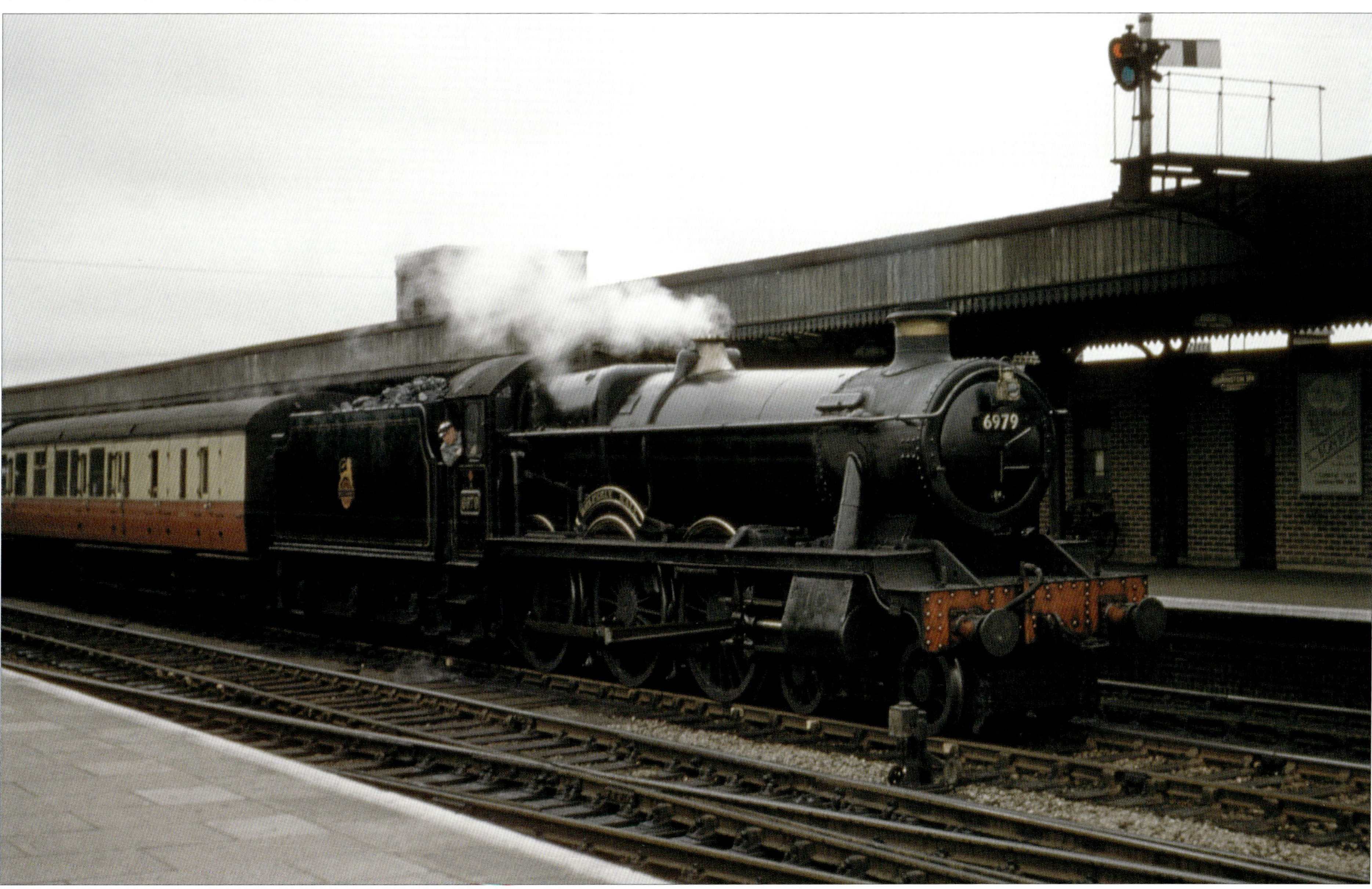

SLIDE 45 | On this cold and dull Saturday morning, the Driver of Banbury-based **6979 Helperly Hall** on an unidentified up local seems distracted by the prospect of having his photograph taken as he waits for the 'right away' at Leamington Spa General. This locomotive spent all of its service life working out of Banbury Shed and is captured here still in its 1950 lined-black livery. When it was withdrawn for scrapping in February 1965, it became one of only two *6959* class *Modified Halls* broken up at *Bird's* of Long Marston (the other being **6963 Throwley Hall**). Incidentally, the tall tower-like structure rising above the station canopy is actually the station lift: used almost exclusively for parcels traffic. Note the desperately slow shutter speed required to successfully capture this scene. *9/7/55 Retina 1A 1/25th F2.8 (Kodachrome)*

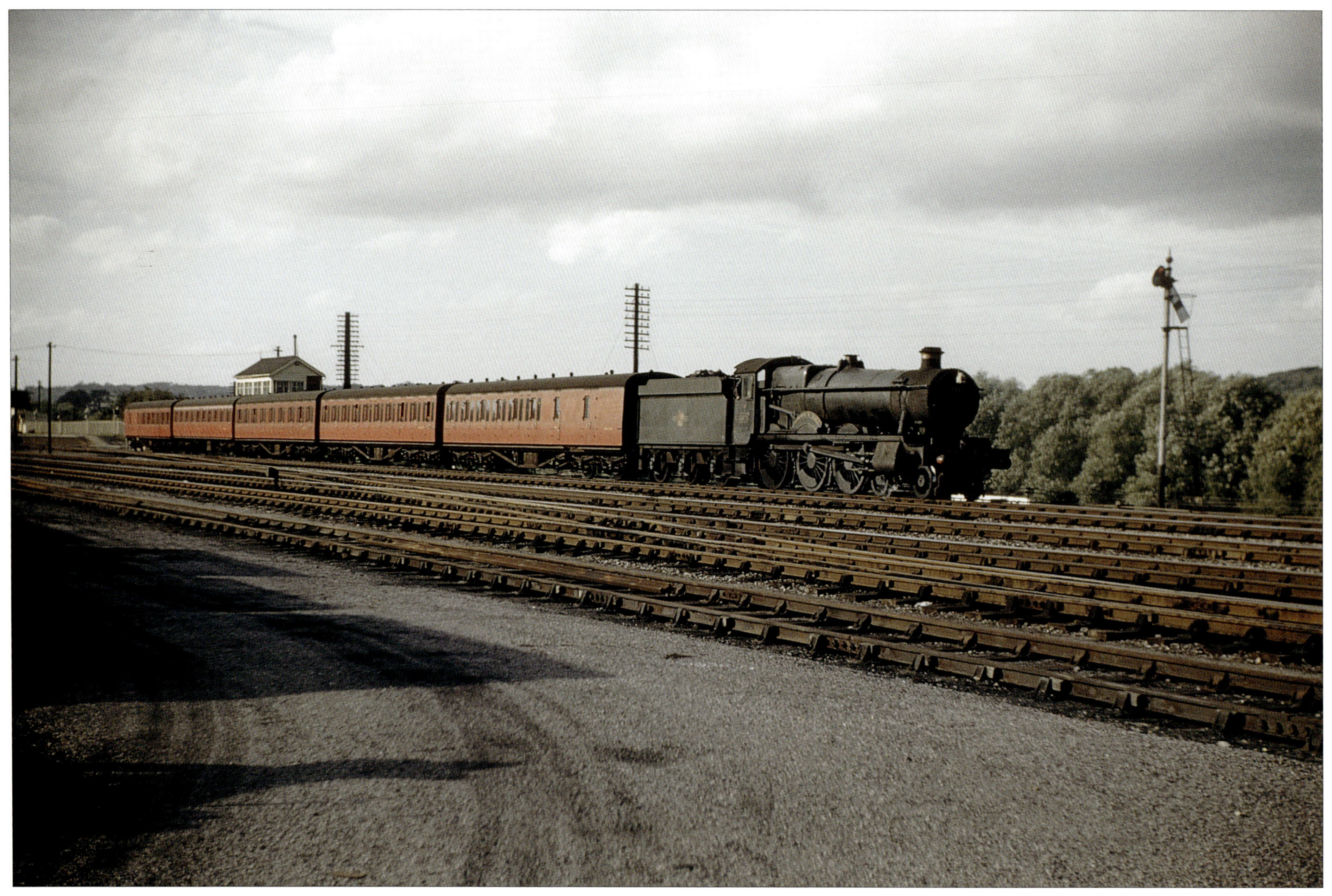

SLIDE 443 | **5978 Bodinnick Hall** pulls away from Tilehurst Station, Reading on the 4.00pm Oxford to Paddington stopping service. At this location, the main line runs parallel to the Thames (a stretch of water known as the *Kentwood Deeps*) and indeed, reflected light from the river can just be seen flickering beneath the front of the locomotive. *5978* was based at Weymouth Radipole at this time, so its presence on this train is unusual to say the least, but we believe it to be working its way back home after undergoing some kind of repairs at Swindon Works. Photograph taken from the once-busy goods yard; the Goods Shed here being demolished as recently as 2013 to make way for a new footbridge. *7/9/57 Leica IIIA (Kodachrome)*

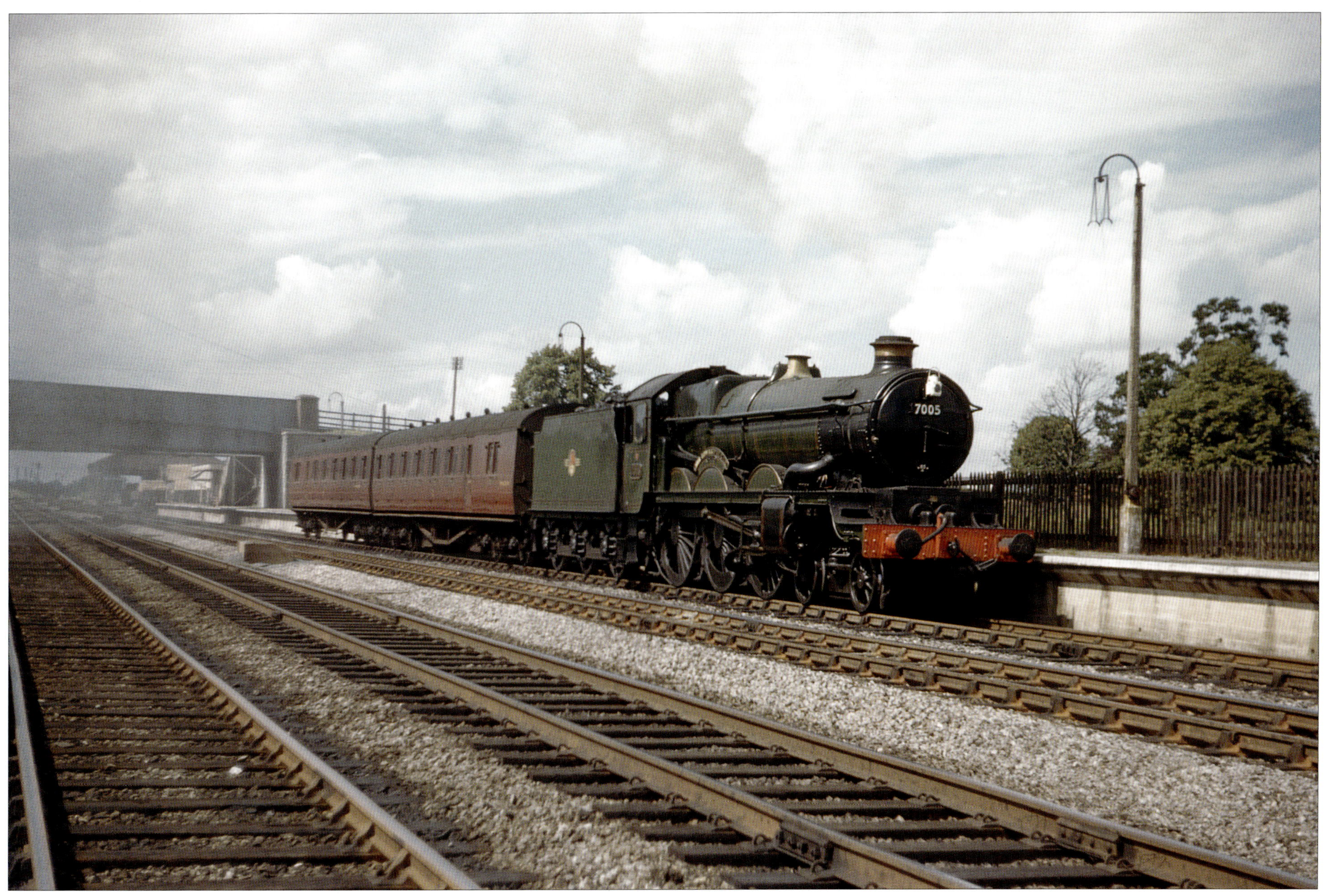

SLIDE 1100 | *Castle* class **7005 Sir Edward Elgar** strolls through Challow Station with a two-coach stopping train for Didcot. It has spent the last week running-in prior to its return home to Worcester Shed after undergoing a heavy general overhaul at Swindon which included the fitting of a new boiler and replacement *Hawksworth* 4,000 gallon tender. *7005* entered service in 1946 as the second incarnation of *Lamphey Castle*, being renamed in August 1957 to mark the centenary of the composer's birth. It was actually the second steam locomotive to carry Elgar's name: the first being *Dean Bulldog* class *3414*, entering service in 1906 as *3704* and named *A.H. Mills*. It was renumbered in 1912 and renamed in 1932, just six years prior to its withdrawal. *16/8/60 (Kodachrome)*

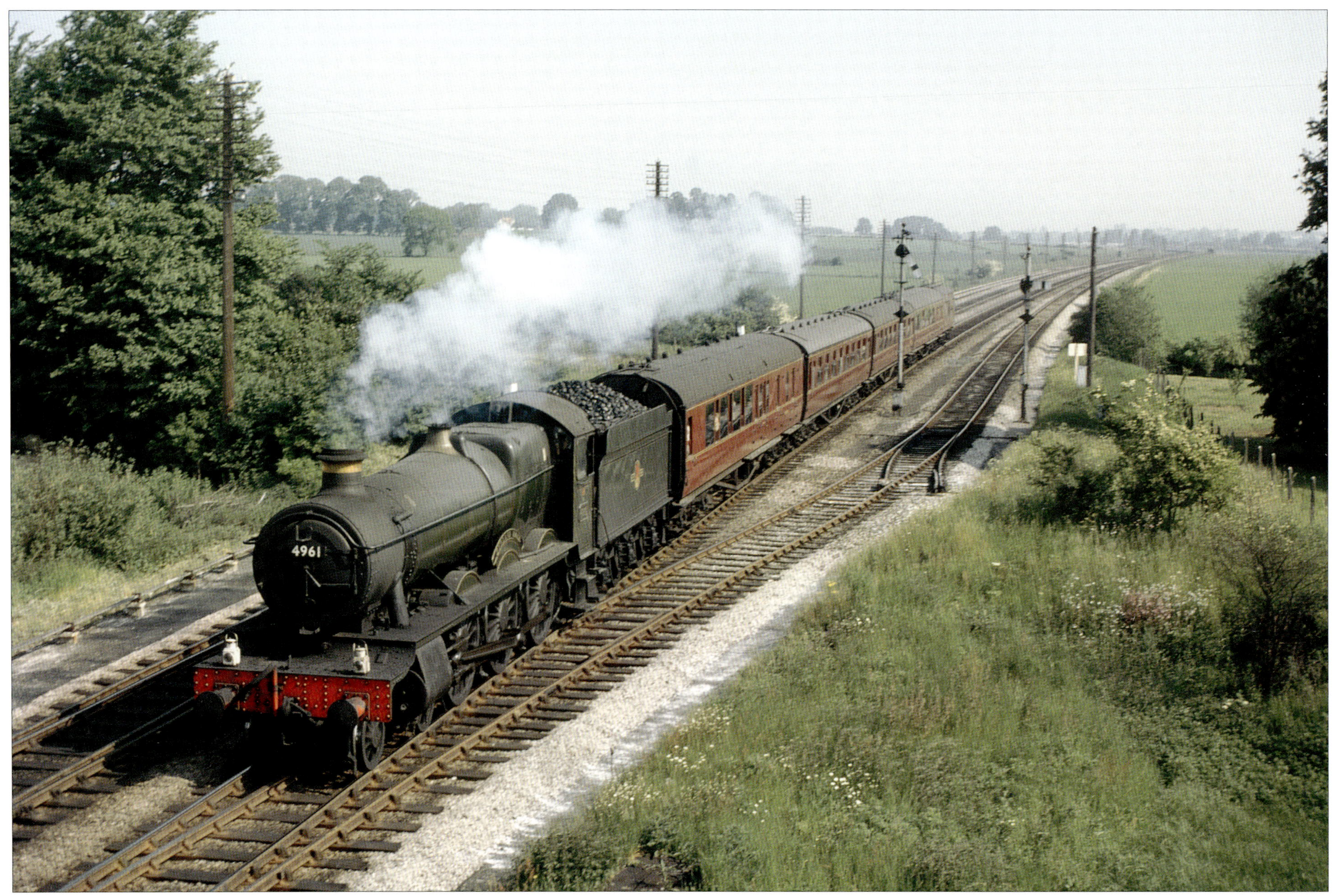

SLIDE 1408 | Looking north from the minor road bridge just a few hundred yards from Radley Station on the outskirts of Abingdon, we see Westbury-based **4961 Pyrland Hall**, less than six months from withdrawal, heading south with a Banbury to Reading semi-fast service. Note the empty horse box at the rear of the train (had it been occupied, it would almost certainly have been placed at the head of the rake for extra stability and comfort for the horse. Two years after this photograph was taken, the relief lines here that were laid during the early part of the Second World War and stretched as far north as Hinksey Yard, were taken up. *9/6/62 (Kodachrome)*

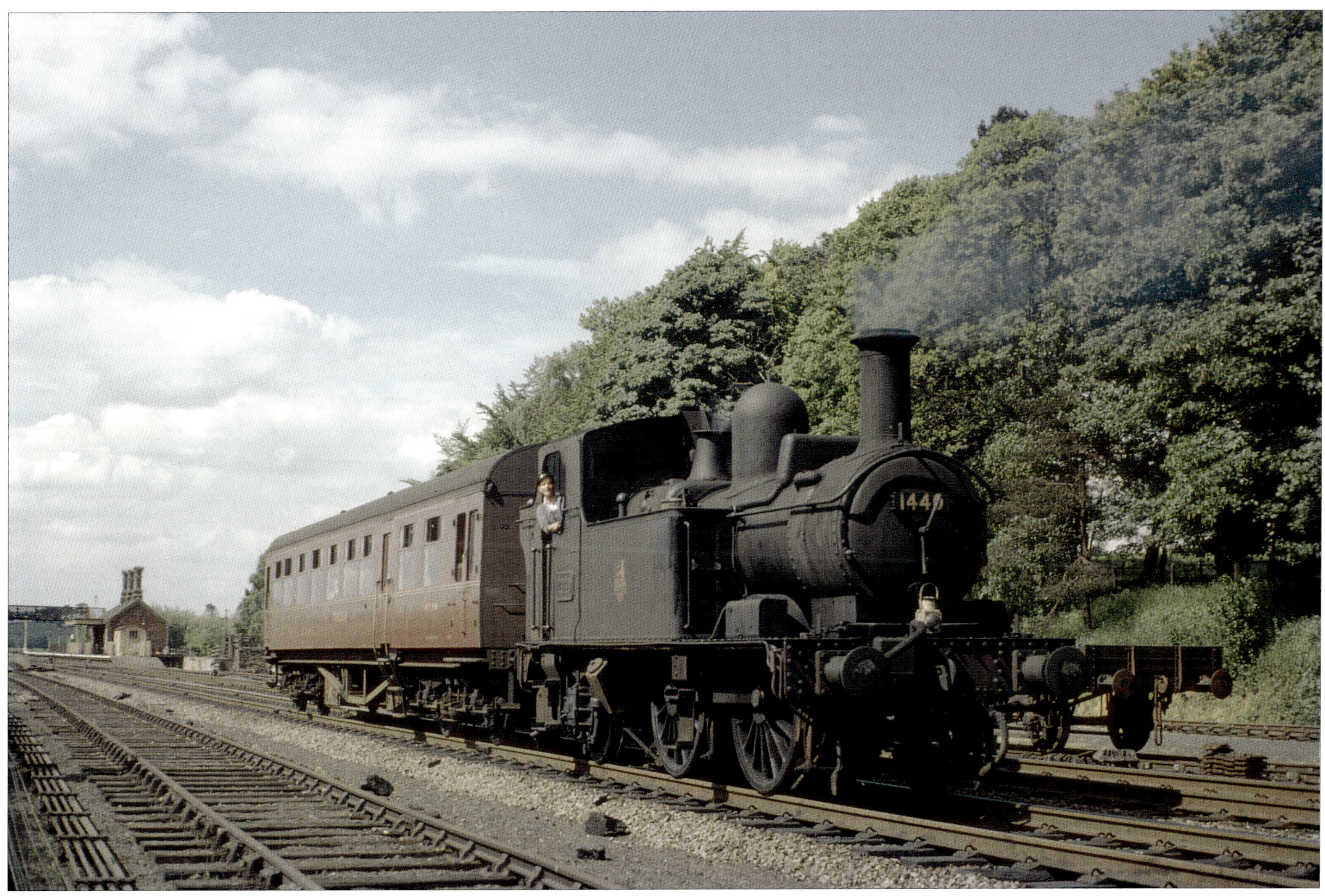

SLIDE 1421 | *Collett* 0-4-2T **1440** has just been transferred from Horton Road shed to Banbury and is captured here propelling auto trailer *Thrush* into King's Sutton on the Bicester to Banbury push-pull service. Note the 'saddle' behind the chimney indicating that *1440* is fitted with a top-feed boiler. Despite the line between Oxford and Banbury being built by the *GWR* between 1845 and 1850, the station at King's Sutton didn't actually open until 1872. By 1887, the arrival of the *Banbury & Cheltenham Direct Railway* coming in from the west (via Kingham, Chipping Norton and Hook Norton) had turned King's Sutton into a junction. By the end of the first half of the twentieth century however, plans were afoot to terminate passenger services between Chipping Norton and King's Sutton. This was actioned in 1951 and thirteen years later, the branch also became closed to freight traffic. *16/6/62 (Kodachrome)*

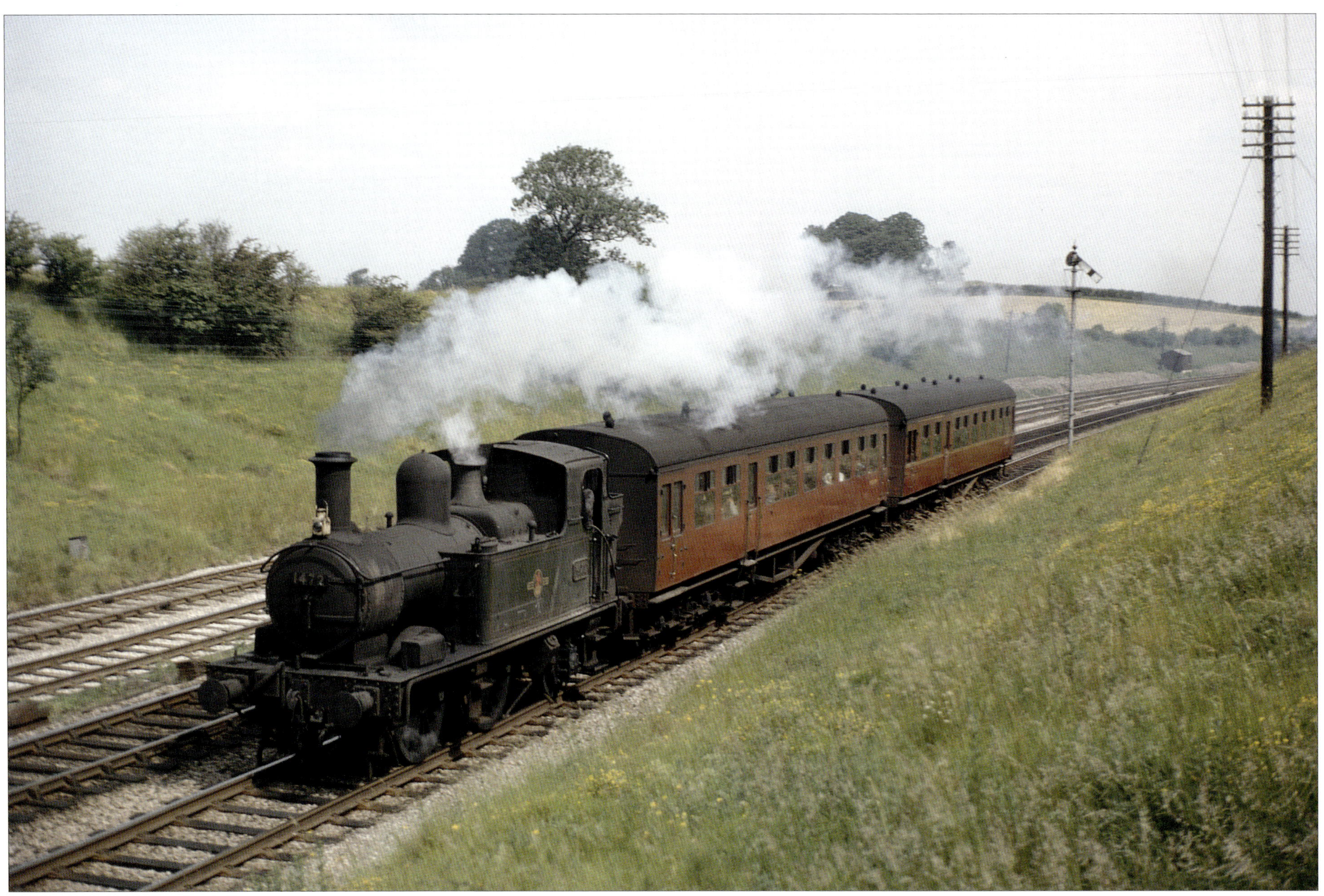

SLIDE 1447 | Horton Road's *Collett* 0-4-2T **1472** with two seemingly well-populated auto trailers charges up the bank towards *Black Bridge*, between Standish Junction and Stonehouse with a Gloucester to Chalford stopping service. The freshly-ballasted tracks on the far side of the cutting constitute the Bristol to Gloucester main line. The *1400* series of locomotives were originally designated the *4800* class, but when the *GWR* decided to convert twelve members of the *Churchward 2800* class and eight of the *2884* class as a part of the oil-firing experiment, it was decided that those locomotives should take the *4800* nomenclature. Thus, the existing seventy-five tank locomotives already carrying this numbering sequence were reclassified *1400–1474* and when the oil-firing trials ended in 1948, their original numbers were not reinstated *(see slide 643 on page 40)*. *30/6/62 (Kodachrome)*

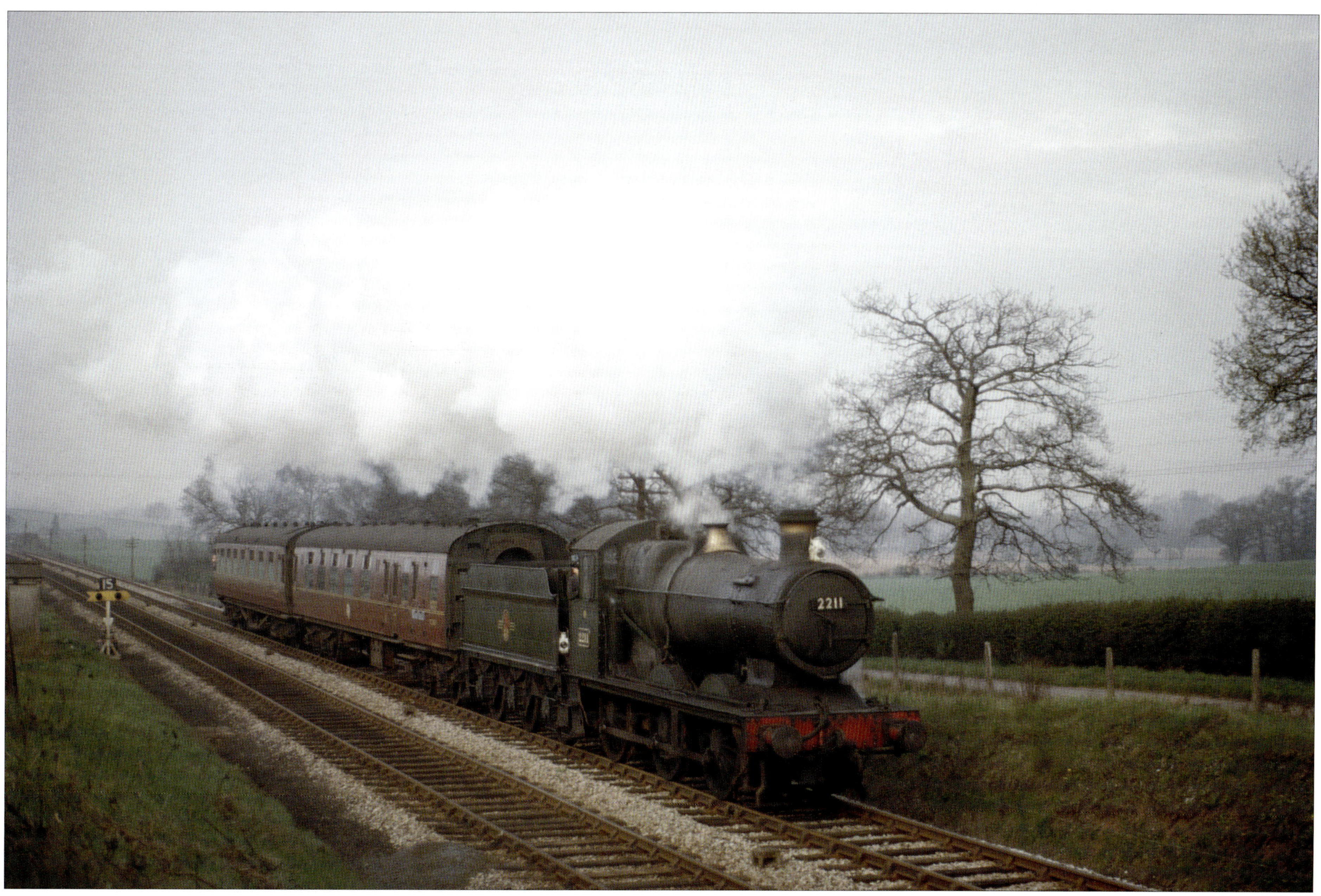

SLIDE 1587 | The remnants of the persistent Winter snows have only recently disappeared from the fields, but the low temperatures are still evident in this atmospheric image. Captured accelerating away from its brief stop at Bearley, five miles north of Stratford-upon-Avon, Leamington-based *2251* class **2211** heads towards *Edstone Crossing* with the 8.43am Stratford-upon-Avon to Leamington Spa service. The 15mph temporary speed restriction arrow warning board we see on the down line was in force due to a weak occupation bridge near Bearley West Junction that for many months was awaiting so-called 'urgent' repair work. Today, this section between Hatton and Bearley is reduced to single track. The minor road we see on the right that briefly runs parallel to the line at this location is *Langley Road*, leading down to the *Golden Cross* junction with the ex-*A34* trunk road. *27/4/63 (Kodachrome)*

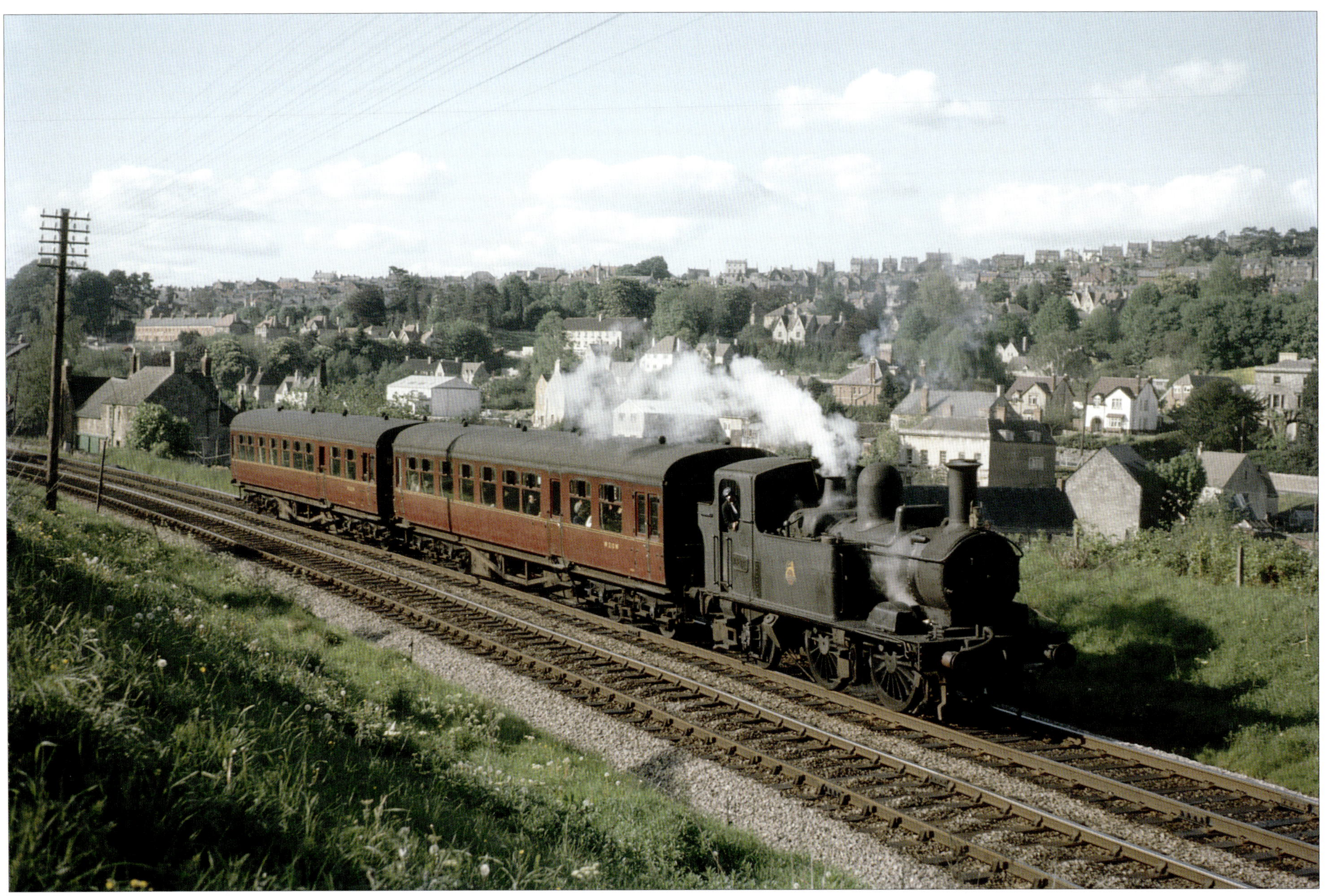

SLIDE 1721 | The final locomotive of its class; Gloucester Horton Road's *Collett* 0-4-2T **1474** with two well-filled auto coaches, trundles along the *Golden Valley Line* just south of its last stop at Stroud, with the all stations and halts push-pull service from Gloucester to Chalford. The train is captured here on the final approach to its next stop at Bowbridge Crossing Halt, where the tracks run parallel to the then-disused *Thames & Severn Canal*. This was to be the last Spring of operation for stopping passenger services on this line and it was also the final Spring of operation for *1474*. It was withdrawn from service in September of this year and broken up just two months later by *Bird's* of Morriston, Swansea. *18/4/64 (Kodachrome)*

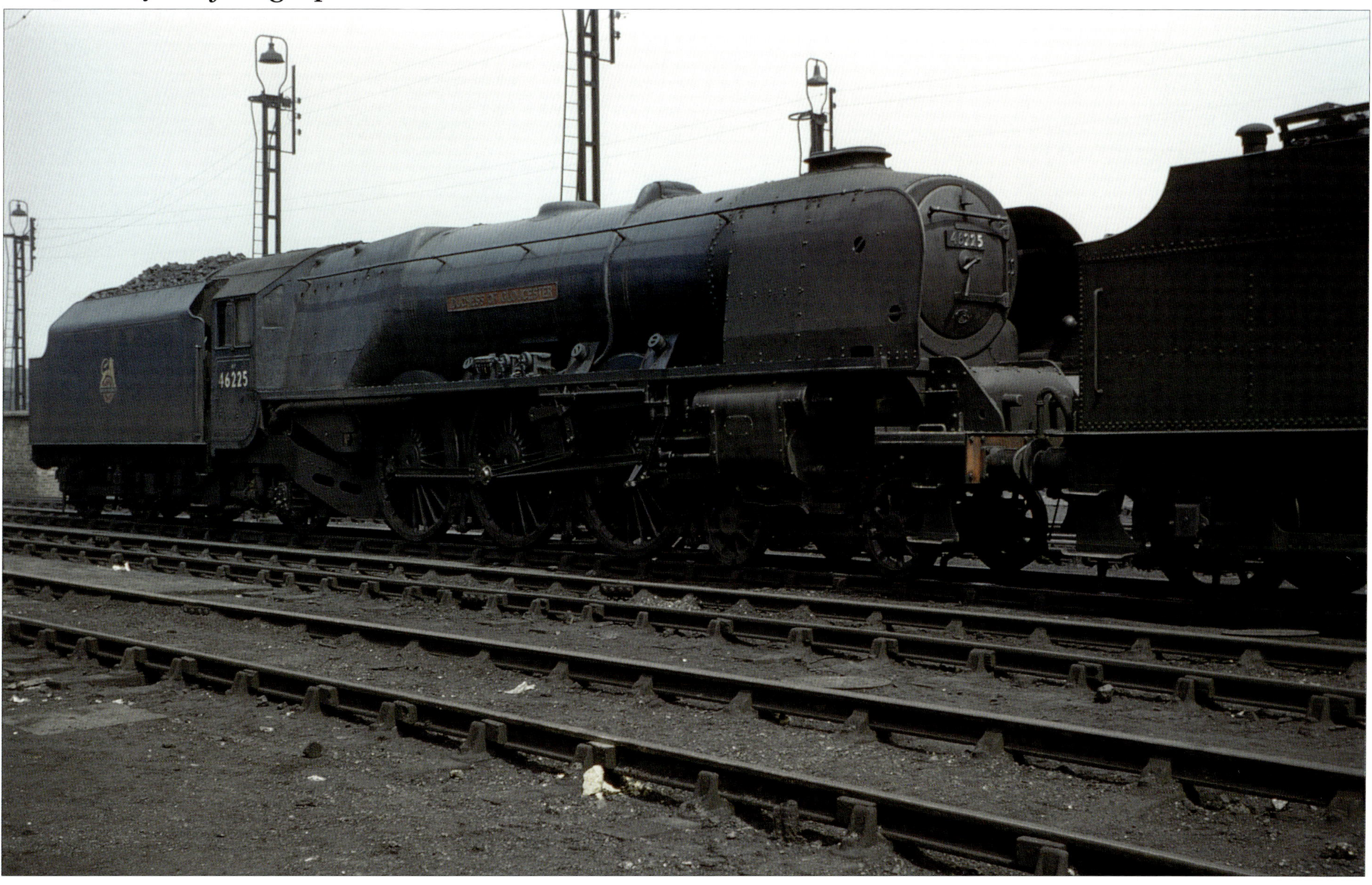

SLIDE 08 | *Stanier Coronation Pacific* **46225 Duchess of Gloucester**, still in its initial *BR* blue livery is on home territory at Crewe North. Built at Crewe and entering service in May 1938 as *LMS 6225*, this locomotive like many of its class, didn't retain this 1950 colour scheme for much longer. During the war years, its original single chimney had been replaced by the double chimney and blast pipe that we see here and during its next overhaul in January, 1955, it will see further modifications, including the replacement of its vintage sloping smokebox front and a repaint in lined *BR* green. *46225* would undergo yet two further changes of livery prior to withdrawal in October 1964: *BR* lined maroon in August 1958 and *LMR* lined maroon in January 1960. It would eventually be broken up by *Arnott Young* of Troon in December 1964. *30/5/54 Agfa Silette (Kodachrome)*

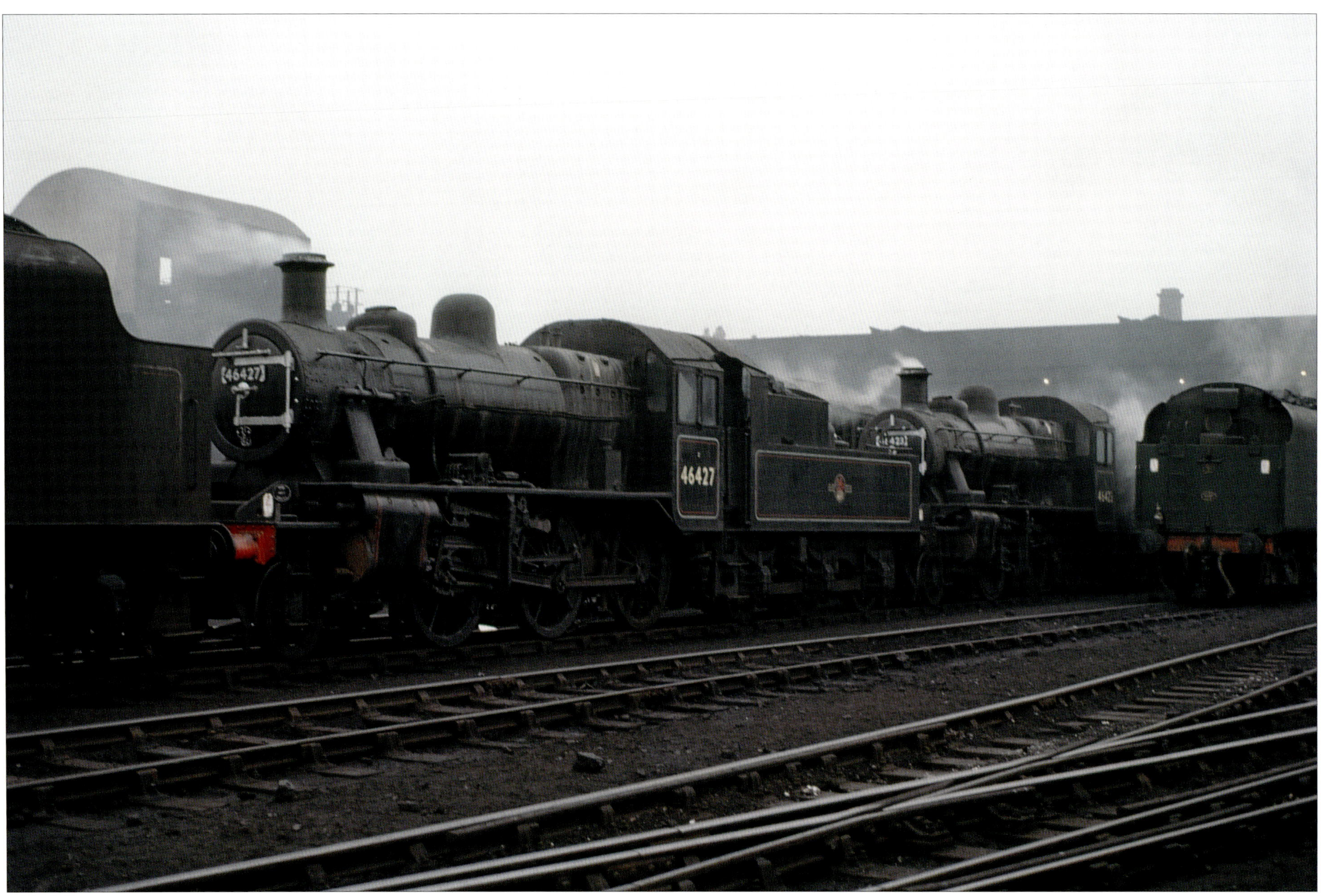

SLIDE 1199 | Shedmates *BR*-built *Ivatt* 2MT *Moguls* **46427** and **46423** simmer away at Aston Shed, Birmingham braving the cold easterly wind as they await their next duties; the background dominated by the imposing concrete coaling tower and huge louvre-roofed locomotive shed. Henry 'George' Ivatt, the last Chief Mechanical Engineer of the *LMS*, designed the class 2 2-6-0 locomotive for light mixed-traffic duties as a replacement for ageing 0-6-0s which had historically formed the backbone of the low-powered locomotives within the *LMS* fleet. The 2-6-0s with their greater range (their tender held 3,000 gallons of water and four tons of coal) were well-suited to their task and, after early teething troubles associated with poor draughting, quickly became popular. Originally introduced in 1946, their manufacture continued (with minor modifications) into *BR* days as the *BR Standard* class 2MT. Both the *LMS* and *BR* 2MT variants were often affectionately referred to by crews and shed staff by the nickname *Mickey Mouse*. *25/3/62 Canonflex (Kodachrome)*

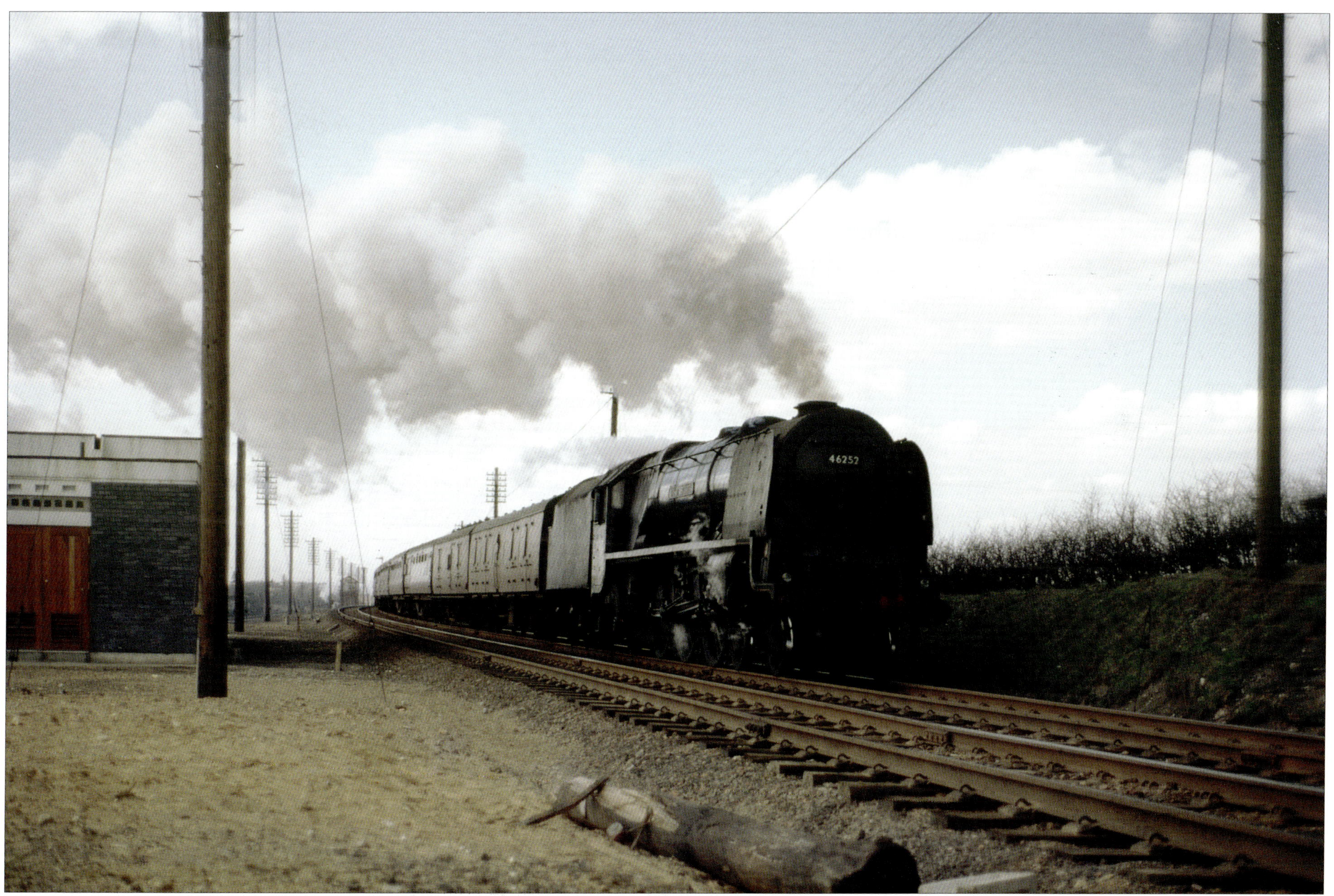

SLIDE 1292 | Carlisle Kingmoor's *Coronation Pacific* **46252 City of Leicester** on an unidentified up express heading south from Rugby has just passed Hillmorton Signal Box (visible in the distance) on the Rugby to Euston main line. Although looking slightly 'blue' in this photograph, purely down to reflected light, *46252* is actually in the *BR* green livery it received in 1952 and retained until it was withdrawn from Camden Shed in June 1963. Built in 1944; one of a batch of only four of its class in this year, *(4)6252* was involved in a near disaster in the early hours of November 19th, 1951 whilst approaching Polesworth Station, Warwickshire. It was derailed whilst entering the crossover from the fast line to the slow at too high a speed whilst hauling a heavy Glasgow Central to Euston express. Despite eight of the twelve coaches derailing behind the locomotive, only two of the one hundred and seventy-four passengers suffered any significant injury. *14/4/62 Leica IIIA (Kodachrome)*

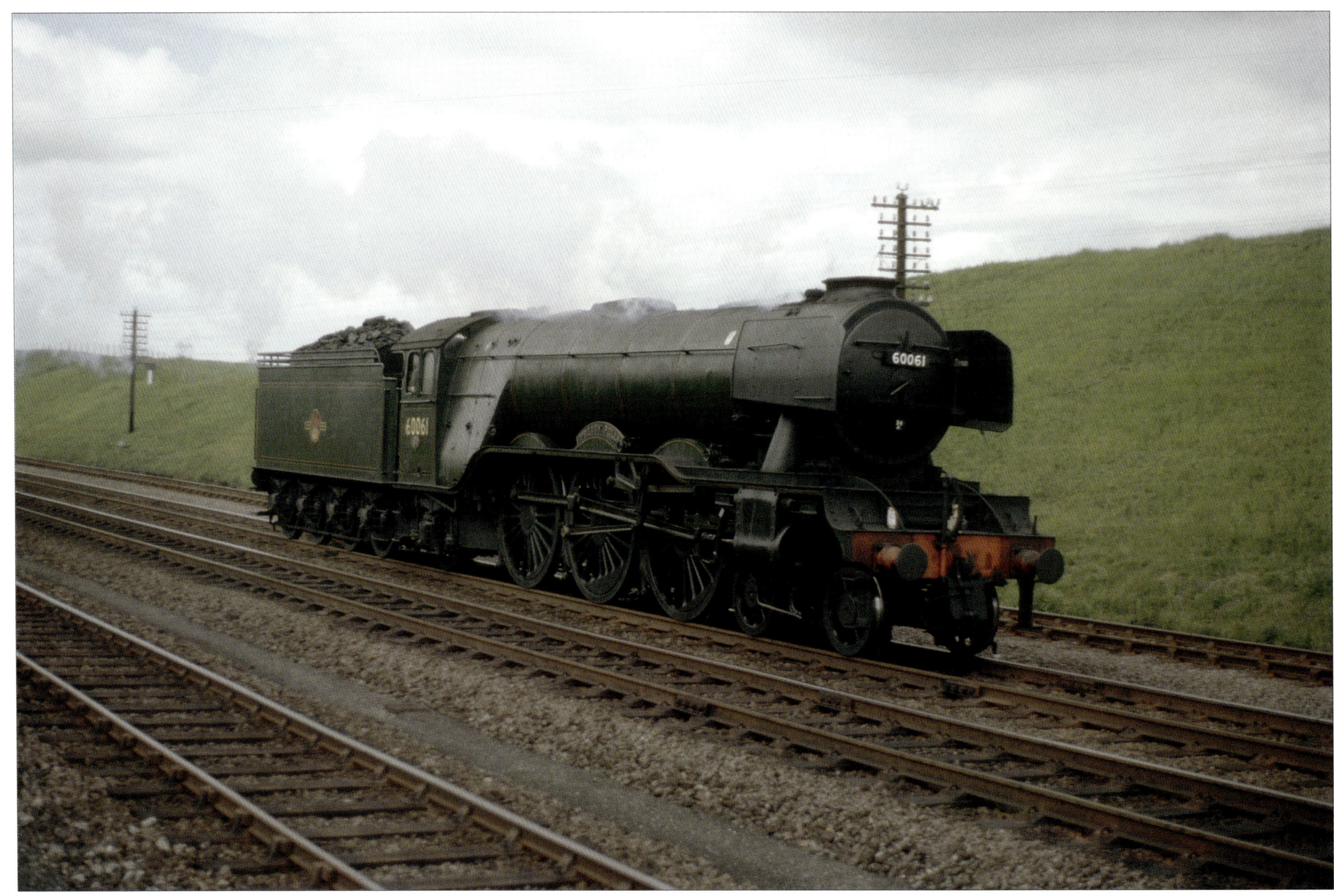

SLIDE 1390 | King's Cross-based ex-*LNER A3 Pacific* **60061 Pretty Polly** is caught running down Stoke Bank, between Little Bytham and Grantham. This locomotive was observed earlier in the day on an unidentified six-coach passenger train which we now believe to have been carrying military personal to *RAF Waddington* and it is seen here later returning light engine to King's Cross. Tom and fellow-photographer Gordon England travelled across to the East Coast Main Line on this day, primarily to photograph *A4* **60022 Mallard** on the outward leg of the *RCTS/SLS Aberdeen Flyer* railtour. This, they did achieve, but unfortunately due to the light being so poor, Tom chose not to waste a single frame of colour film on it; capturing it only in black-and-white with his *Contessa-Nettel*. Thankfully, the weather improved as the day went on. *2/6/62 Leica IIIA (Kodachrome)*

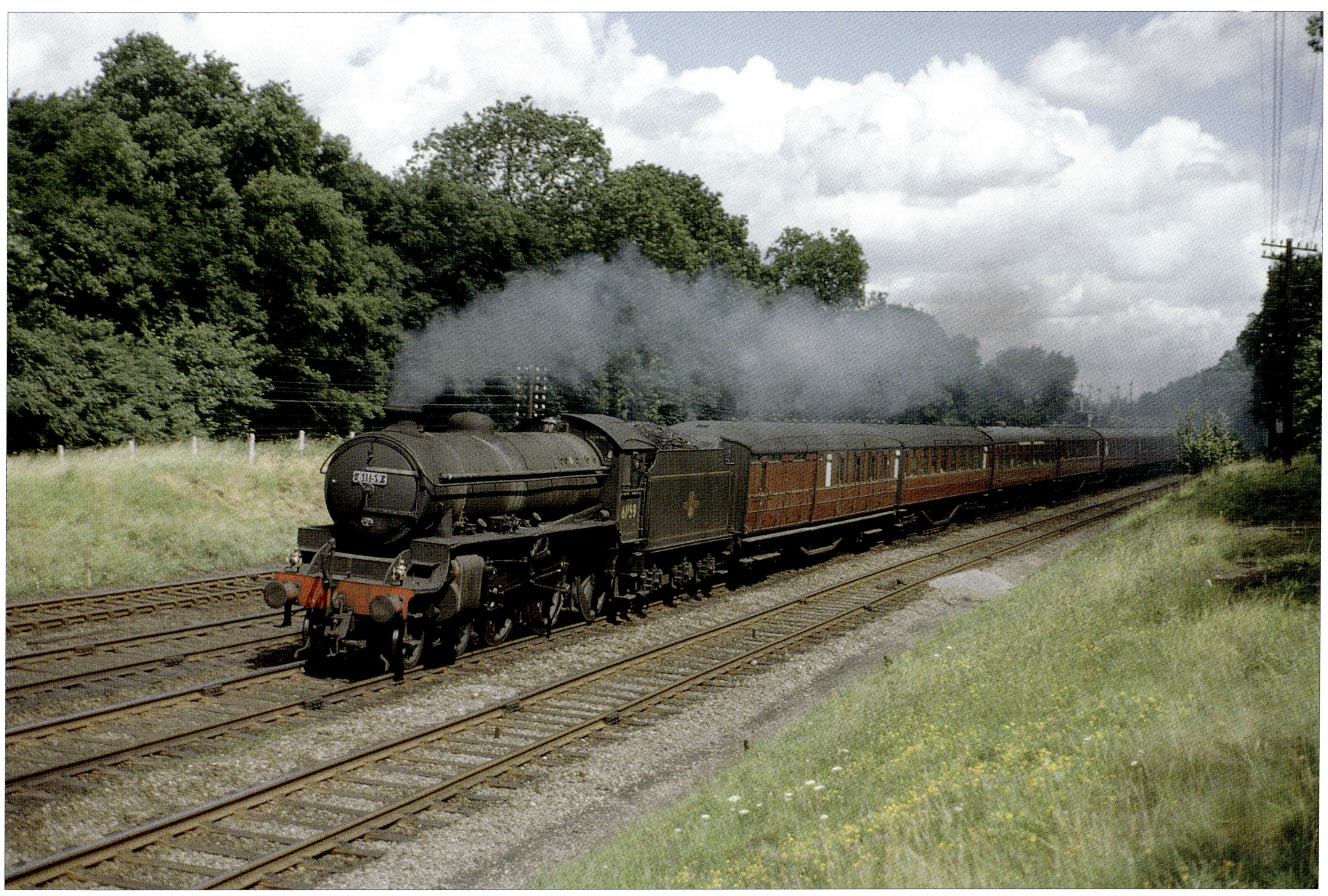

SLIDE 1458 | Immingham-based *Thompson B1* class 4-6-0 **61159** is captured on a *Butlin's* Skegness to King's Cross excursion train just south of Hatfield Station (some of the associated signal arrays just visible in the distance). At this location the East Coast Main Line begins to curve almost due south, briefly running parallel to the *Great North Road*: at almost the exact point of the Hatfield rail crash of October 17th 2000. A *GNER InterCity 225* on the 12.10pm to Leeds was derailed at high speed when a fatigued rail fractured as the train passed over it, resulting in four fatalities and over seventy injured, including *GNER* staff. The aftermath of the crash and subsequent inquiry were also to have far-reaching repercussions throughout the rail industry itself. *21/7/62 Leica IIIA (Kodachrome)*

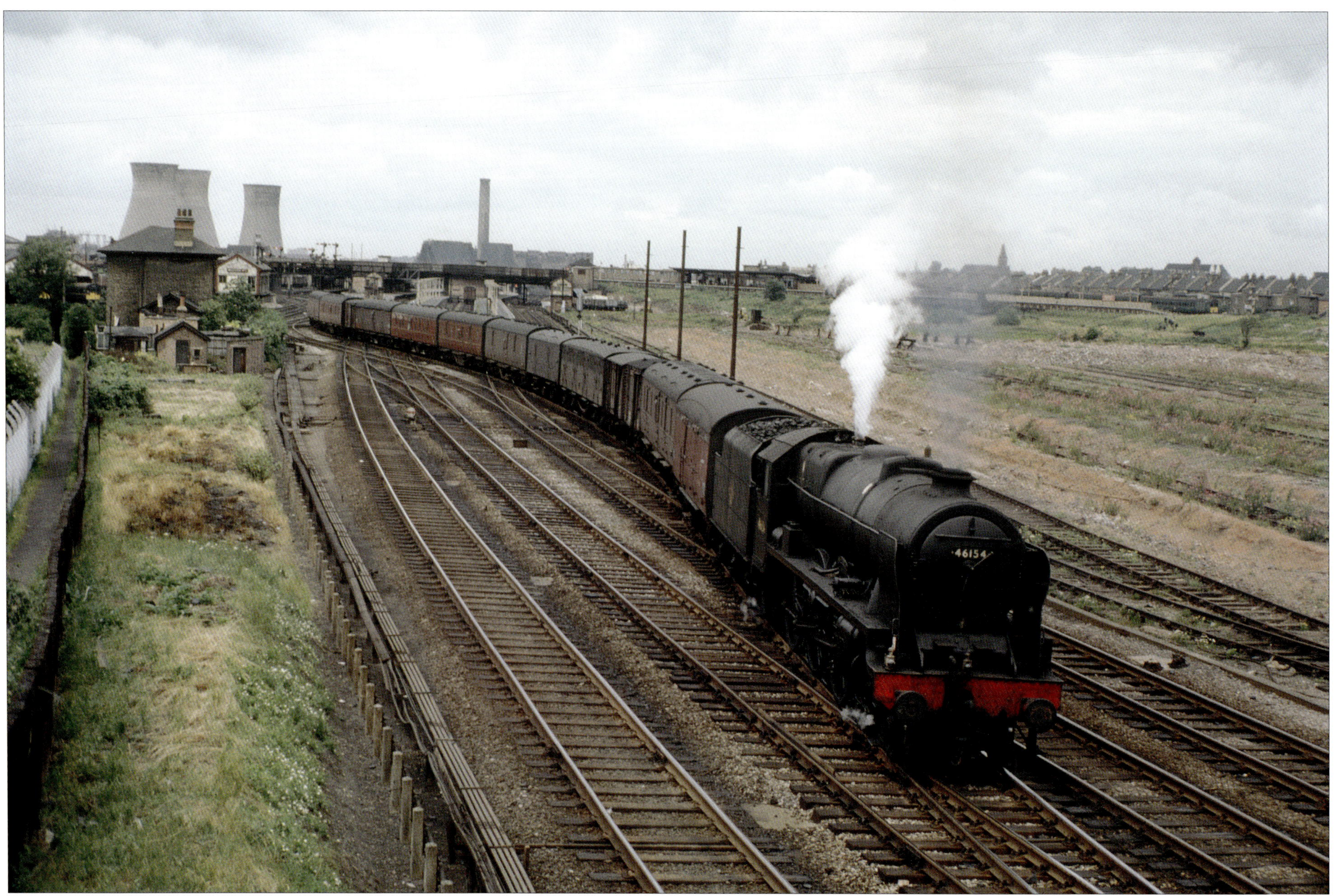

SLIDE 1461 | Ex-*LMS Royal Scot* 4-6-0 **46154 The Hussar** has recently been reallocated to Willesden Shed after a brief spell at Holyhead. It is captured here with an up parcels train, threading its way from the North London Line to access the main line at Willesden No. 4 Signal Box, just West of Willesden Junction (Low Level) Station. The skyline here was dominated by the Acton Lane power station and the distinctive Gothic silhouette of the *Harlesden Baptist Church*, Acton Lane (to the right of the plume of escaping steam). Also just visible on the right, the twin spires of the nearby *All Souls Church*, silhouetted against the *Our Lady of Harlesden R.C. Church*. Willesden Junction (High Level) Station can be seen to the right of the intersection bridge crossing behind the signals. The desolate area occupying the right-hand middle ground of this image, populated by disused tracks, rubble and *Rosebay Willowherb*, is the site of the recently demolished carriage shed. Photograph taken looking west from the *Scrubs Lane Bridge. 21/7/62 Leica IIIA (Kodachrome)*

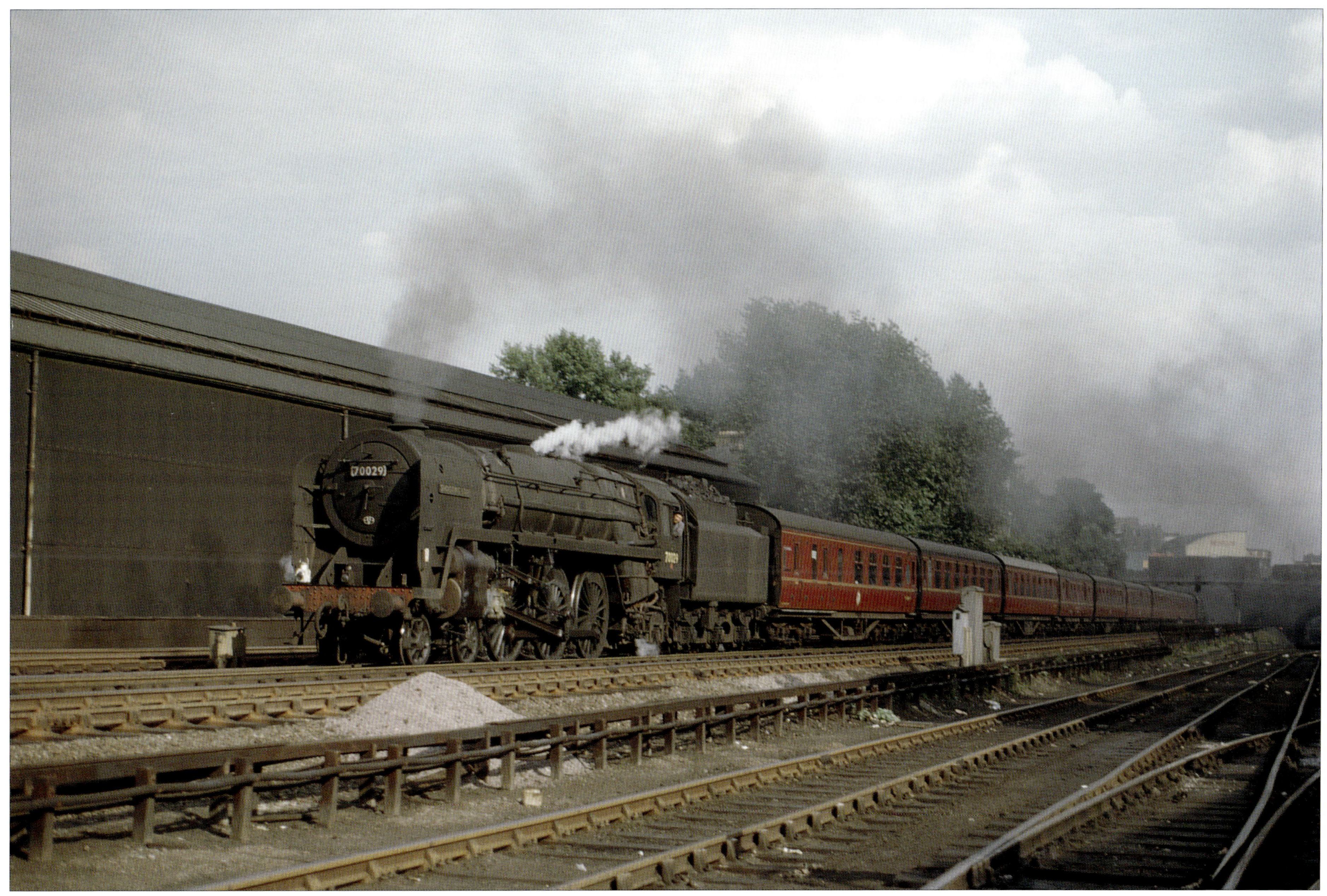

SLIDE 1466 │ At around 5.20pm on this Monday evening, Aston-based *BR Standard* class 7 **70029 Shooting Star** heads up Camden Bank from Euston with a train of empty coaching stock destined for the carriage shed at Camden. The first coach is labelled *1Z16* and indeed, this rake had come in approximately an hour earlier behind *Stanier Princess Royal* class **46209 Princess Beatrice**: comprising an unidentified Liverpool Lime Street to Euston express. Unfortunately, Tom was unable to photograph this train as it came in, because it was completely obscured by a down express exiting Euston and passing directly in front of him before he had the opportunity to relocate. It is interesting to compare the *LMR type-2* smoke deflectors on *70029*, with the earlier *WR* interpretation of the same modification illustrated in *slide 436 on page 4*. Also note that the locomotive is still fitted with its original *GWR*-style central lamp iron, which will be removed approximately a year later *(see also slide 1468 on following page)*. *23/7/62 Leica IIIA (Kodachrome)*

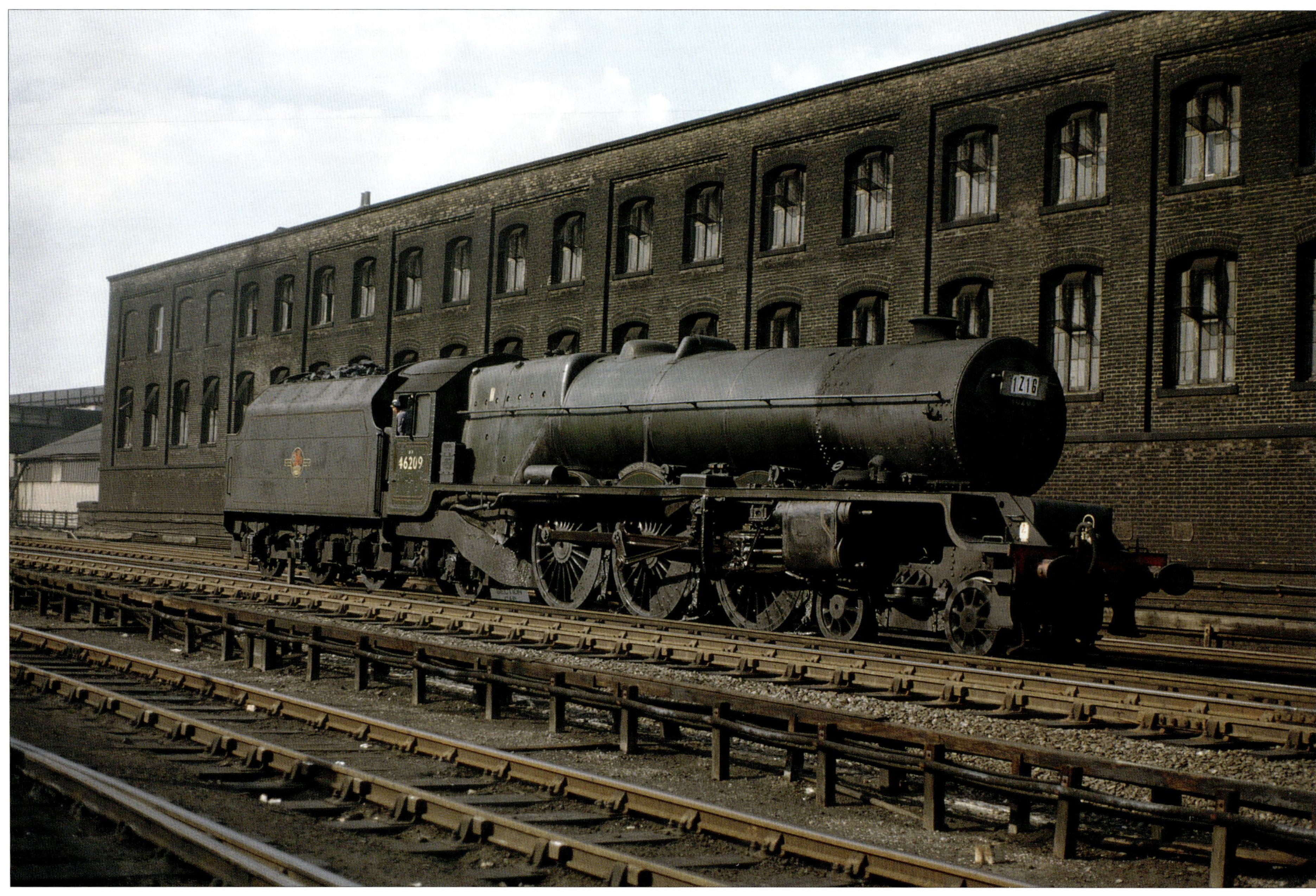

SLIDE 1468 | Within a minute or so of the previous image being captured, Camden's own *Stanier Princess Royal* class 4-6-2 **46209 Princess Beatrice** reverses light engine back up from Euston to its home shed after coming off train *1Z16* that it has brought in from Liverpool. One of the last of its twelve-strong class to enter service in August 1935, *46209* was only two months from withdrawal when the above photograph was taken. After a short period of storage at Camden, it was returned to its birthplace at Crewe for breaking up (during November 1962). Note in this image, the interesting oil-spray patterning on the wheels caused by the action of centrifugal forces on the lubricant during periods of spirited running. *23/7/62 Leica IIIA (Kodachrome)*

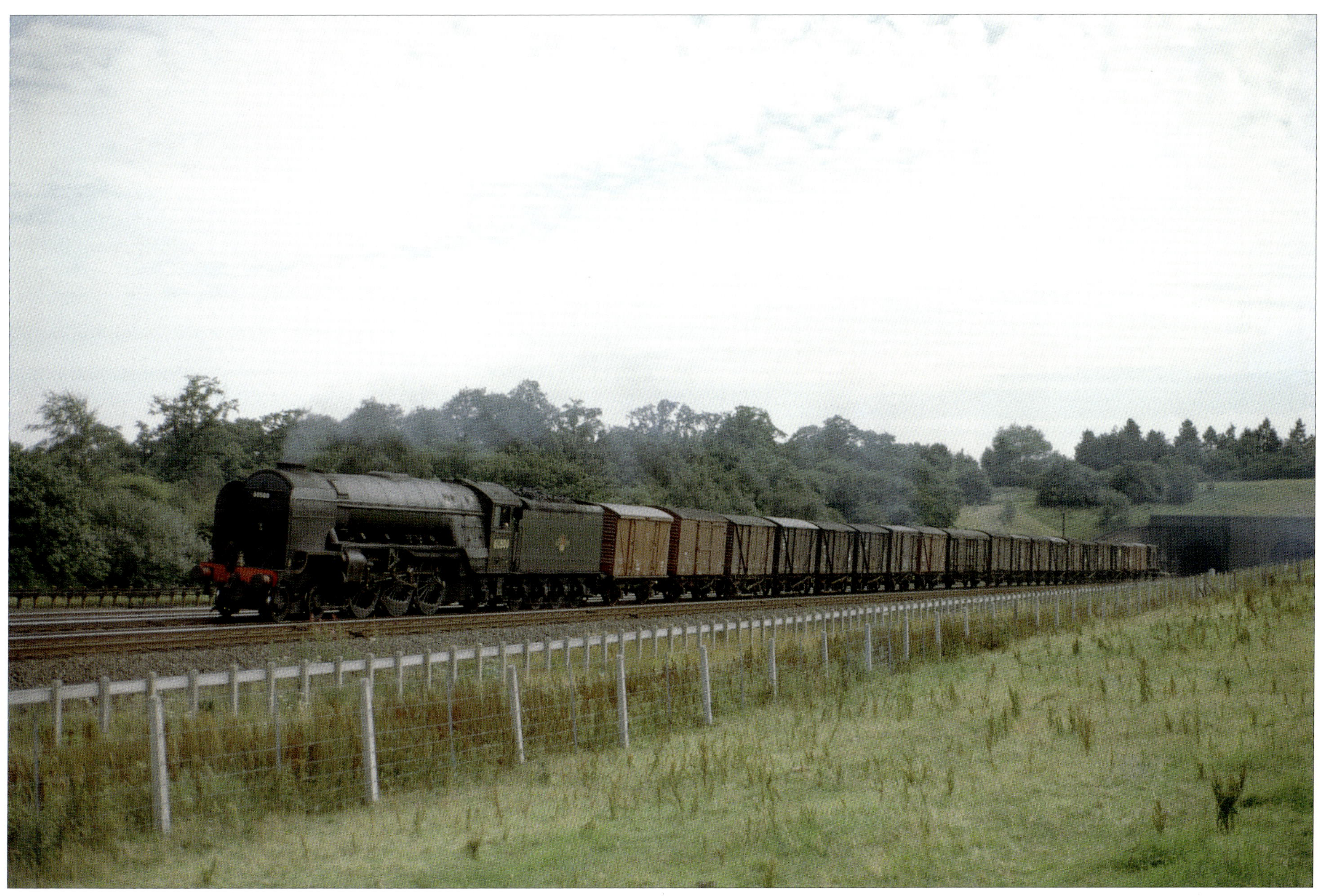

SLIDE 1478 | The 200th locomotive to roll out of Doncaster Works, leader of its class *and* the only one to see service during the tenure of its designer, ex-*LNER A2/3* class *Pacific* **60500 Edward Thompson** exits Hadley Wood North Tunnel with a fully fitted freight. Although the manufacture of fourteen further locomotives of the class proceeded under the auspices of Arthur Peppercorn, Thompson's successor, the building of further members of the class was curtailed subject to a re-evaluation of their design. Peppercorn's 'improved' design was ultimately to became the standard *A2* class. Spending the majority of its service life working out of King's Cross and New England, Peterborough, *60500* was withdrawn just under a year after this photograph was taken and broken up at Doncaster where it had been built in May 1946. *27/7/62 Leica IIIA (Kodachrome)*

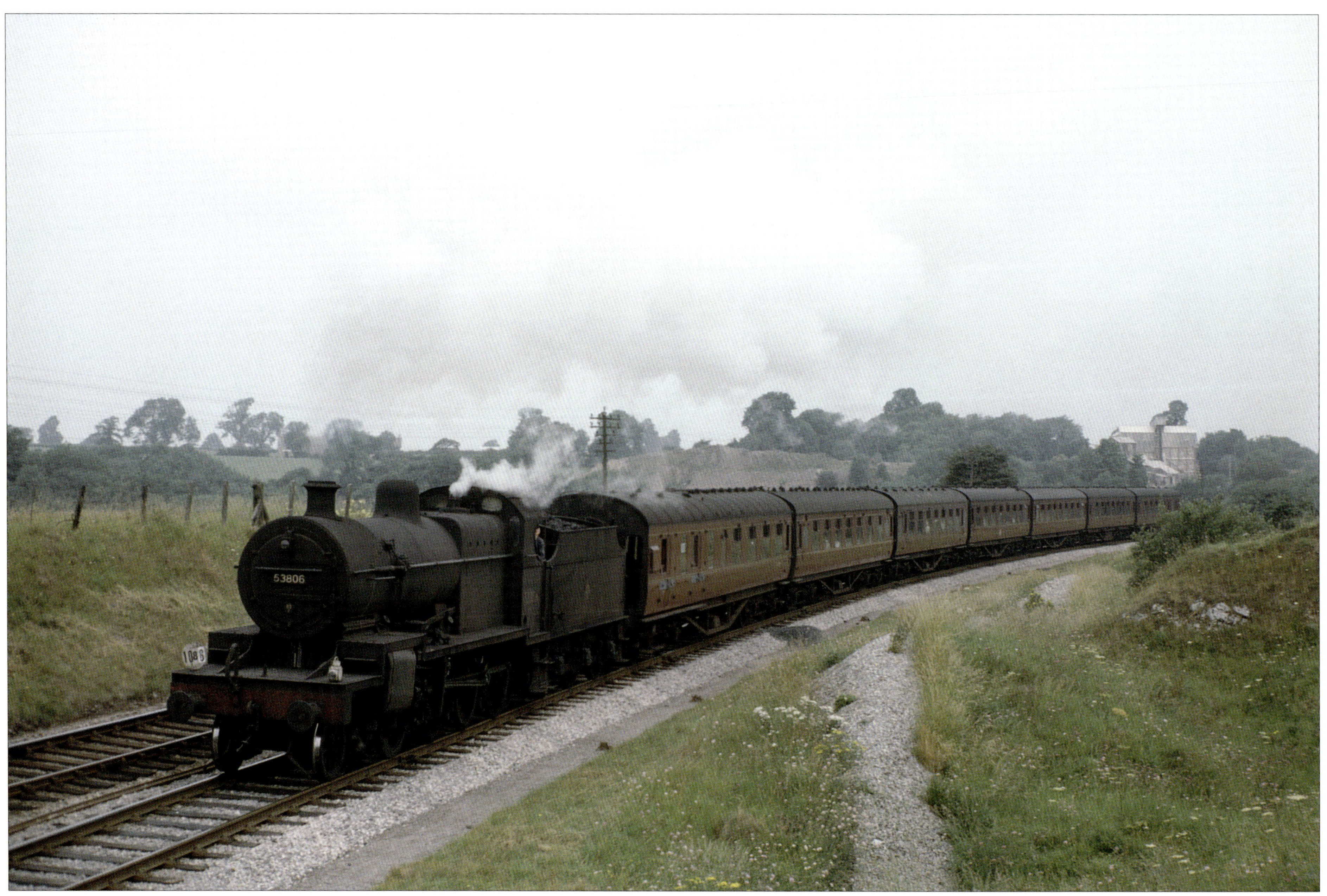

SLIDE 1484 | Bath Green Park's *Fowler* 7F **53806** on a Walsall to Bournemouth relief train heads south on the ex-*S&D* near Binegar, approximately three miles south-west of Chilcompton, Somerset. Built by *Robert Stephenson & Hawthorn Ltd.* and first entering service as *86* in 1925, *53806* was the first of the second batch of five locomotives ordered and fitted with the larger *G9BS* boilers (the initial batch of locomotives being fitted with the *G9AS* boilers of the *Midland Compounds*). Interestingly, *53806* was also the first of its class to be built, like all subsequent machines, with left-hand drive. The withdrawal of the class began in 1959, but *53806* made up one of the four that were to remain in service until January 1964. It was eventually broken up by *Cashmore's* of Newport approximately six months later. *28/7/62 Leica IIIA (Kodachrome)*

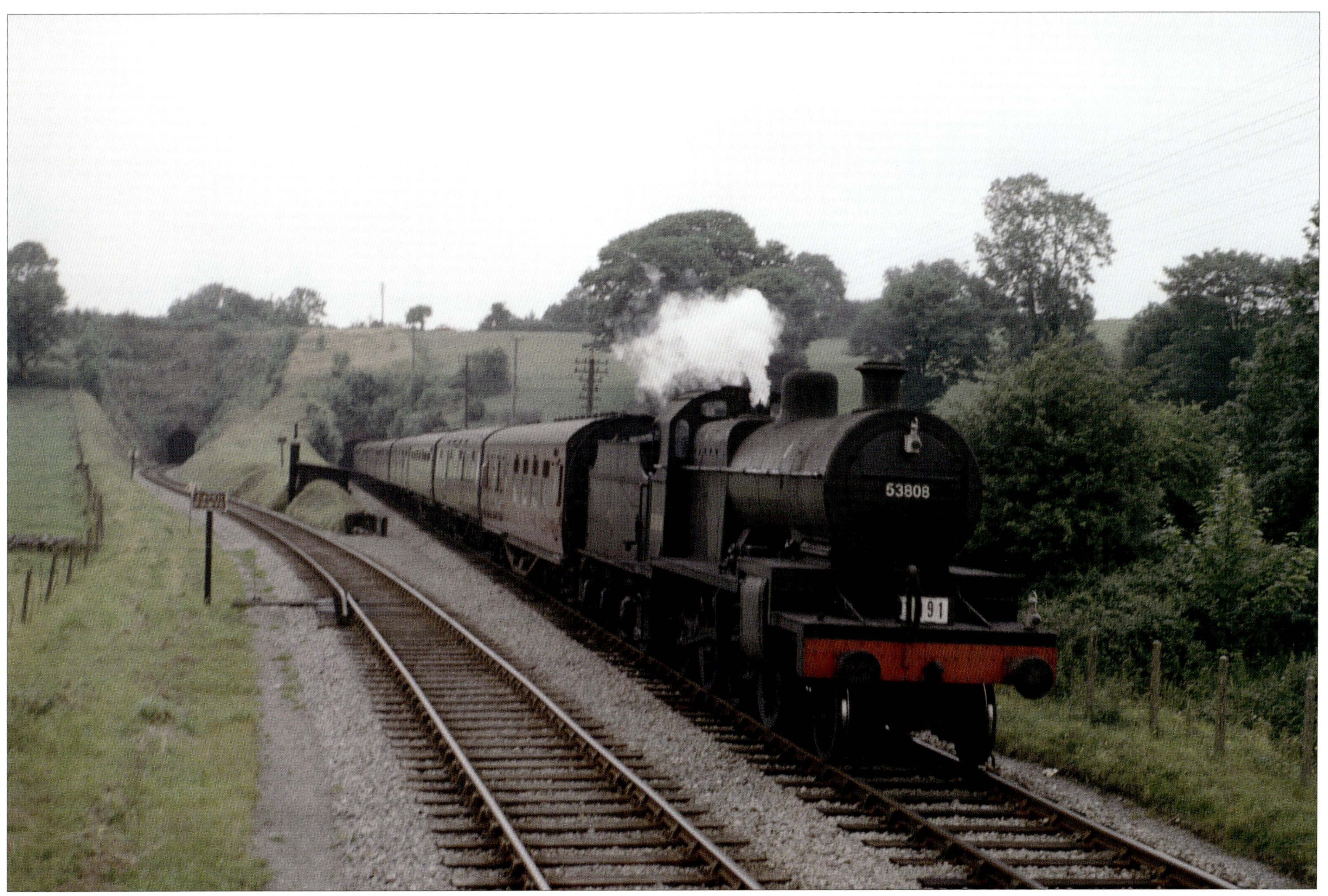

SLIDE 1487 | The now-preserved, Bath Green Park-based *Fowler* 7F **53808** exits the southerly portal of the Windsor Hill 'down' tunnel, just north of Shepton Mallet on a Nottingham to Bournemouth express. The train is about to traverse the *Forum Lane* bridge. Necessitated in 1872 when the *S&D* built a single-line extension linking a new junction at Evercreech with the *Midland Railway* at Bath, this single tunnel was ultimately found to be inadequate and a continued increase in traffic throughout the 1880s prompted the doubling of the line and consequently, the boring of the second 'up' tunnel. Shortly after services on the *S&D* between Bath and Bournemouth finally came to an end on March 7th 1966, followed by a prompt lifting of the tracks, Windsor Hill's original (and longer) down tunnel became a test-bed for Concorde's *Rolls Royce/Snecma Olympus* engines. *28/7/62 Leica IIIA (Kodachrome)*

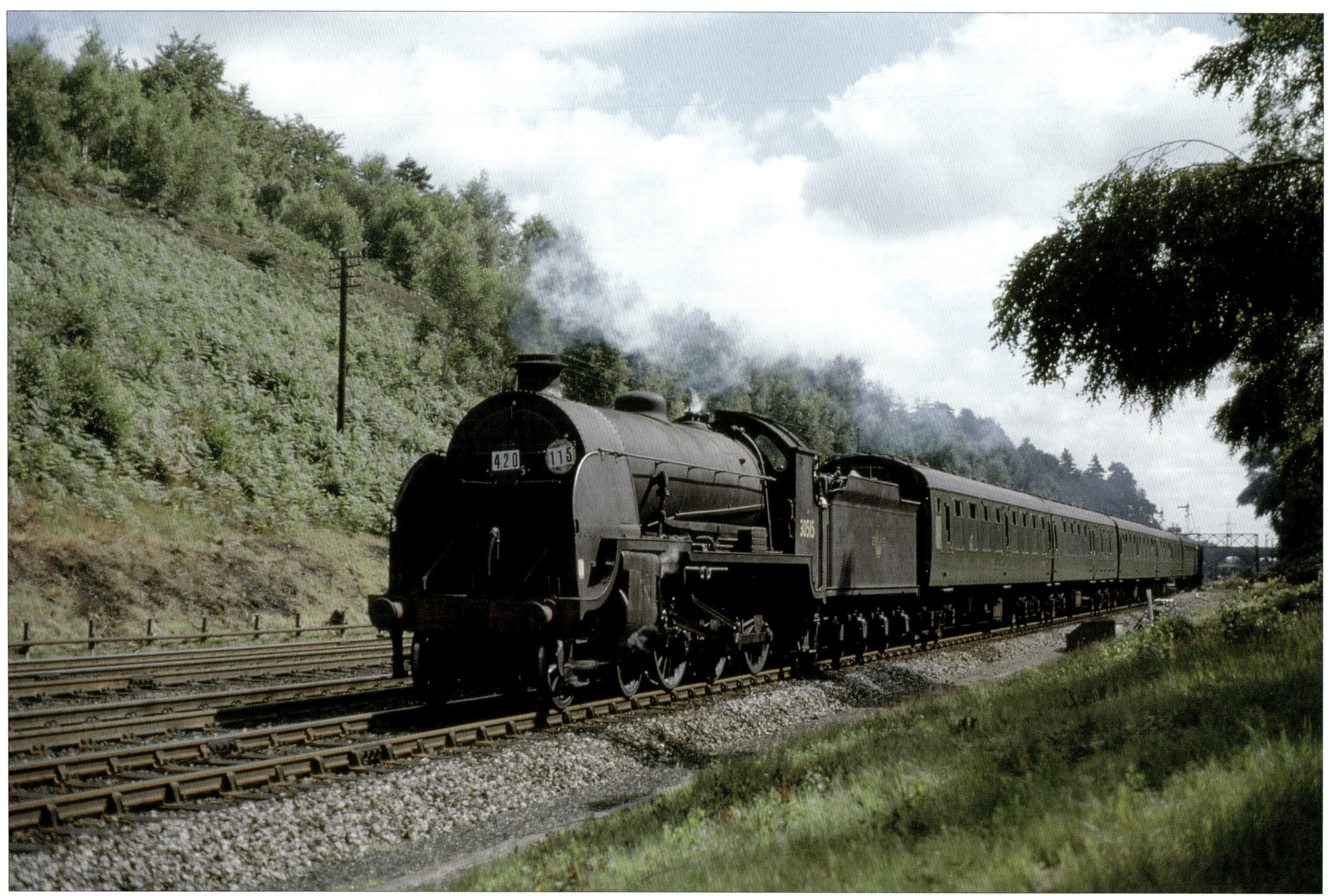

SLIDE 1499 | Feltham's *Urie/Maunsell S15* class **30515** accelerates away from its last stop at Winchfield on a Waterloo to Basingstoke stopping train. *30515* was actually the final production *S15* built at Eastleigh in 1921 for the *LSWR* to Robert Urie's original specification, prior to Richard Maunsell's reappraisal of certain aspects of the locomotive's design. Reduced diameter cylinders, higher boiler pressure, plus cab and footplate reconfigurations were all lauded by locomotive crew as great improvements on what was already considered a sound workhorse. Despite the basic *S15* class design being only a year or so younger than that of its larger-wheeled *N15 King Arthur* class cousins, the *S15* proved to have more longevity, primarily down to its dual freight/passenger capabilities. The last member of this class in service was **30837** which was eventually withdrawn from Eastleigh in September 1965. *4/8/62 Leica IIIA (Kodachrome)*

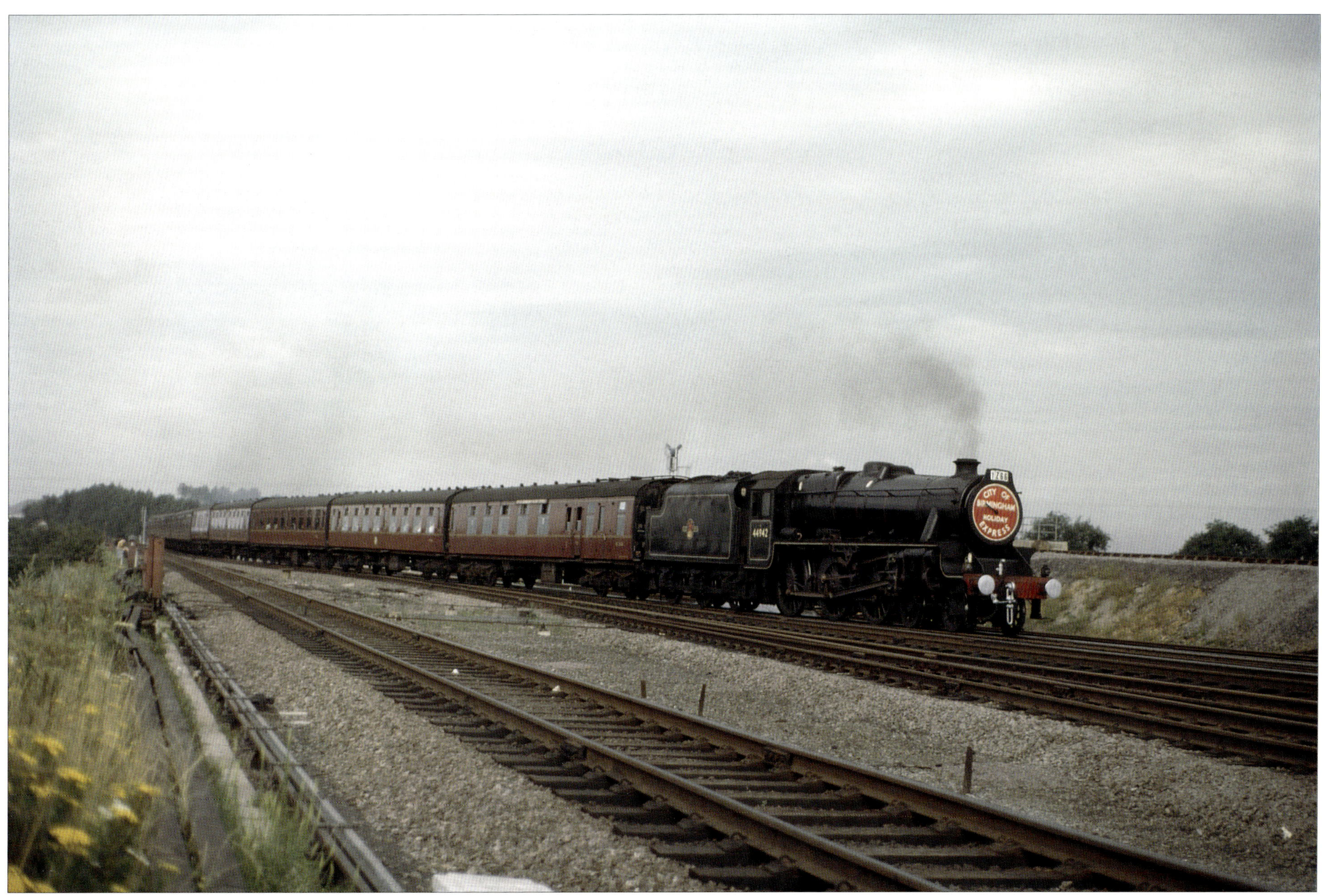

SLIDE 1503 | On this Bank Holiday Monday morning, the men at Aston Shed have turned out *Stanier Black Five* **44942** in exemplary condition for the south-bound *City of Birmingham Holiday Express*. This service ran from Birmingham New Street during the 'Factory Fortnight' industrial close-down, providing day-trips for workers and their families to popular locations such as London, Hastings and Skegness. *44942* spent almost a decade working out of Aston and during this period was regularly observed on these excursions. The train is captured here crossing *Bridge 265* (spanning Lower Street/Moors Lane, Hillmorton) on the Rugby to Euston main line approximately two miles north-west of Kilsby Tunnel and is just about to pass Hillmorton Signal Box. The line in the foreground leads into Hillmorton Sidings and the embankment visible in the background carries the line to Northampton. *6/8/62 Leica IIIA (Kodachrome)*

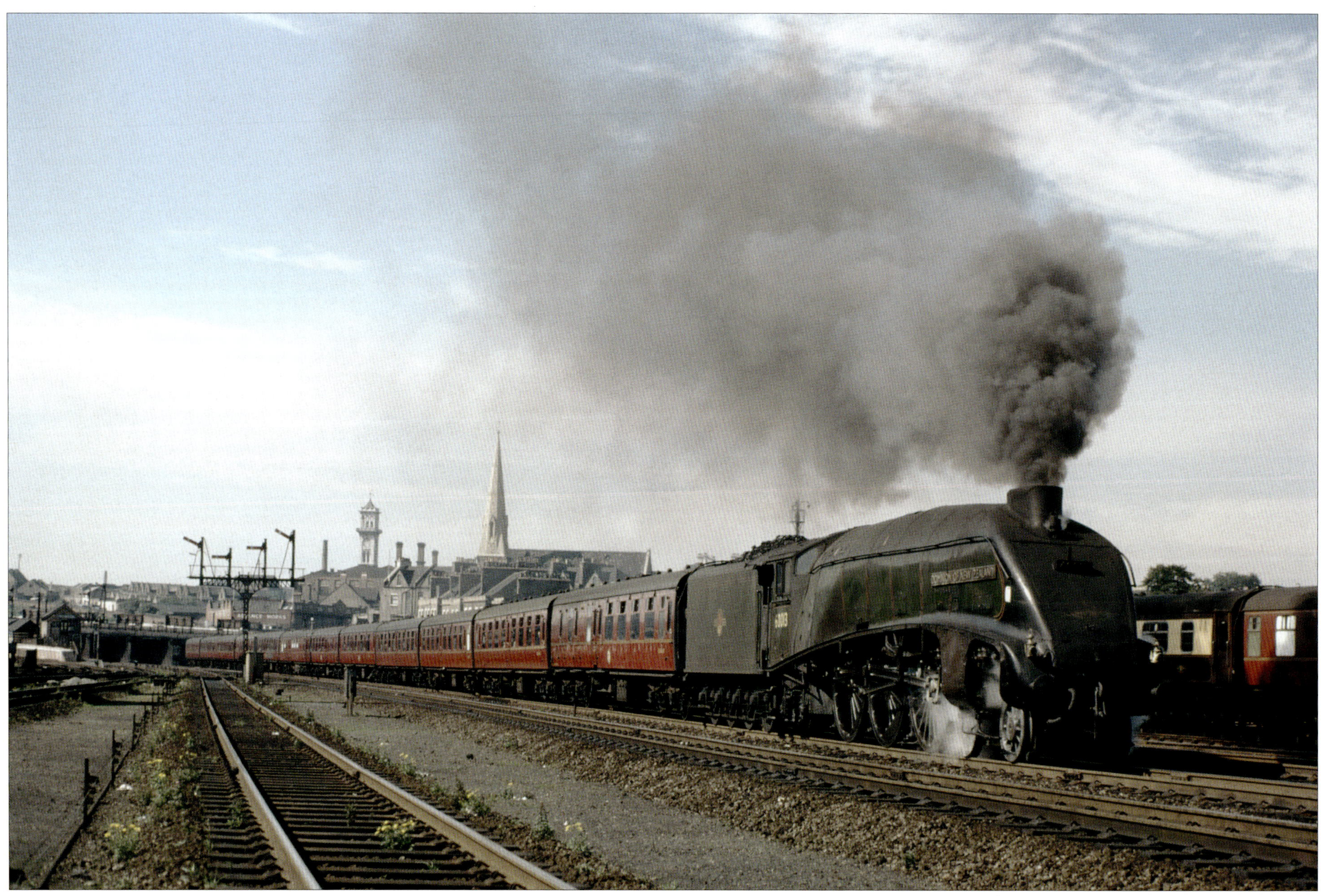

SLIDE 1525 | *Gresley A4 Pacific* **60013 Dominion of New Zealand** *(ex-LNER 4492)* is on home territory as it heads up the bank, past Holloway South Box with the 10.40am King's Cross to Newcastle Central service. In the distance we see the iconic clock tower of the former *Caledonian Cattle Market* and the distinctive spire of the contemporary *Wesleyan Methodist Church*, on the intersection of Hillmarton Road and Caledonian Road, Lower Holloway which would be demolished in 1976 as part of a redevelopment initiative. When the above photograph was taken, *60013* had less than a year to go prior to withdrawal. In April 1963 it returned to Doncaster Works where it had been built in 1937, only to be dismantled within a week of its arrival. *19/8/62 Leica IIIA (Kodachrome)*

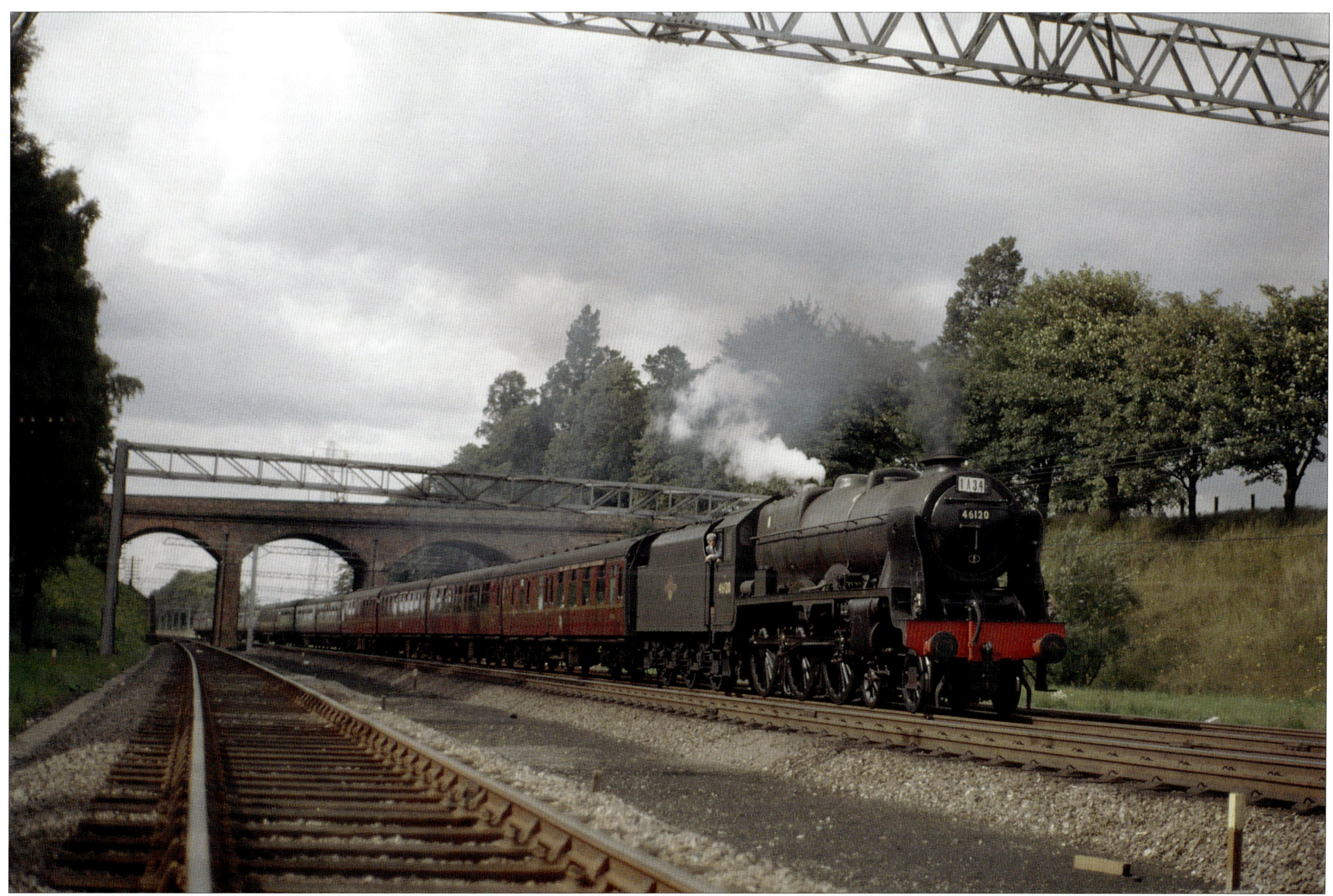

SLIDE 1532 | Llandudno Junction's *Royal Scot* class **46120 Royal Inniskilling Fusilier** hauls the up *Lakes Express* south under *Brinklow Road*, Easenhall, near Rugby. This locomotive had quite a chequered history: not actually having been involved in any significant incidents, but during its *LMS* past had been regarded by successive crews as a *'wrong un'*. Rough-riding was a common problem with this class; attributed to the stiff bogie side-control springs which, if combined with excessively worn rear axle-box facings, would cause *nosing* or lateral oscillation of the locomotive, particularly when travelling at speed. During the late 1940s *(4)6120* was put through a series of exhaustive tests on the *LMS* dynamometer car, which resulted in class-wide modifications being made to the bogie assemblies. To add insult to injury, *(4)6210* was still vilified as a particularly rough ride and it wasn't until its driving wheels were analysed on the balancing machine at Crewe Works, that it became apparent they had not been balanced correctly during its 1944 rebuild. Replacement coupling rods had also been ill-fitted. *25/8/62 (Kodachrome)*

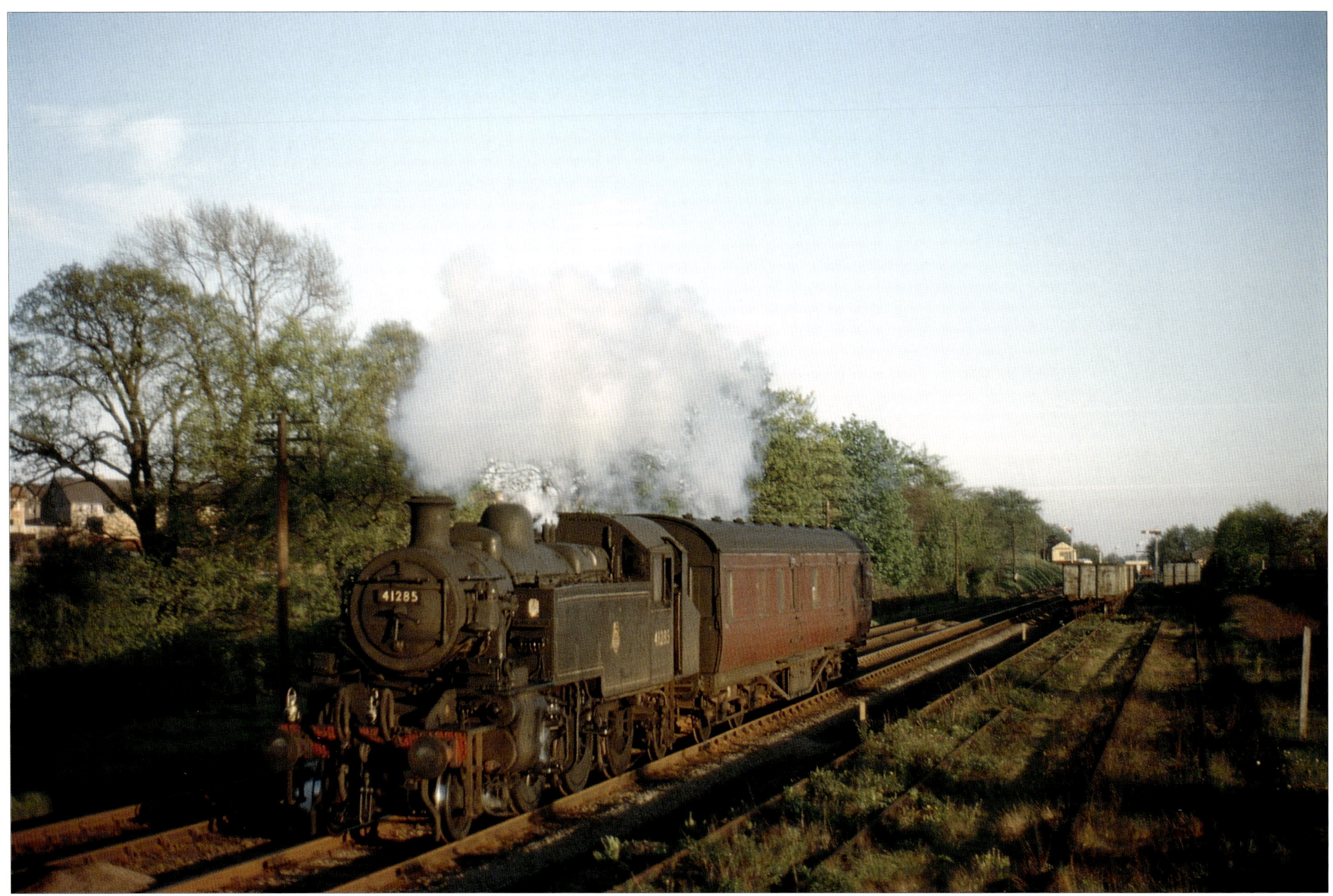

SLIDE 1610 | Leamington-based *Ivatt* 2MT 2-6-2T **41285** with a single parcels van heading for Coventry passes the overgrown goods sidings just north of Milverton Station, between Leamington Spa and Warwick. The signal box that controlled the approach to the station, locomotive shed and goods yard is just visible in the distance on the bank shouldering the up line. The original Warwick Milverton station (or what was then known as *Leamington Station*) had formed the terminus of the *LNWR* single-line branch between Coventry and Leamington. Having originally opened in 1844, this station was replaced in 1883 by a completely new structure erected just north of the site of the original buildings and it is this incarnation of the station (despite going through several name changes) that remained in operation until finally falling victim to the *Modernisation Plan* in 1965. ?/5/63 *(Kodachrome)*

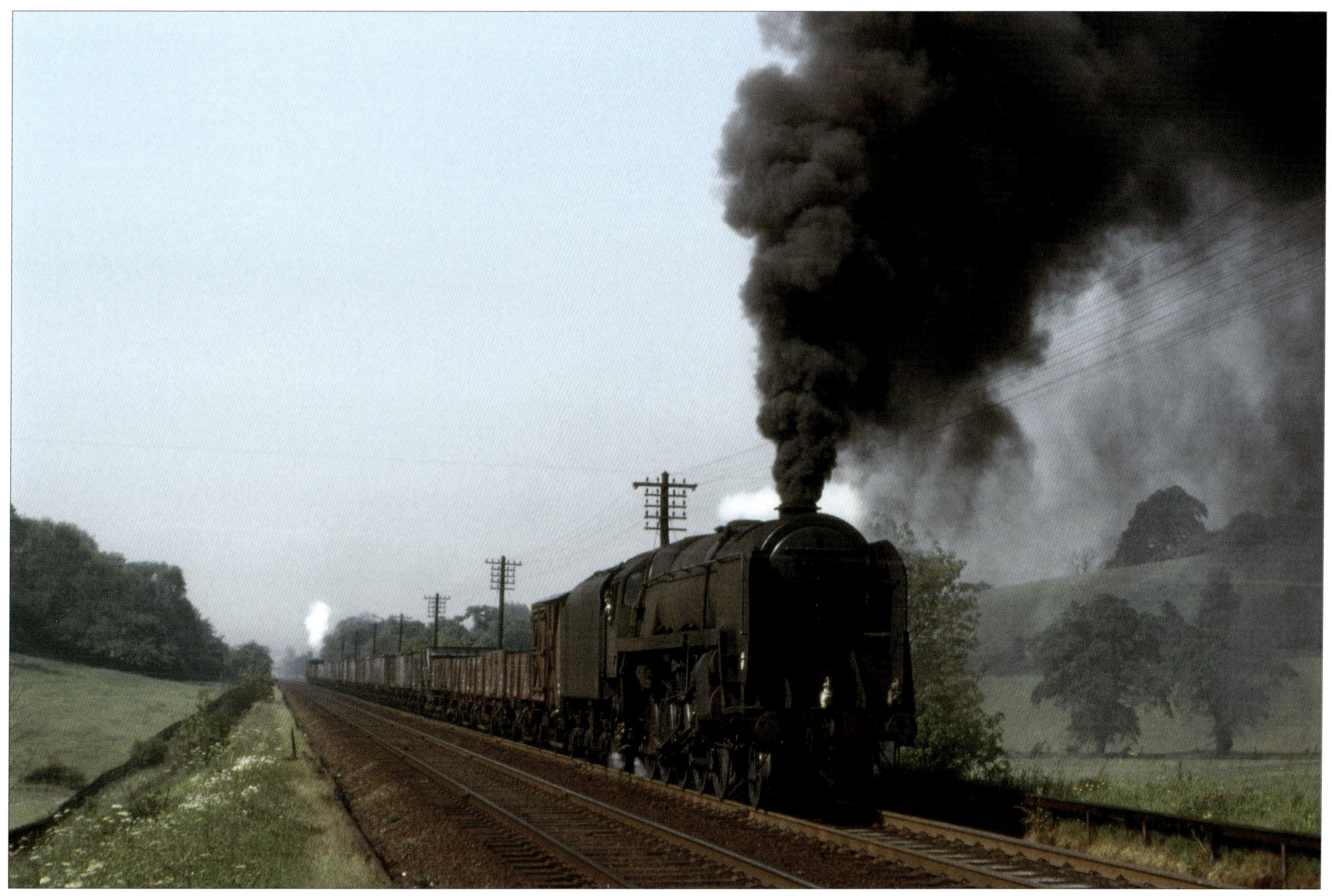

SLIDE 1641 | Saltley-based *BR Standard* 9F **92129** fills the cloudless summer sky above the Lickey Incline with black smoke as it grinds uphill towards Blackwell, north-east of Bromsgrove, Worcestershire with a partly fitted freight from South Wales, bound for the marshalling yard at Washwood Heath. Note the plume of exhaust from the banker visible in the distance (an unidentified *Hawksworth 94xx* class Pannier Tank). *92129* remained at Saltley for another year before being reallocated to Banbury Shed, where it was regularly observed working the South Wales-bound ironstone trains. It was eventually withdrawn for scrapping from Carlisle (Kingmoor) in July 1967 and broken up by *Motherwell Machinery & Scrap*, Wishaw, North Lanarkshire four months later after a service life of just over a decade. *8/6/63 (Kodachrome)*

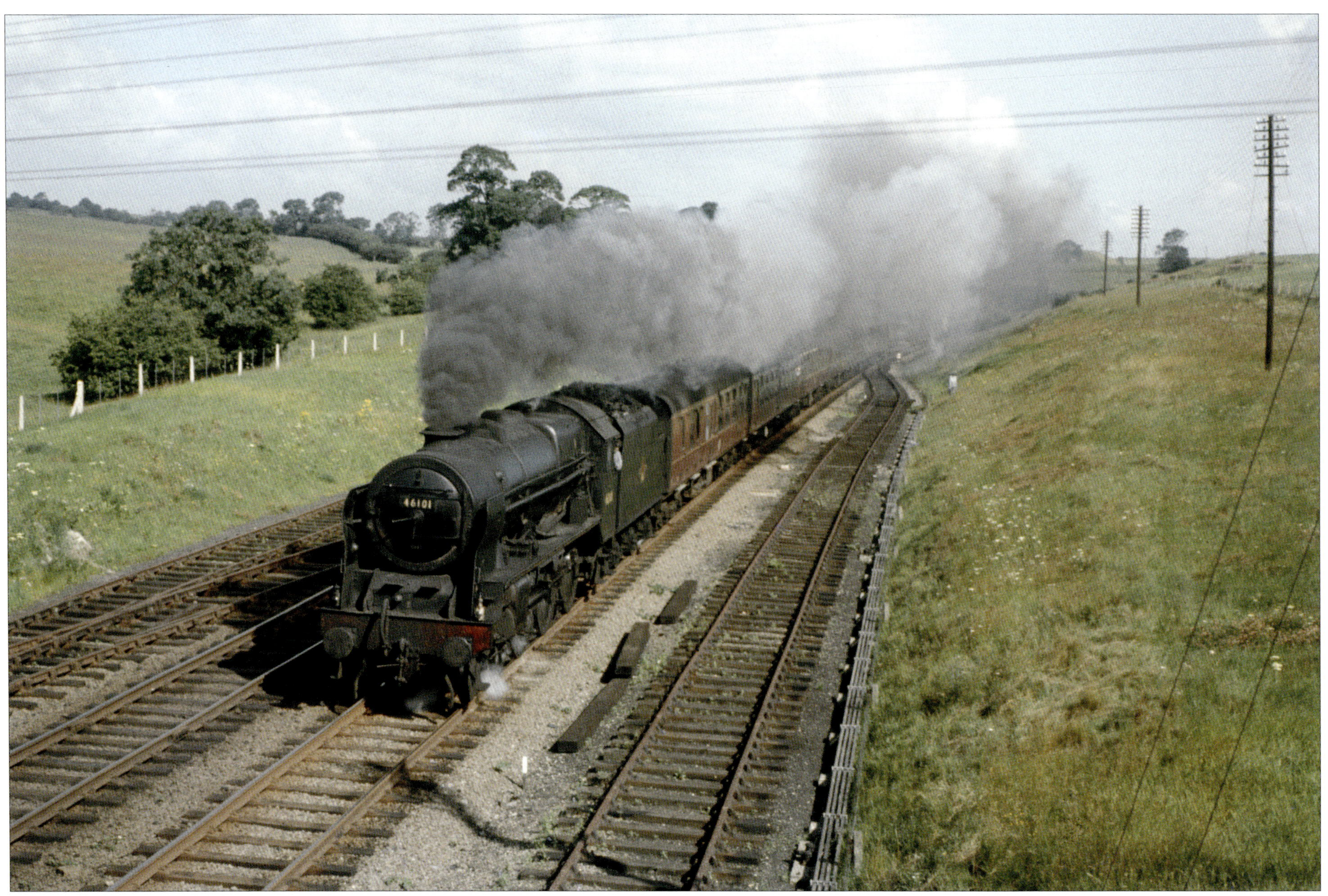

SLIDE 1673 | The Fireman appears to have been working unusually hard as Annesley-based **46101 Royal Scots Grey** exits Catesby Tunnel near Charwelton on the *Great Central* hauling an unidentified Nottingham Victoria to Marylebone express. The *Great Central* had fallen under the control of the *LMR* five years previously and, intent on running services down with a view to eventually closing the route, some worn out and highly unpopular ex-*LMS Royal Scot* class locomotives were drafted in, including the one we see here. Built in Glasgow by the *North British Locomotive Company* and entering service in September 1927, *46101* was living on borrowed time when this photograph was taken. It was withdrawn for scrapping from Annesley Shed less than three months later and broken up by *Slag Reduction Co. Ltd.*, on the outskirts of Rotherham during April of the following year. *26/7/63 (Ansco)*

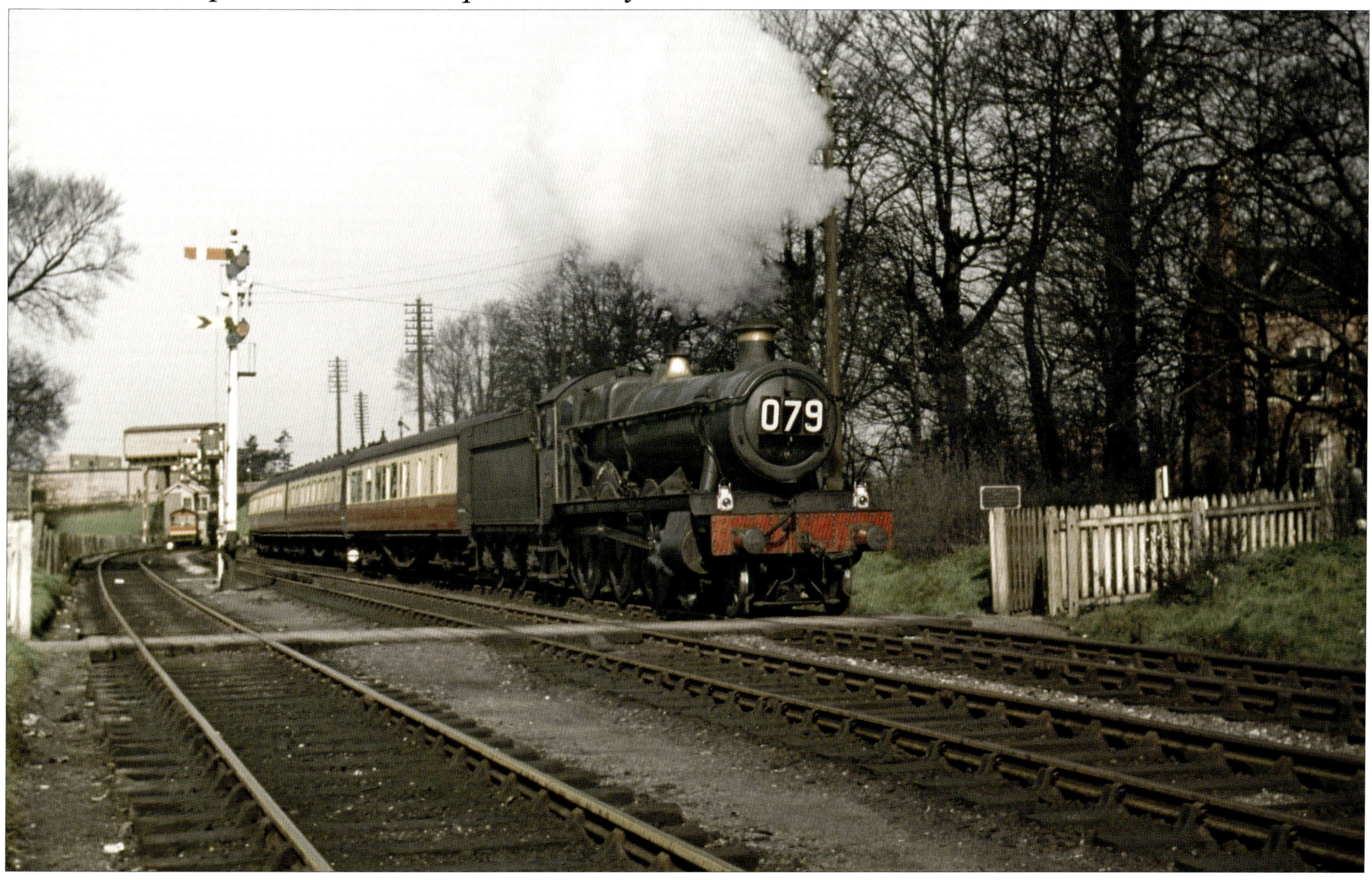

SLIDE 167 | The start of 1957 was to turn out quite an eventful time for the 'Birmingham line'. On February 25th a minor collision at Leamington Spa caused the temporary re-routing of all trains between Paddington and Wolverhampton via Stratford and Oxford (which at least gave the *Kings* a well-earned rest!) Less than a fortnight later, an earth slippage near Harbury Tunnel created a similar disruption to timetabled services. **5984 Linden Hall** has recently been reallocated to Tyseley Shed from Worcester and is captured on this cold Tuesday morning crawling through Stratford on the 6.45am Wolverhampton to Paddington. It is just about to cross the first *Shottery Fields* pedestrian crossing on its way south-west to access the Worcester to Oxford main line via the junctions at Honeybourne. Within a twenty-four hour period, services were to return to normal. *5684* remained at Tyseley for a little over six months after this photograph was taken, before being returned to Worcester. *12/3/57 Periflex (Gevacolor 26)*

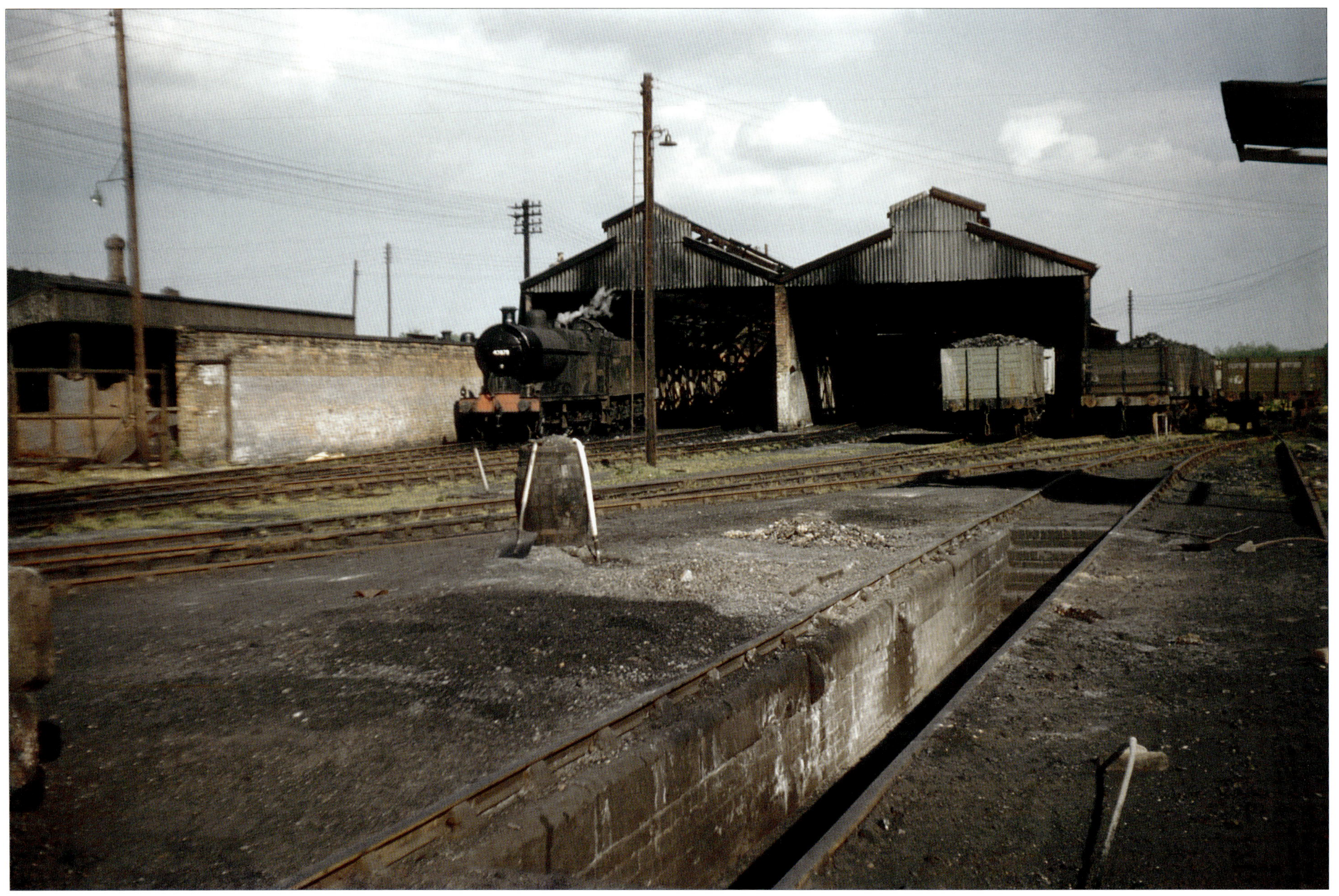

SLIDE 233 | The locomotive shed and former workshops of the *Stratford-upon-Avon & Midland Junction Railway* were located in *Old Town*, adjacent to the station. Originally opened in 1876 by the *East & West Junction Railway* the facilities were heroic in proving that an impoverished railway company could somehow keep its trains running whilst seemingly forever on the brink of bankruptcy. When the *LMS* took over in 1923, they promptly closed all repair facilities and replaced the motley *SMJ* fleet with standard ex-*Midland* locomotives. The shed continued as a depot for a small number of locomotives and as an important crew changing point for Bedford and Gloucester. After the official cessation of passenger services in April 1952, the shed soon lost its own locomotive fleet and was relegated to a service point for visiting ones only. This sleepy early-evening scene shows *Fowler 4F* **43878** from Saltley Shed as the sole occupant. Two months later on July 22nd, the shed became officially closed for good. The slight distortion in this image seems to have been caused by the film somehow fouling on the sprockets. *6/5/57 Periflex (Kodachrome)*

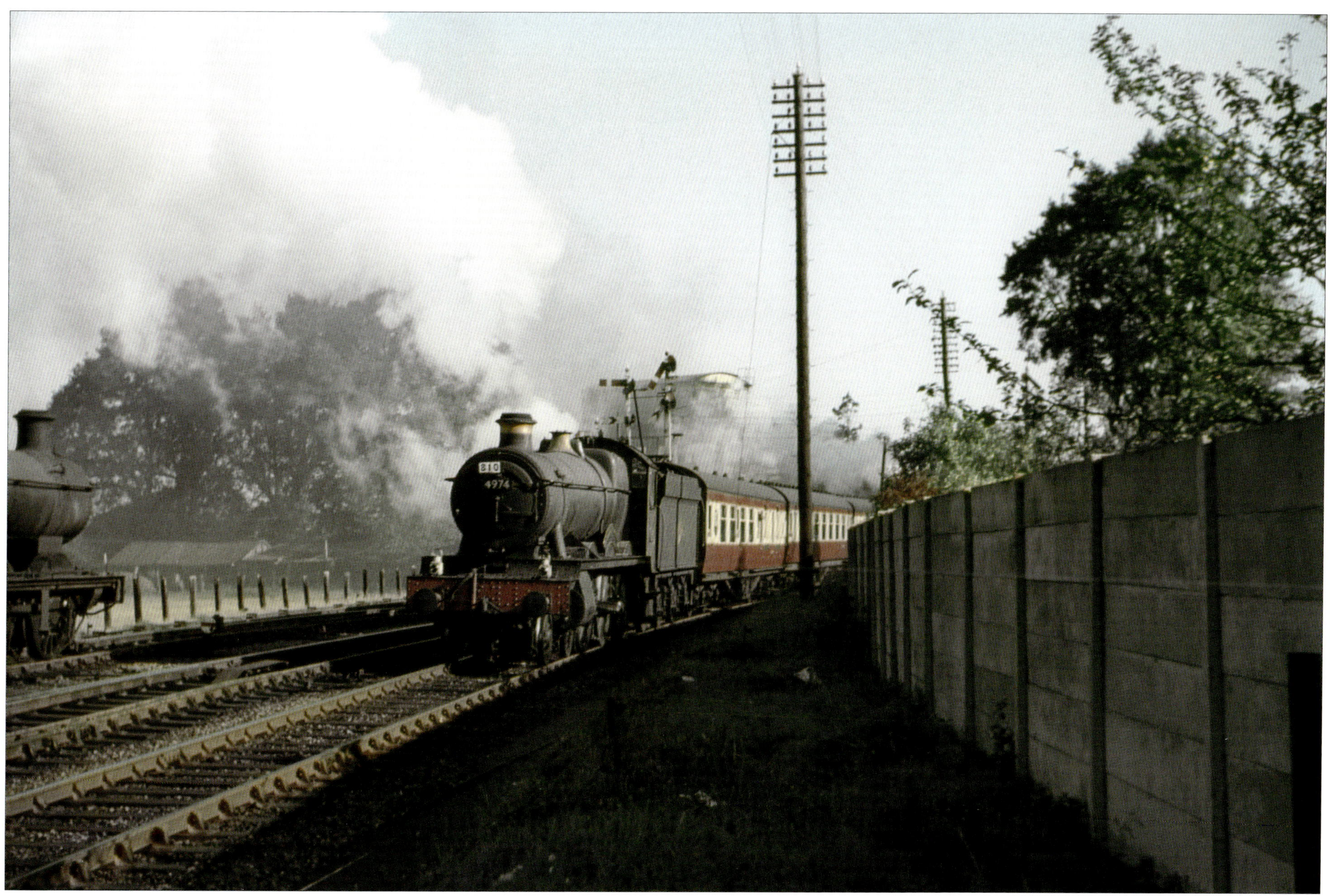

SLIDE 306 | On this humid and misty Saturday morning, Cardiff Canton's **4974 Talgarth Hall** heads south under the *Alcester Road* bridge with the 7.00am SO Birmingham to Penzance service, the atmospherics enhancing the locomotive's exhaust and escaping steam almost to the point of obscuring the water tank in the background. Just visible on the left of this image, in the up refuge siding just south of Stratford-on-Avon West Signal Box, is *Collett 2251* class 0-6-0 **2257** awaiting its first banking turn of the day. Looking at the condition of *4974* in this shot, one might be forgiven for thinking that it is still sporting its 1950 black mixed-traffic livery, but in reality it had been outshopped by Swindon in pristine lined-green livery only two months previously. We know this because Tom photographed it on April 14th in the yard at Swindon immediately after overhaul. *15/6/57 Periflex (Gevacolor 26)*

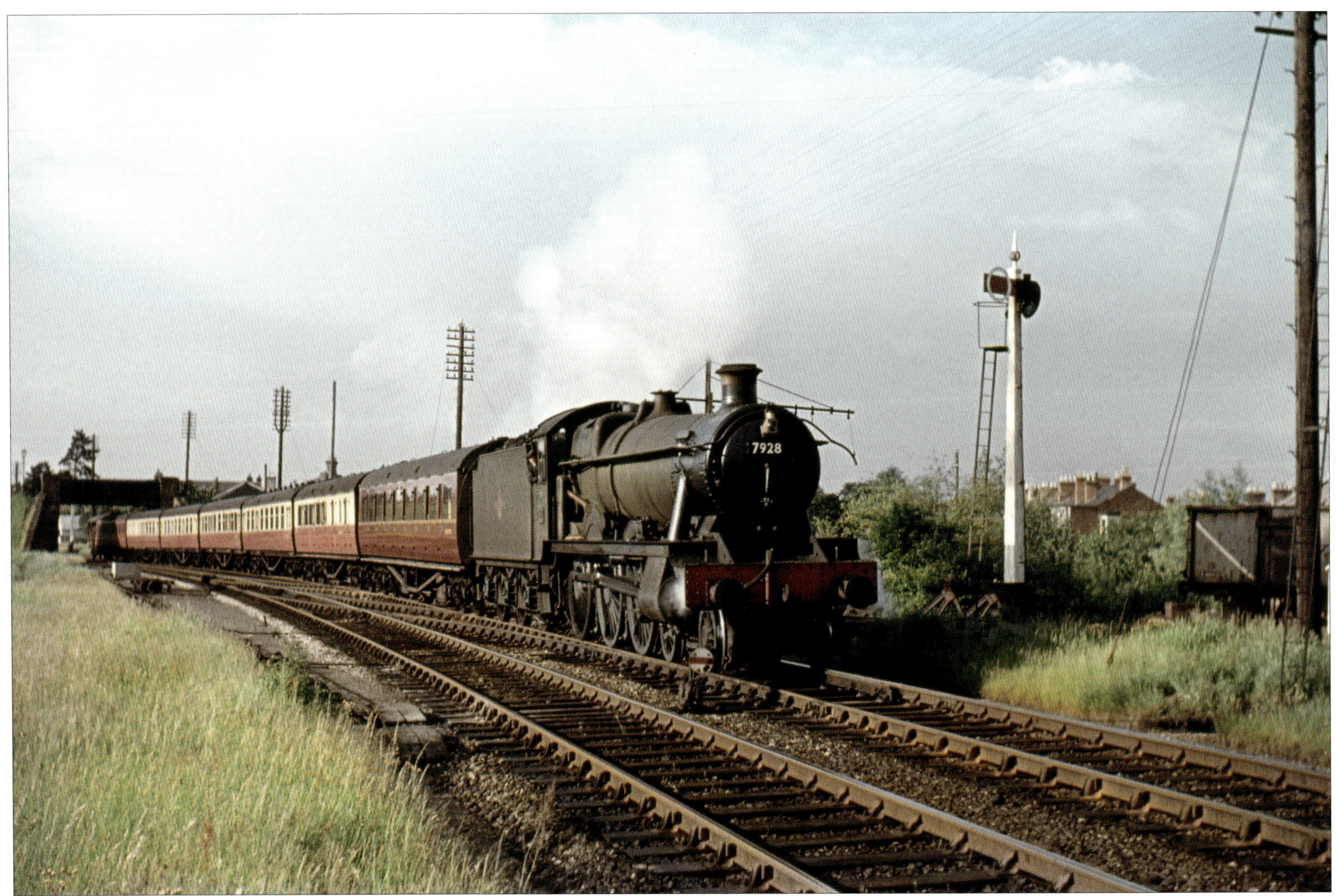

SLIDE 493 | A fortuitous ray of sunlight in an otherwise brooding sky illuminates Worcester stalwart **7928 Wolf Hall** as it heads home, threading the *Sanctus Road* bridge with the 6.39pm from Stratford. The train is just passing the run-down ex-*SMJ/LMS* sidings in *Old Town*. Note that, despite being a 'one-shed-loco' *7928* has at some point been serviced by Caerphilly Works; evidenced by the red-painted reversing rod, just visible beneath the grime. This practice was unique to Caerphilly and it clearly ruffled some feathers, as in November 1958 they were officially instructed to cease in an unambiguous directive from the top brass at Swindon. This photograph was taken from almost exactly the same viewpoint as *slide 1661* reproduced on page 69. *31/5/58 Leica IIIA (Agfacolor CT 18)*

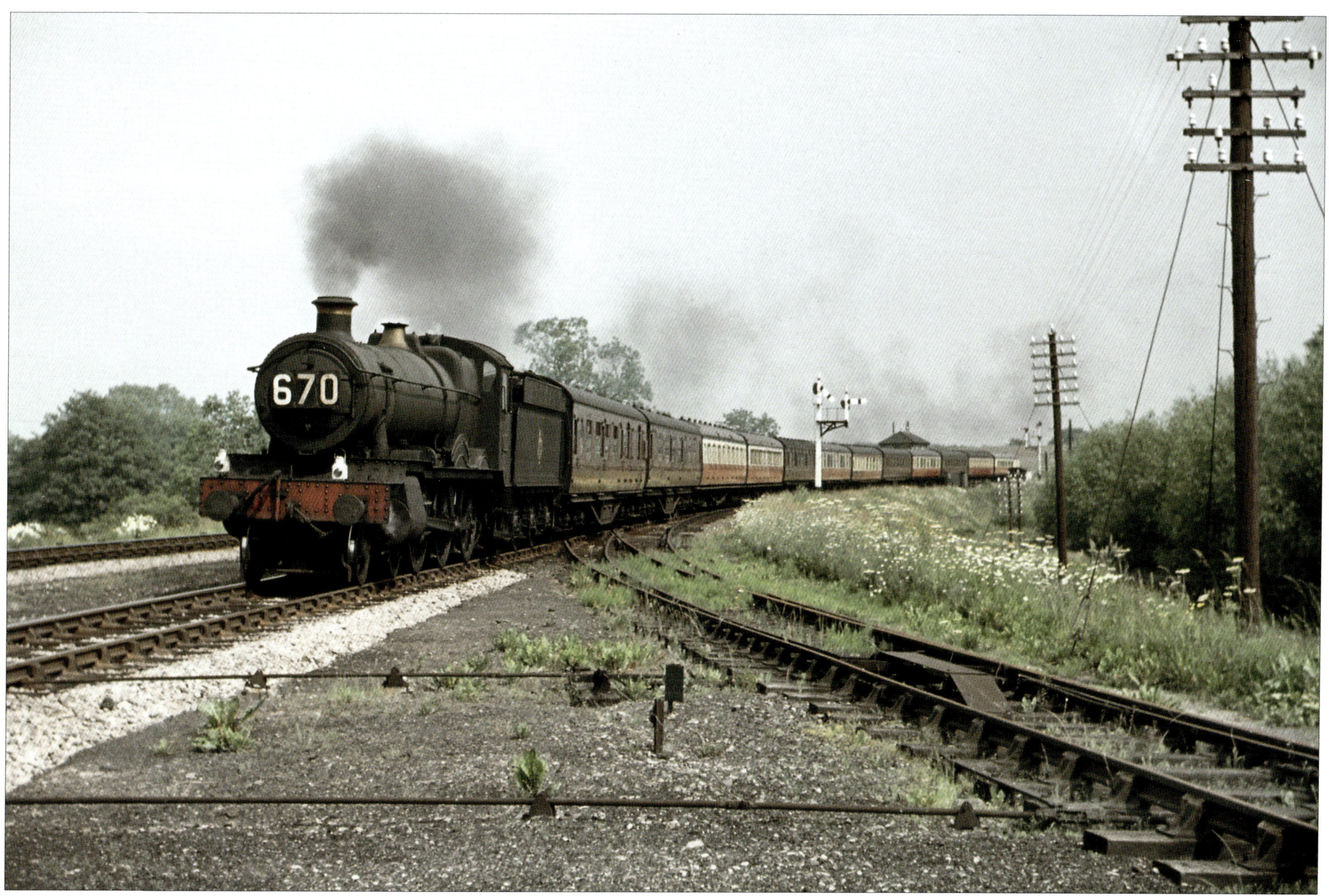

SLIDE 507 | Pontypool Road's grubby **6812 Chesford Grange** on the 7.40am SO St. Austell to Wolverhampton has just passed Bearley North Box and traversed *Salters Lane* on its way north-west. The tracks visible in the right foreground constitute the all-but-derelict branch line to Alcester with tubular *GWR*-pattern point rodding still extant. Note the unusually wide gap between the up and down main line at this location; necessary to accommodate one of the piers of the thirteen-span *Edstone Aqueduct* (behind the photographer) which carries the *Stratford-upon-Avon Canal* over the *North Warwickshire Line*. The timber-constructed Bearley North Box visible in the background of this shot controlled both junctions at this location: Bearley North Curve and the Alcester branch. *14/6/58 Leica IIIA 1/500th F3.5 (Agfacolor CT 18)*

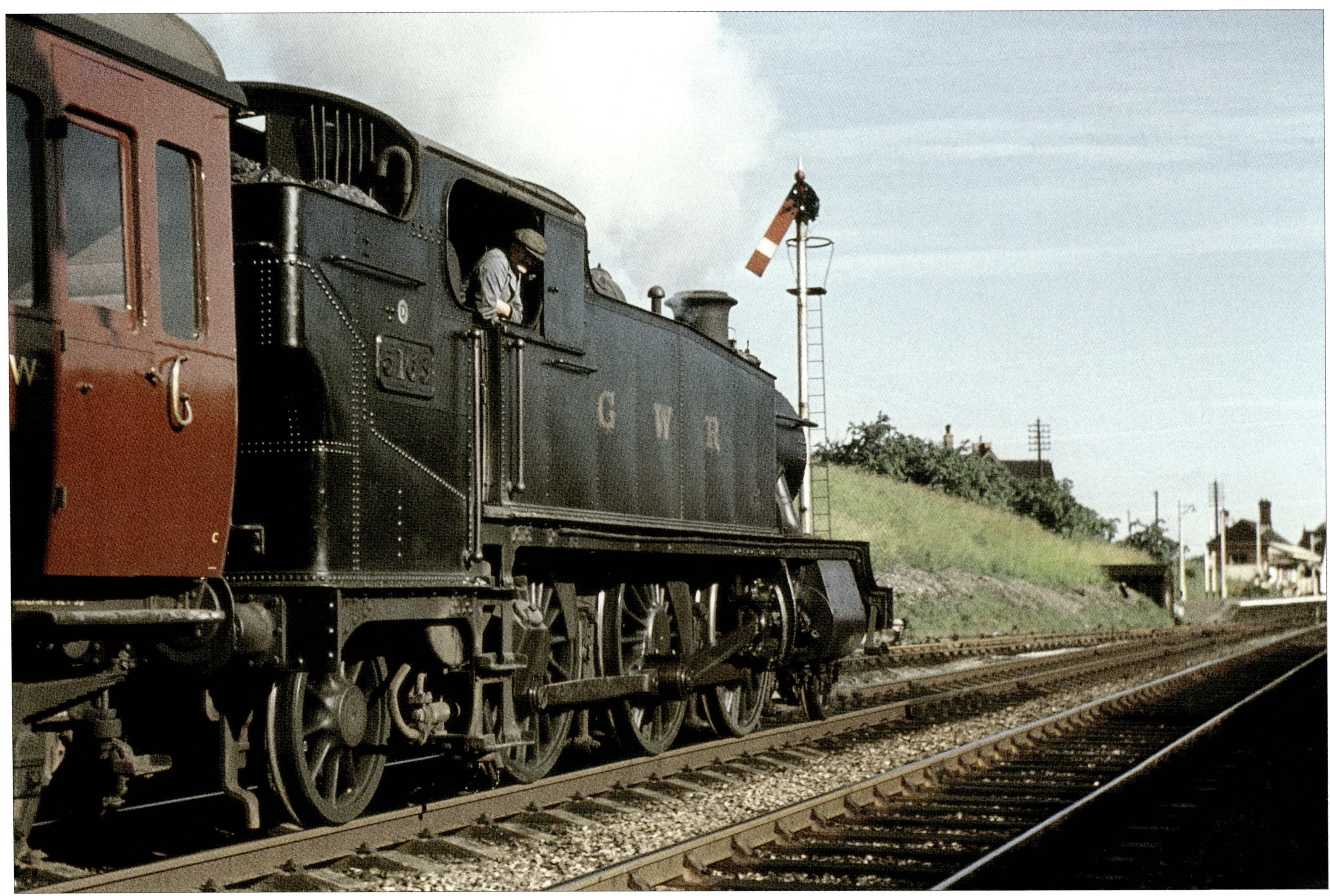

SLIDE 545 | Looking remarkably clean and still with prominent *GWR* transfers that date back to the late 1940s, Tyseley-based *5101* class 2-6-2T **5163**, passes the up goods refuge on the approach to Wilmcote Station on an early morning stopping train from Stratford to Birmingham Snow Hill. These locomotives were perfectly suited to suburban passenger traffic, involving regular stopping, but fast acceleration and it is no surprise that many of the class were deployed throughout the *Midlands* primarily for this very purpose. 5163 spend most, if not all of its *BR* years working out of Tyseley from where it was withdrawn just over a year after this photograph was taken. *14/7/58 Leica IIIA 1/500th F4.5 (Agfacolor CT 18)*

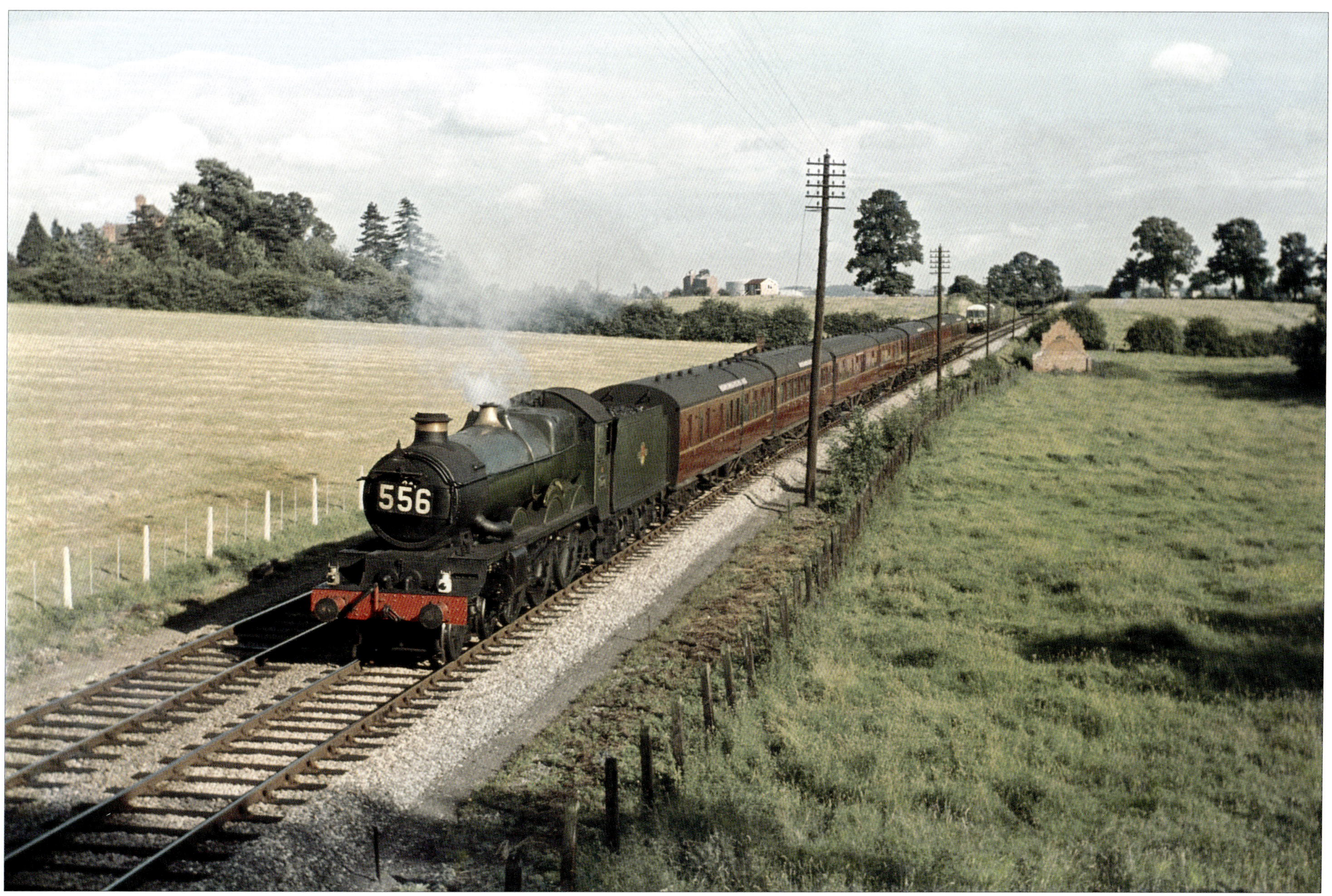

SLIDE 579 | At around 6.35pm on this glorious Wednesday evening, Stafford Road's *Castle* class **5046 Earl Cawdor** heads north out of Stratford towards the *Bishopton Lane* bridge on the 12.15pm SX Kingswear to Wolverhampton service. The locomotive has clearly been fitted with the reversed *Cornishman* headboard, suggesting it had worked the down Wolverhampton to Penzance train as far as Bristol and having been turned round quickly, is seen here returning the headboard back home for the following day's down *Cornishman* service. Note that in the distance, we can see that the express has just passed a *DMU* on a Leamington stopping train consisting of two 'bubble cars' coupled together. *30/7/58 Leica IIIA 1/500th F4.5 (Agfacolor CT 18)*

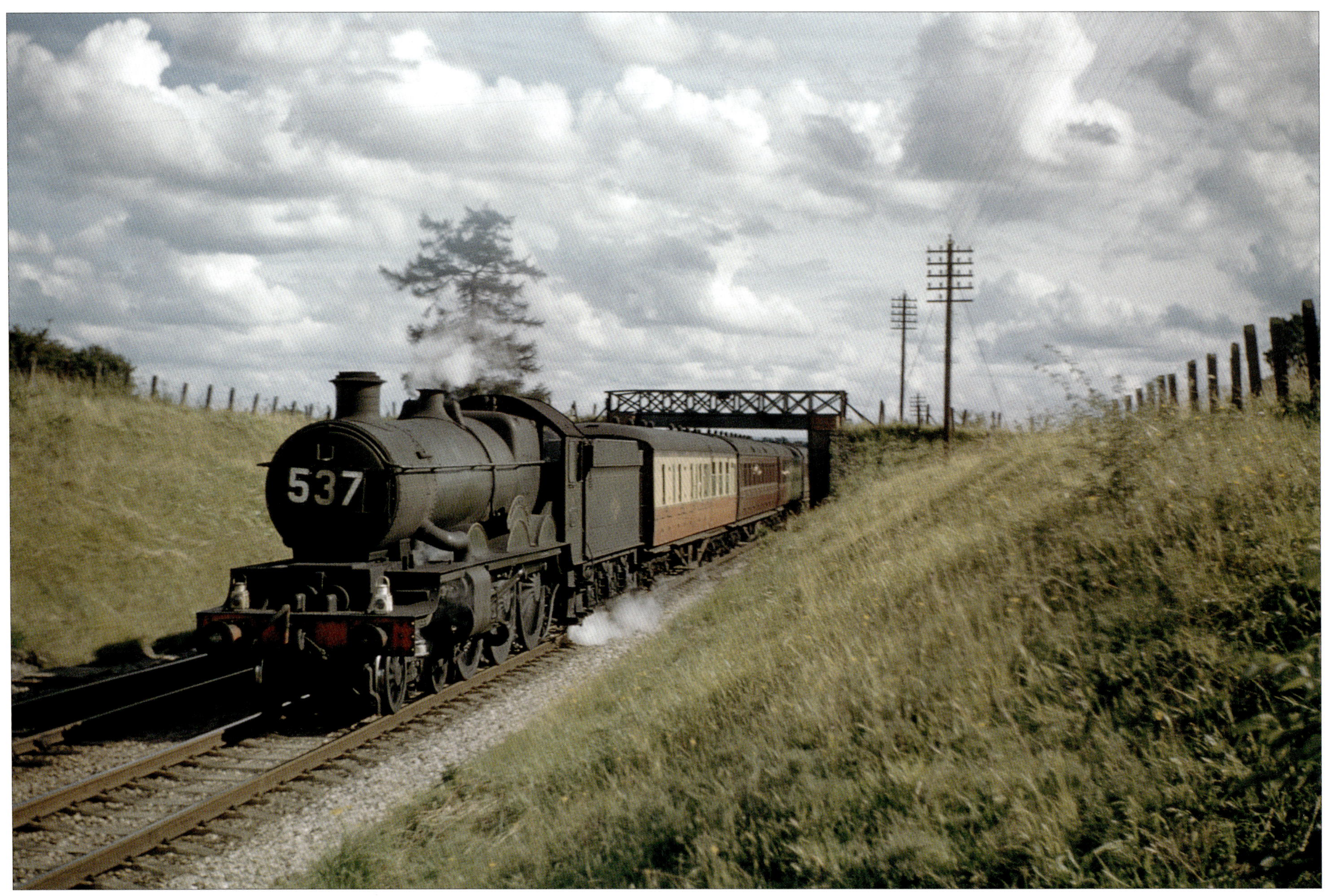

SLIDE 620 | Just about up to the summit of the 1 in 75 climb from Stratford, Bristol Bath Road's **5054 Earl of Ducie** *(ex-Lamphey Castle)* threads Wilmcote's *Canada Bridge* with the 10.35am SO Paington to Wolverhampton service. At this date, *5054* (along with **5058 Earl of Clancarty**) was one of the last of the *Castles* to retain the original-build 'tall' chimney, when most other contemporary members of the class had lost theirs during the first few years of Nationalisation *(see also slide 748 on page 6)*. What is also evident in this photograph is the generally dowdy appearance of the locomotive. Indeed, at this time after a busy Summer's schedule, an overhaul was already overdue; its last substantial visit to Swindon Works had been at the beginning of the previous year. *23/8/58 Leica IIIA 1/200th F2.5 (Kodachrome)*

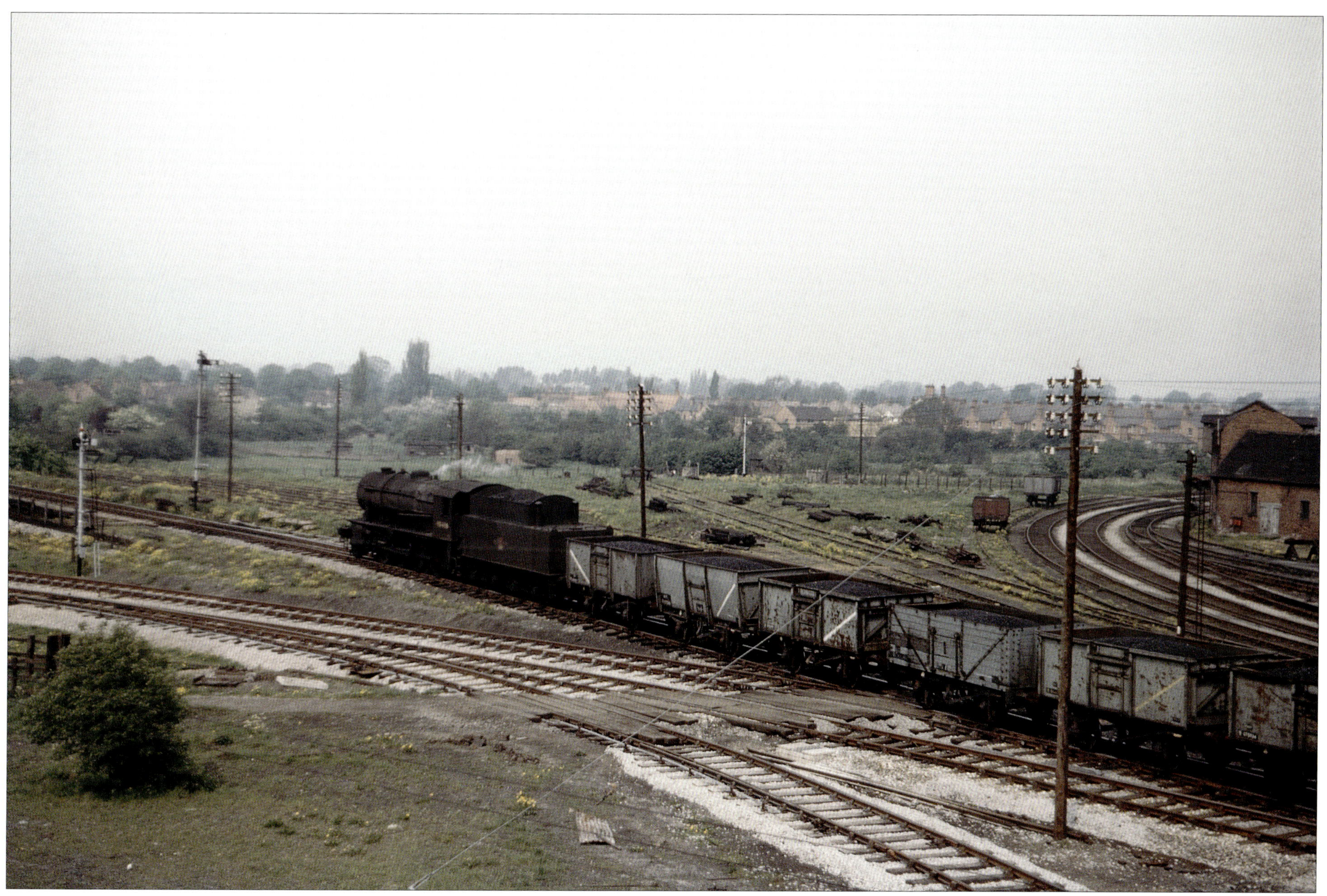

SLIDE 1032 | There are only a few days left before the final closure of the route between Stratford-upon-Avon *Old Town (ex-SMJ/LMS)* and the junctions at the village of Broom, approximately nine miles away. Here we see one of the final west-bound coal trains to use the route prior to the opening of the new east-to-south chord line visible in the foreground. With the start of the 1960 Summer timetable, all traffic will be directed south at this point, joining the ex-*GW* route to the south-west, via Honeybourne and Cheltenham, thus consolidating the Broom line's redundancy. At the head of this train is *WD/8* 2-8-0 **90486** from Woodford Halse. Photograph taken from the top of the Station's water-softening tower. This structure was dangerous and desperately in need of repair at the time this image was captured, but with the locomotive shed having been closed almost three years previously and the station buildings all but derelict, the tower's maintenance was not a consideration. *8/5/60 Leica IIIA (Kodachrome)*

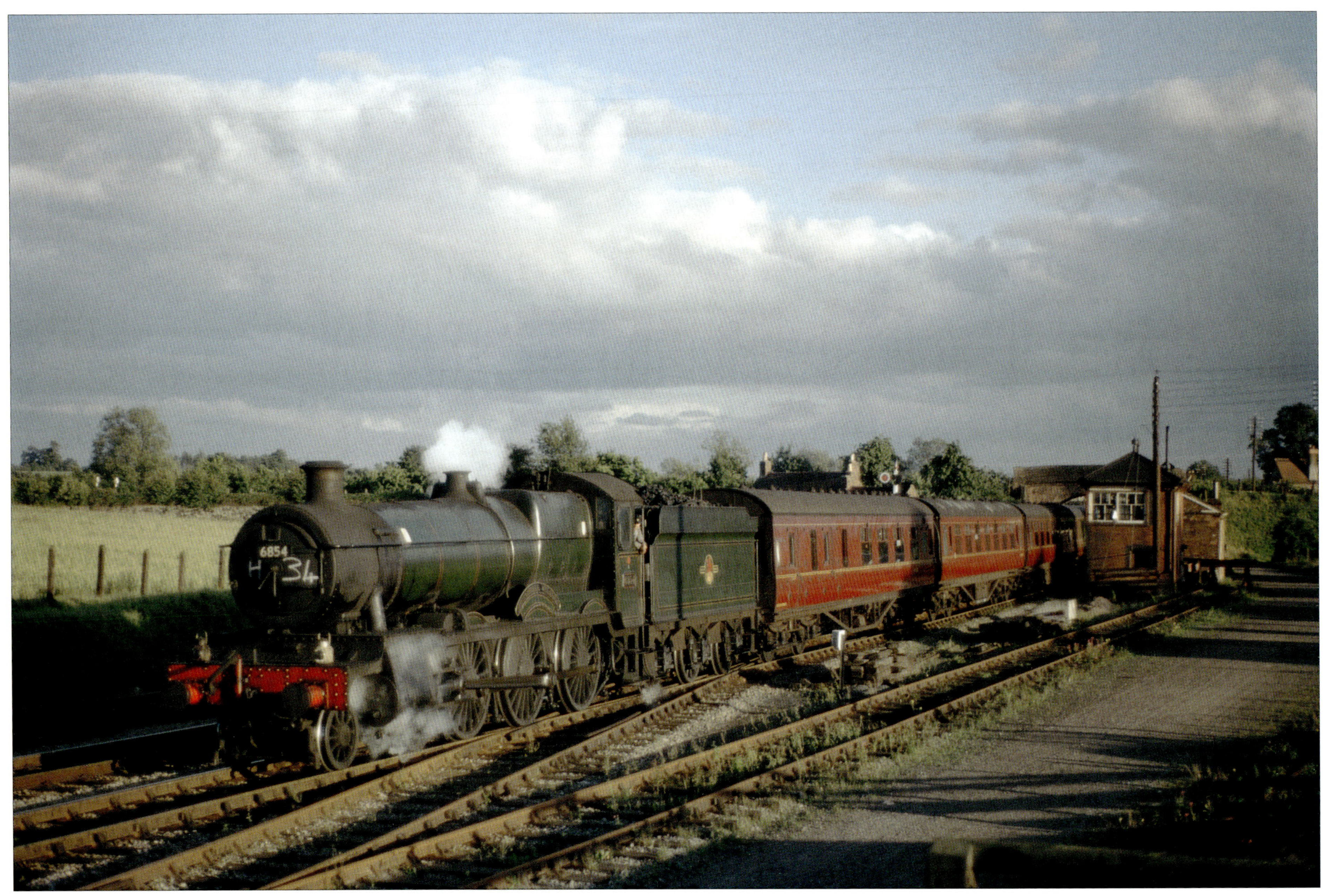

SLIDE 1534 | It looks as if Oxley's shed staff have had the first half-hearted attempt at cleaning **6854 Roundhill Grange** after a busy Summer. It is seen here disturbing the Saturday evening slumber of the small goods yard at Wilmcote with the 11.15 SO Newquay to Wolverhampton. After spending the first year or so of the decade being passed between sheds in the *West Country* and Cornwall, *6854* remained in the Midlands for the final three years of its working life. It was withdrawn from Tyseley Shed in September 1965 and became one of only six locomotives of its class to be broken up comparatively locally, at *Bird's* of Long Marston approximately five miles south-west of Stratford-upon-Avon *(see slide 1201 on page 78). 25/8/62 Leica IIIA (Kodachrome)*

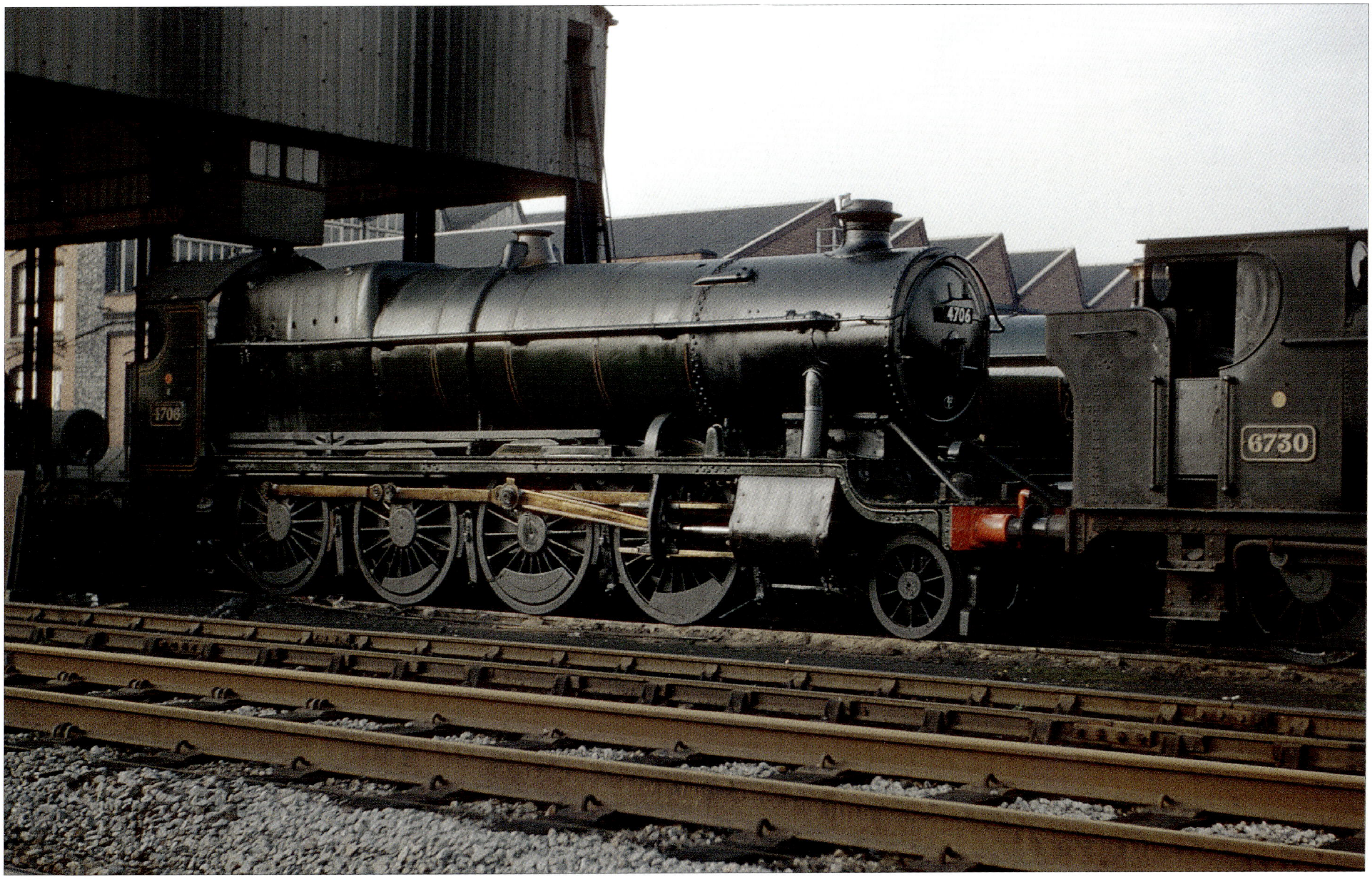

SLIDE 733 | Arguably George Churchward's finest masterpiece was the nine-strong 2-8-0 *47xx* class, limited only by its weight and an 'officially' imposed speed restriction of 60mph. Here we see **4706** minus its tender in lined livery at Swindon after minor repairs. It has not undergone a full repaint, but has been cleaned and after steam-testing and running in, will return primarily to night freight and relief passenger duties at St. Philip's Marsh. Entering service in March 1923, *4706* was one of five of its class built without the external 'snifter' valves built into the outer faces of the steam chests. After withdrawal in 1964, it became one of only two of its class actually cut up at Swindon (the other being **4702**): the rest were sold off to private breakers *(see also slide 1502 on page 79)*. Also in the above shot, we see *Collett 57xx* class 0-6-0PT **6730** which is sat awaiting its fate having been withdrawn from Newport Pill over a year previously. It will eventually be sold to *R.S. Hayes* of Gloucester where it will fall foul of the cutter's torch in February 1960. *2/11/58 Leica IIIA (Kodachrome)*

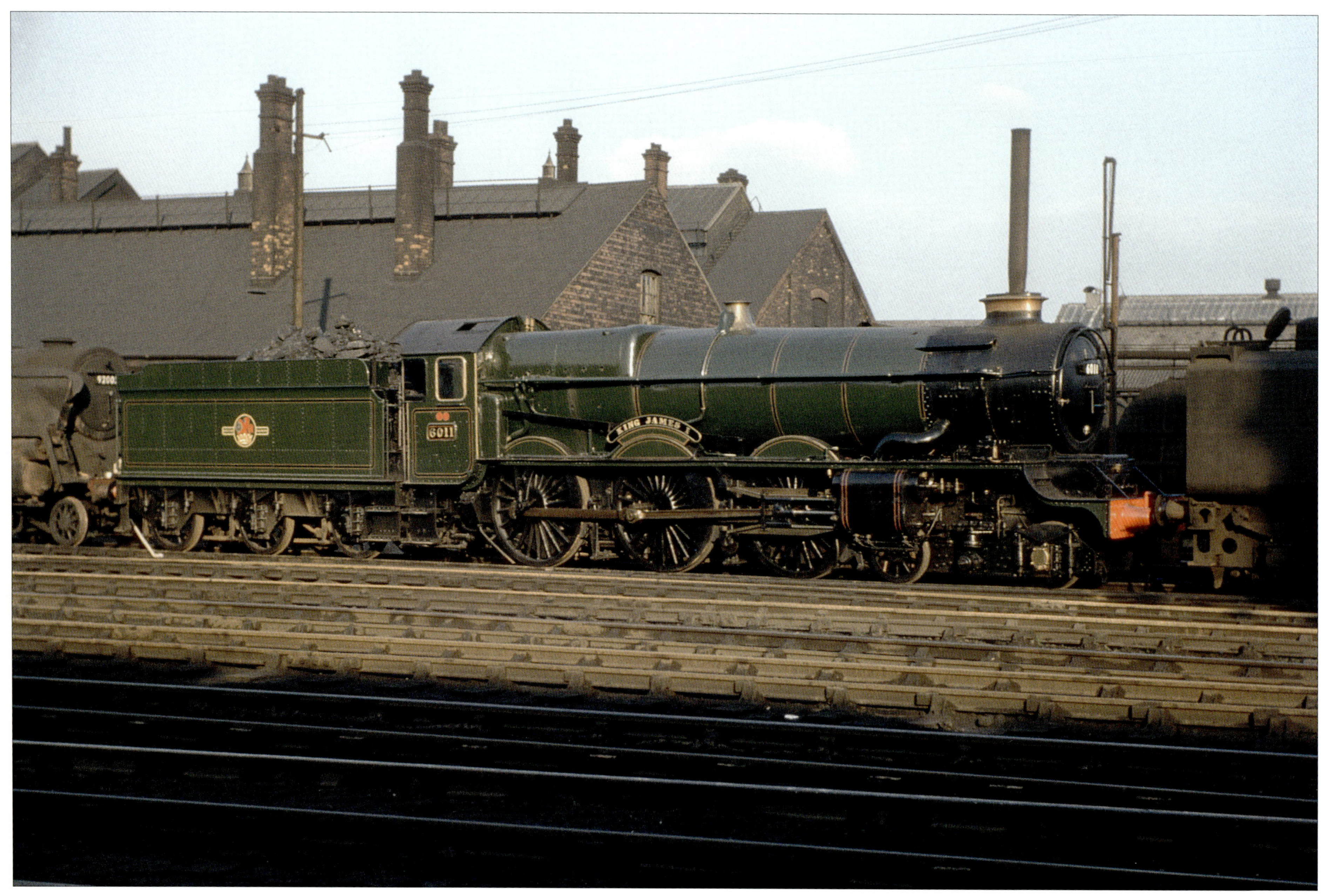

SLIDE 743 | As the low November sun casts increasingly long shadows as if to signify Winter's imminent approach, **6011 King James I** in ex-works splendour at Swindon looks a picture basking in the yellow pastel rays as it awaits a return to traffic at Stafford Road after overhaul. In 1954, *6011* had been one of the first of its class fitted with the *Alfloc* water treatment system designed to minimise limescale deposits on the boiler tubes, demanding regular washouts *(see slide 1528 on page 10)*. Treatment of the water theoretically allowed the *King* to run for thirty days prior to the boiler requiring attention. Behind *6011*, looking somewhat less elegant and showing more than a degree of front-end damage, stands Ebbw Junction's *BR Standard* 9F **92002**, awaiting entry to the works for repairs. Unfortunately, despite extensive research, we have not been able to ascertain the circumstances of this damage which looks to be consistent with a low-speed collision of some kind. *21/11/58 Leica IIIA (Kodachrome)*

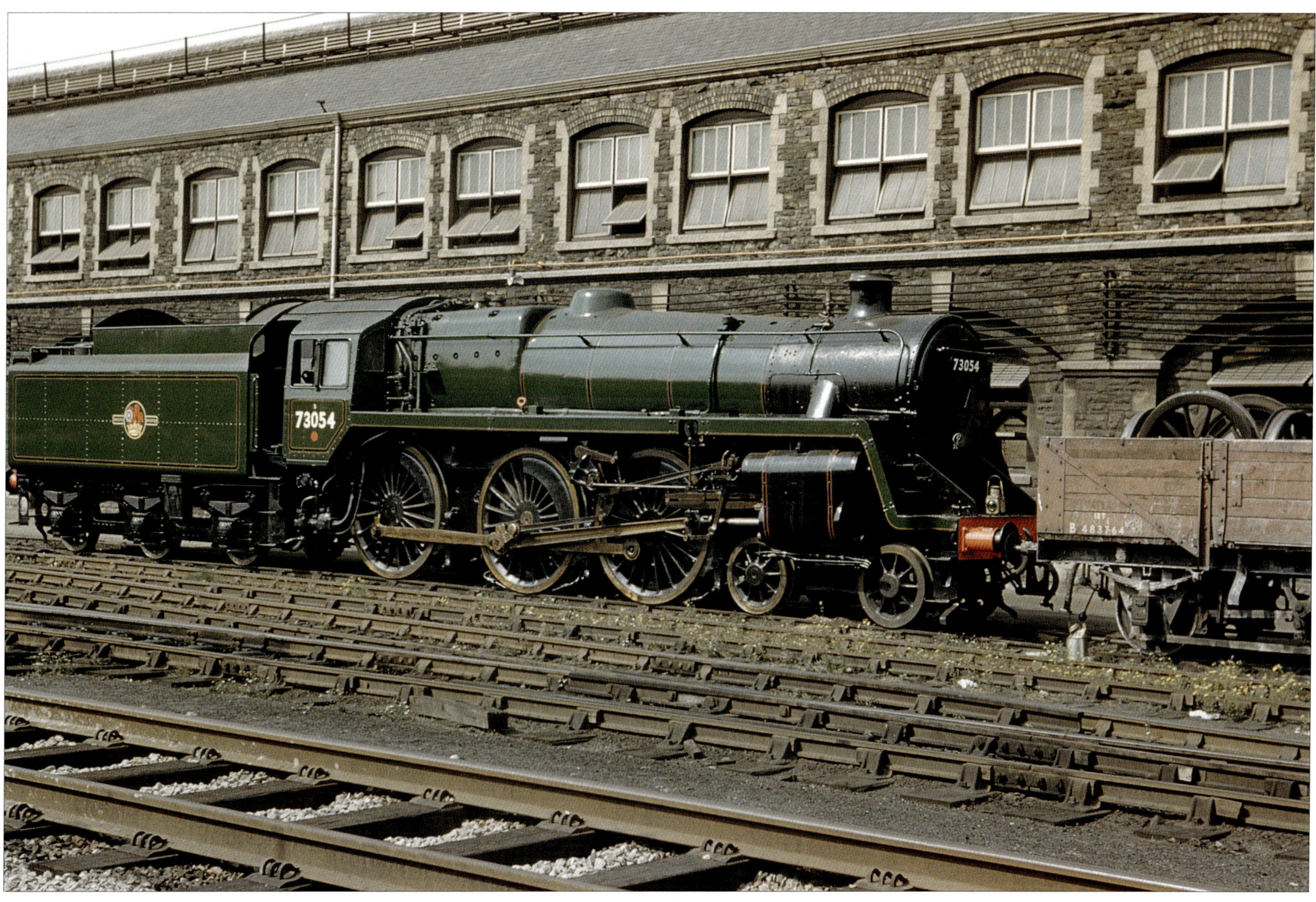

SLIDE 935 | Bristol Barrow Road's *BR Standard* class 5 **73054** has been given the 'full works' treatment at Swindon. This was the first repaint this locomotive was to receive in its comparatively short working life of just over eleven years. It was built at Derby Works and entered service in June 1954, initially staying in the north of England, working out of Leeds Holbeck and Derby sheds. It was transferred to the *West Country* in 1957, spending the final four years at Bath Green Park, from where it was withdrawn in August 1965. It is interesting to note in this photograph that only the lower edge of the running plate has been lined. This practice seemed to be peculiar to Swindon: those locomotives that received similar repaints at Eastleigh Works had lining applied to both top and bottom edges of the running plate and indeed, later photographs of *73054* (taken post-1963) are indicative that it did receive a further full repaint at Eastleigh at some time during that year. *6/9/59 Leica IIIA (Kodachrome)*

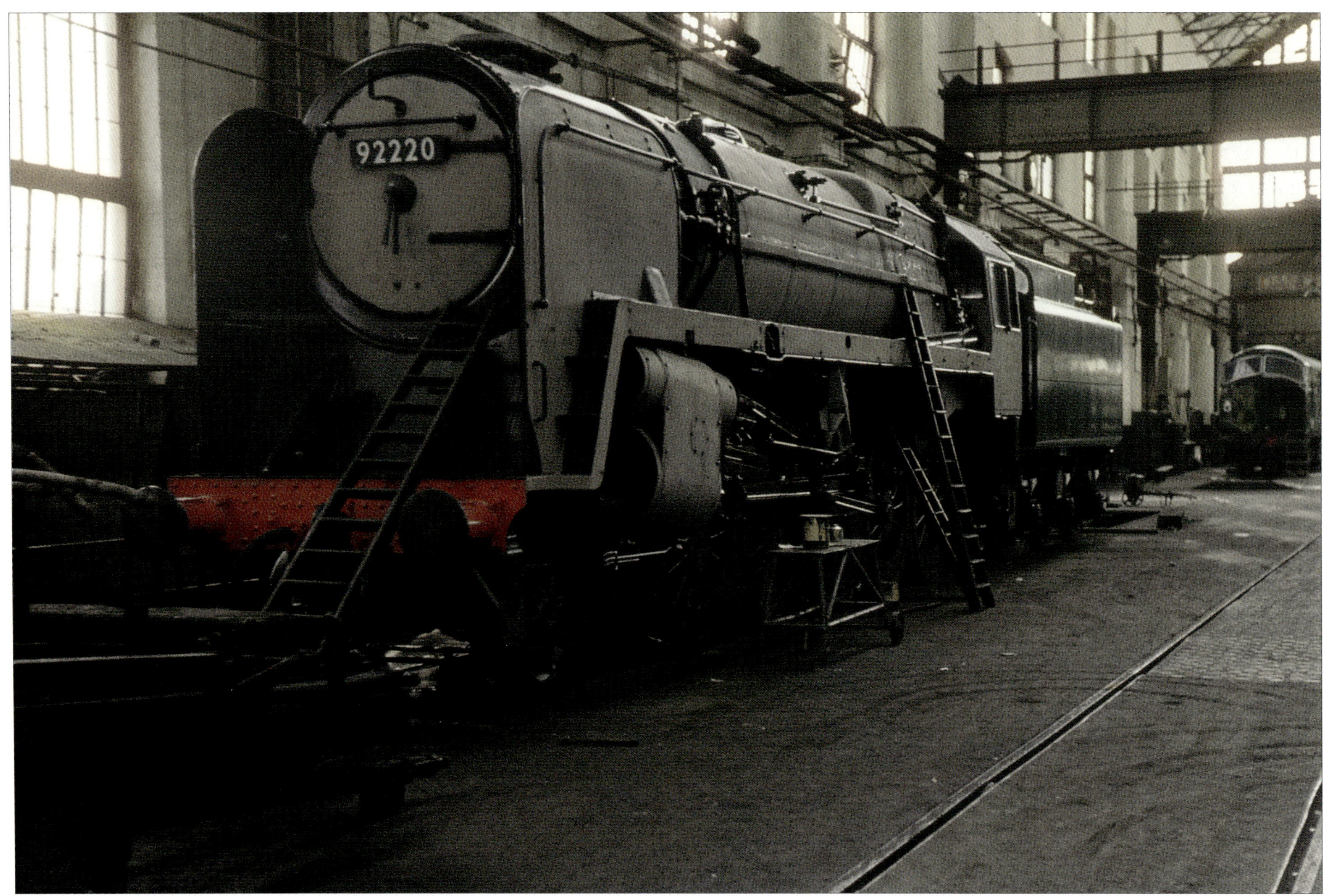

SLIDE 989 | Just under a month before the official *'Last Steam Locomotive built for British Railways'* unveiling ceremony at Swindon, *Standard* class 9F **92220 Evening Star** is seen here completed inside the works, but waiting final painting, lining and fixing of nameplates. Note that its unique copper-capped chimney has been masked off with a cloth material to minimise the risk of blemishes and splashes of paint. At the end of March it will begin its short five-year service life working out of Cardiff Canton. Despite being earmarked for preservation at the point of construction, it is suspected that *92220's* early withdrawal from service was hastened by damage sustained to its buffer beam as a result of a shunting accident during its final months at Cardiff East Dock. *21/2/60 Leica IIIA (Agfacolor CT 18)*

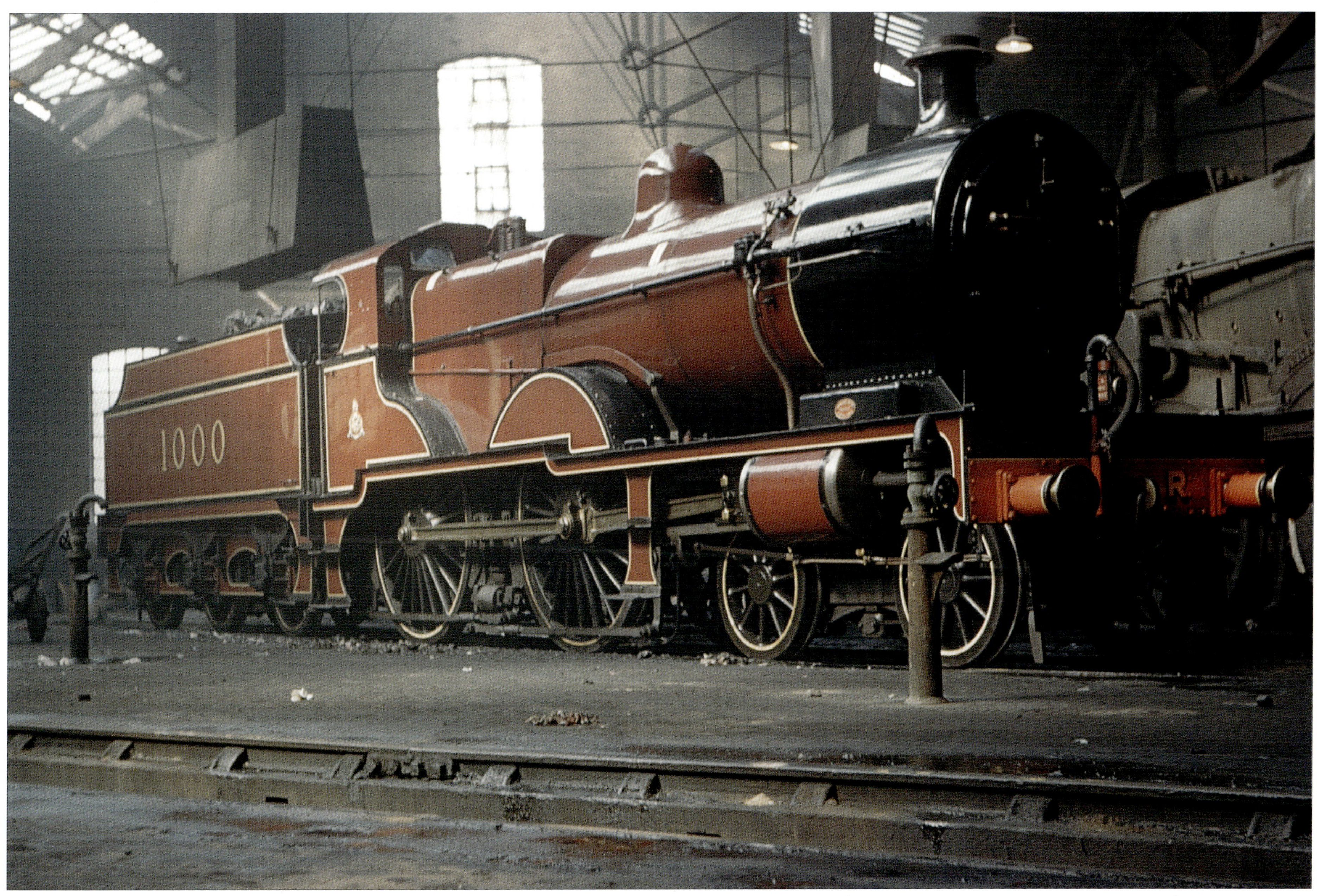

SLIDE 1138 | A very unusual sight in any ex-*Great Western* shed: ex-*MR/LMS Compound* 4-4-0 **1000** still in steam, rests facing the east turntable at Swindon whilst on *RCTS* railtour duties *(see also slide 1129 on page 51 and slide 928 on page 47)*. By way of a contrast, Swindon's own **5986 Arbury Hall** *(ex-oil burner 3954)* lurks in the shadows, seemingly ashamed of its comparatively unkempt appearance. After several months of storage at Derby, the *Compound* (as *BR 41000*) was officially withdrawn in September 1951 and set aside for preservation, though very little actual remedial work was carried out for over seven years. Of the forty-five members of this class built, only thirty-seven actually made it into *BR* ownership: the last in service being **41025**, which was withdrawn from Gloucester Barnwood in January 1953 and broken up at Derby Works almost immediately. *11/9/60 Leica IIIA (Kodachrome)*

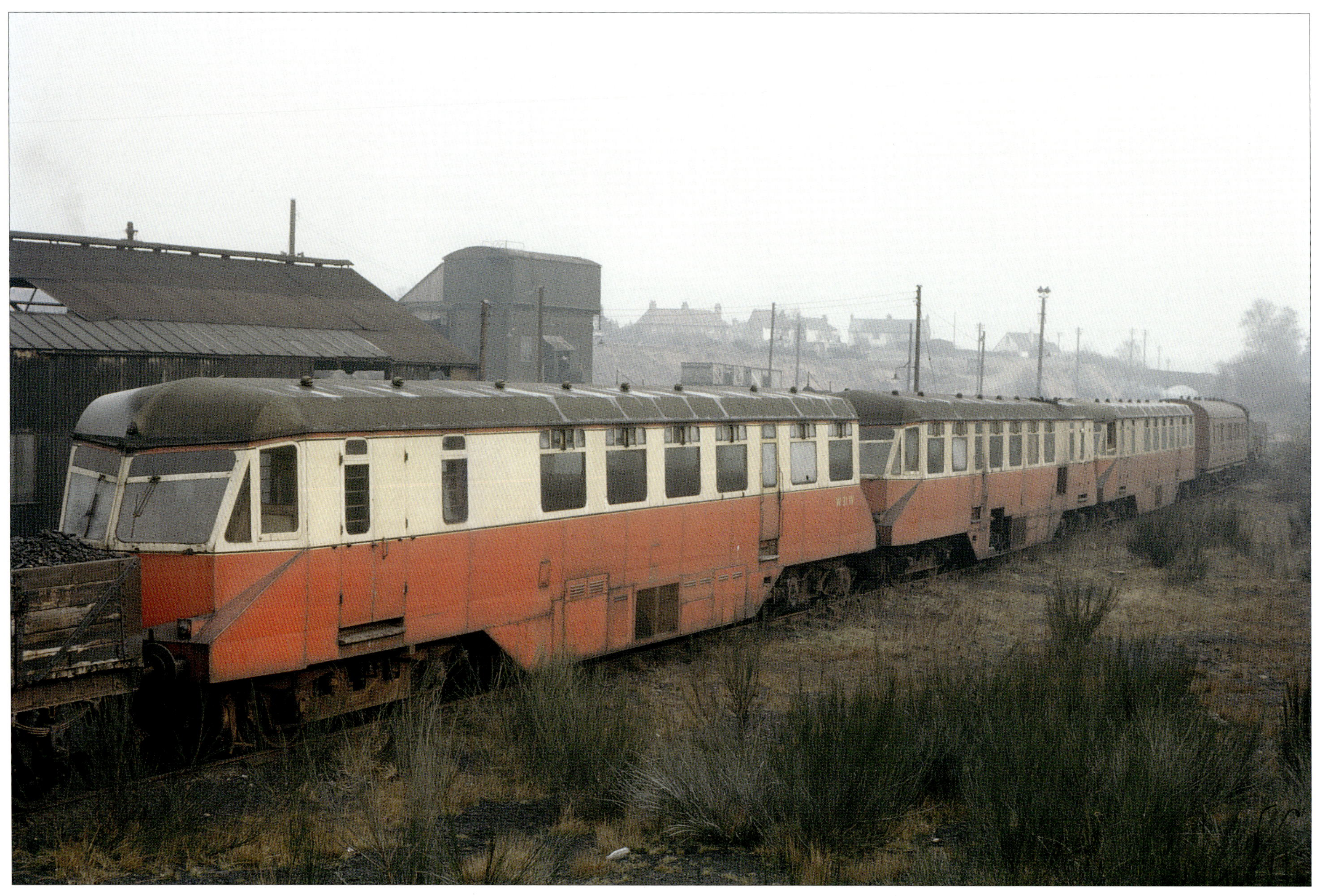

SLIDE 1197 | A cold and damp March morning at Kidderminster Shed sees retired *AEC* railcars **W31W**, **W25W** and **W22W** languishing on a storage siding, all facing an uncertain future. As we now know, *W22W* was to have a reprieve from the cutter's torch. Built in 1940 *(power and transmission by AEC, Southall and chassis/bodywork at Swindon)* it first saw service at Newport. Its twilight years were spent in the Worcester area, from where it was withdrawn in late 1961 and stored for several months where we see it pictured here. The following five years saw *W22W* put into storage at Swindon, from where it was purchased for preservation by the Midland Group of the *Great Western Society* in 1967. Initially working on the *Severn Valley Railway* and eventually moving to *Didcot Railway Centre*, it is currently the only operational member of its class. Kidderminster Shed, as we see it here, was situated in the Aggborough region of the town, just south of the *Hoo Road* bridge (which we can see in the distance). Built in 1932, it replaced the original smaller shed that was situated nearer Kidderminster Station, around quarter-of-a-mile north east of this location *(see slide 221 on page 74)*. 25/3/62 *Leica IIIA (Kodachrome)*

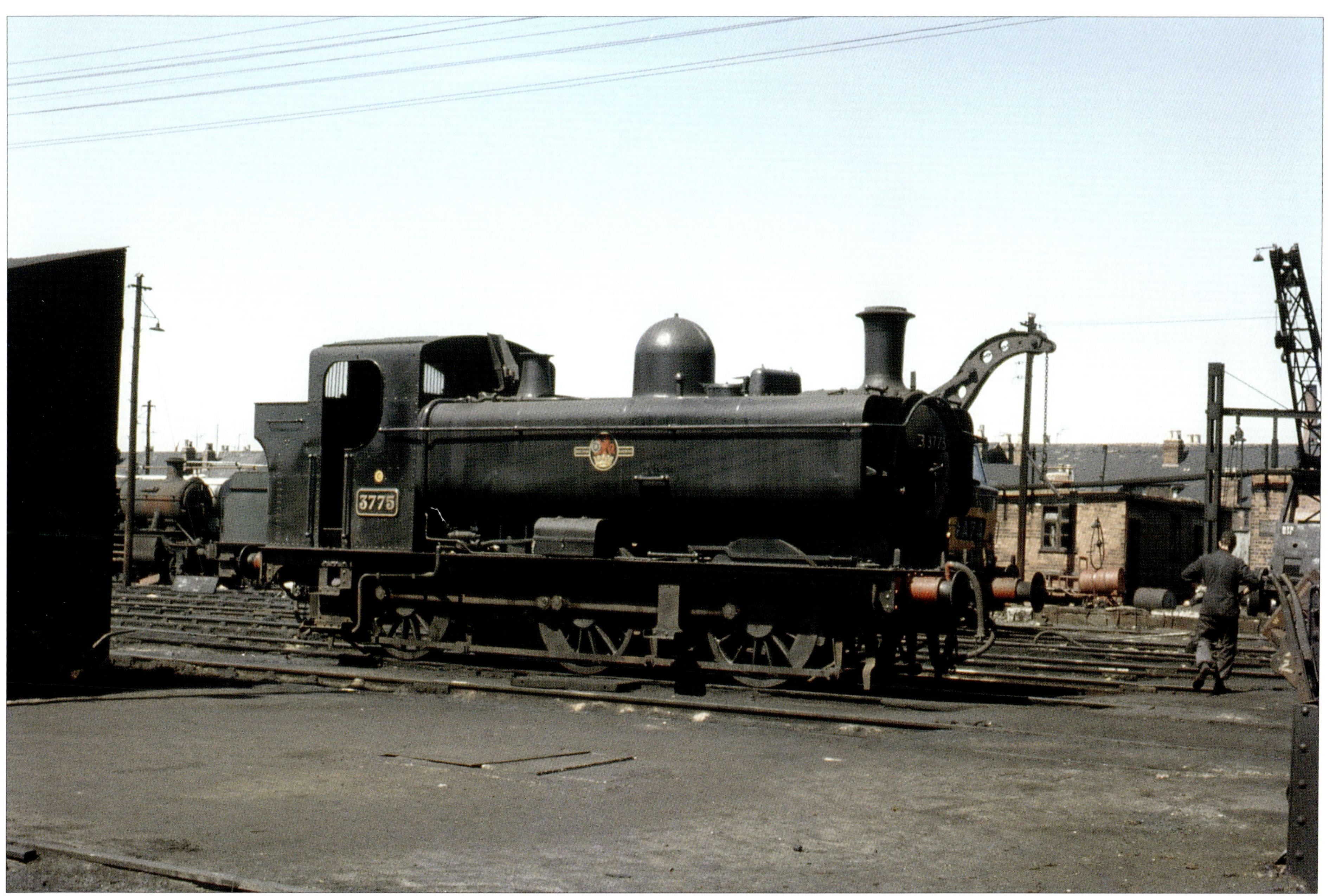

SLIDE 1656 | *Collett 57xx* class 0-6-0PT **3775** is pictured here at Gloucester Horton Road. This locomotive was one of the second batch of the *37xx* series built at Swindon during the late 1930s, following on consecutively from the *97xx* series. Chalked on the left-hand wall in this image, barely legible, are the words: *'WALLY: 4104 FAILED'*. We don't know who Wally was, but *4104* refers to the *5101* class 2-6-2T that was shedded at Horton Road between April 1963 and May 1964, when it was withdrawn for scrapping and sold to *Cashmore's* of Newport. Ironically, despite working out of Horton Road for a further two years after this photograph was taken, *3775* also fell foul of the cutter's torch at *Cashmore's* during April 1966. Unfortunately, Tom didn't record the identity of the class 35 'Hymek' in the background. *21/7/63 Leica IIIA (Ansco)*

13 | Numerical index of Locomotives.

17(W) *p74*
123 .... *p48*
1000 .... *p47, 51, 121*
1010 .... *p34*
1027 .... *p72*
1365 .... *p46*
1440 .... *p85*
1472 .... *p86*
1474 .... *p88*

22(W) *p74, 122*
25(W) *p122*
26(W) *p74*
29(W) *p74*
21C114 .... *p33*
2211 .... *p87*
2257 .... *p109*
2811 .... *p77*

31(W) *p122*
3171 .... *p42*
3440 .... *p42, 43, 44, 45, 48*
3775 .... *p123*
3819 .... *p75*
3839 .... *p40*
3864 .... *p32*
3903 .... *p67*
3951 .... *p39*
3954 .... *p121*
30515 .... *p100*

30837 .... *p100*
34014 .... *p33*
34105 .... *p69*

4056 .... *p13*
4075 .... *p17*
4082 .... *p2*
4085 .... *p7, 8, 36*
4087 .... *p2*
4088 .... *p2*
4090 .... *p42, 44*
4091 .... *p24*
4103 .... *p14*
4234 .... *p71*
4358 .... *p42, 43, 44*
4492 .... *p102*
4702 .... *p117*
4706 .... *p117*
4853 .... *p40*
4907 .... *p67*
4961 .... *p84*
4974 .... *p109*
4978 .... *p1*
4979 .... *p68*
4988 .... *p23*
4991 .... *p37*
41025 .... *p121*
41285 .... *p104*
43878 .... *p108*
44942 .... *p101*

45567 .... *p70, 71*
46101 .... *p106*
46120 .... *p103*
46154 .... *p94*
46209 .... *p95, 96*
46225 .... *p89*
46229 .... *p54*
46233 .... *p54*
46252 .... *p91*
46423 .... *p90*
46427 .... *p90*
48012 .... *p76*
48410 .... *p73*

5018 .... *p3*
5028 .... *p36*
5033 .... *p66, 67*
5042 .... *p3, 5*
5045 .... *p21, 49*
5046 .... *p55, 113*
5054 .... *p6, 114*
5058 .... *p114*
5070 .... *p23*
5071 .... *p56*
5084 .... *p2*
5163 .... *p112*
5510 .... *p1*
5567 .... *p70*

5976 .... *p39*
5978 .... *p82*
5984 .... *p107*
5986 .... *p121*
53806 .... *p98*
53808 .... *p99*

601(D) *p25*
6003 .... *p32*
6004 .... *p38*
6005 .... *p18, 20*
6008 .... *p26*
6009 .... *p28, 29*
6010 .... *p29*
6011 .... *p118*
6012 .... *p14, 21*
6013 .... *p35*
6016 .... *p10, 52*
6017 .... *p15*
6018 .... *p53*
6019 .... *p27, 30*
6021 .... *p20*
6022 .... *p16, 24*
6024 .... *p29*
6025 .... *p35*
6027 .... *p19, 22*
6152 .... *p9*

6225 .... *p89*
6229 .... *p54*
6233 .... *p54*
6252 .... *p91*
6366 .... *p64*
6730 .... *p117*
6803 .... *p78*
6812 .... *p111*
6820 .... *(i)*
6825 .... *p54*
6853 .... *p65*
6854 .... *p12, 78, 116*
6931 .... *p38*
6962 .... *p41*
6963 .... *p81*
6979 .... *p81*
60013 .... *p102*
60022 .... *p92*
60061 .... *p92*
60500 .... *p97*
61159 .... *p93*

7000 .... *p31*
7005 .... *p58, 83*
7007 .... *p10*
7013 .... *p2*
7014 .... *p2*

7017 .... *p79*
7026 .... *p11*
7027 .... *p59, 60, 61*
7246 .... *p71*
7305 .... *p63*
7317 .... *p51*
7705 .... *(iii)*
7816 .... *p80*
7818 .... *p62*
7922 .... *p50*
7928 .... *p110*
70022 .... *p4*
70026 .... *p4*
70029 .... *p95*
70577 .... *p76*
73054 .... *p119*
76006 .... *p51*

86 .... *p98*
8012 .... *p76*
8104 .... *p44*

9492 .... *p43*
90486 .... *p115*
90573 .... *p42*
92002 .... *p118*
92129 .... *p105*
92220 .... *p120*

Abbreviations:

AEC - *Associated Equipment Company*, BR - *British Railways*, DMU - *Diesel Multiple Unit*, GNER - *Great North Eastern Railway*, GW(R) - *Great Western (Railway)*, ICI - *Imperial Chemical Industries*, LCGB - *Locomotive Club of Great Britain*, LMR - *London Midland Region*, LMS(R) - *London, Midland & Scottish (Railway)*, LNER - *London & North Eastern Railway*, LNWR - *London & North Western Railway*, LSWR - *London & South Western Railway*, MR - *Midland Railway*, NBL - *Northern British Locomotive (Company)*, NRM - *National Railway Museum*, RCTS - *Railway Correspondence & Travel Society*, REC - *Railway Enthusiasts' Club*, S&D(R) - *Somerset & Dorset (Railway)*, SLS - *Stephenson Locomotive Society*, SMJ(R) - *Stratford-upon-Avon & Midland Junction (Railway)*, WR - *Western Region*.

Standard timetable abbreviations commonly used: SX - *Saturdays Excepted*, SO - *Saturdays Only*, SuO - *Sundays only*.

In all instances where 'Stratford' is mentioned in this publication, it refers to Stratford-upon-Avon, Warwickshire.